THE INSIDERS' GUIDE TO ANTIQUE FURNITURE

by Alan Robertson

illustrations by Linda Combi

for Lucy & Hamish

Bell & Hyman

with very special thanks to: **Rod Dunning**

the highly respected York antique restorer for his time, advice and help on furniture construction and restoration.

Editor (Bell & Hyman): Connie Austen-Smith
Production: Kevin Benson, Gary Boanas
Restoration Photography: Paul Hines
Cover Photography: Ken Shelton
Typography: John Smyth

First published 1985 by Bell & Hyman Limited
37-39 Queen Elizabeth Street, London SE1 2QB

British Library Cataloging in Publication Data
Robertson, Alan
The Insiders' Guide to Antique Furniture

1. Furniture — Collectors and Collecting
2. Furniture — Prices

1. Title
749'.1'0294 NK 2240

ISBN 0 7135 2568 1

Typeset by J. A. Magson Limited, York.

Printed and bound in Great Britain by
William Clowes Limited, Beccles and London

contents

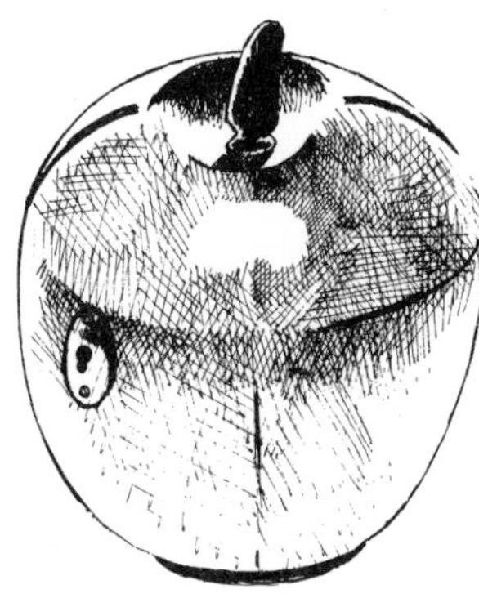

FURNITURE DESCRIPTIONS

In my furniture descriptions I have tried to give you a quick check list of some of the factors that can influence the desirability — or otherwise — of a piece of furniture from the antique trade point of view. This is not a purist's guide — rather one based on the school of hard knock-outs.

It may be helpful to describe or elaborate on the choice of headings:

Quick view: A brief summary of the piece.

Desirable woods: Some woods are what you might reasonably expect to find the piece made in — other woods could be a bonus or otherwise. If the norm were mahogany, walnut might be better. On the other hand, in other examples it might not!

Shape: The normal or common shape, with a mention as to whether the other possible shapes should be considered a benefit.

Handles: Great store is set in the trade by original brass handles. When new handles have to be fitted they can be subjected to such clever treatment as to make their detection extremely difficult.

Restoration: Some furniture presents rather special restoration problems. In this section I have tried to cover some of these briefly.

Fake?: For a wide variety of reasons, some antique furniture is never totally faked. In other cases, the genuine article is the exception.

Configuration: A brief outline of the expected features.

Decoration/inlays: An indication of when these can increase the value and/or desirability.

Best period: From a trade point of view, some Victorian examples might be rated higher than a generic Georgian piece.

Best size: Small is not always beautiful — usually, but not always.

Colour: Colour is always important, but very hard to describe.

Feet: Originality is the thing, but this is very much one of the areas where sympathetic replacement is perfectly allowable.

Features to look for: Some 'little things' which may set the piece apart and make it that much more attractive and valuable.

Potential: Some items are worth more as material for conversion or improvement, some only as raw material for the restorer. Many pieces have potential yet to be realized in terms of desirability, usefulness or fashion.

Interiors/drawers: All may not be obvious at first glance. The piece that hides secret treasures may be worth a fortune.

Most valuable: There is always one example in every furniture group which has set some kind of auction or sale record.

Oddities: The exceptions or design variations on a theme.

In a word (or two): Just that!

POTENTIAL BANDS:

A great many items are undervalued in the antique trade — an even greater number are overvalued. The Potential Band attempts to indicate whether the piece has reached its full value relative to other antique furniture — all further increases in its value being caused by normal inflation, general demand for antique stock and a continually shrinking supply.

Undervaluing frequently reflects the lack of practical use today compared with the original concept. A typical example might be a large **cellarette** or wine cooler, seldom used for its original purpose, and of very little use for anything else. However, high quality materials and a great deal of expertise were involved in its creation.

Compare the same craftsmanship and quantity of materials in a little set of **hanging shelves** of the same period. Their price, piece for piece, would be considerably more. On the other hand, they too score high marks on the potential band as they are rare — due mainly to their easily broken delicate design — and are unlikely to rise in value proportionally to contemporary antique inflation.

FASHION BANDS:

Antiques are very much a fashion business, especially with the great quantity of export sales being made to the United States. There, interior designers and the glossy home interior magazines dictate fashion, style and consequently, demand. Fashion starts slowly at the 'top end' and filters down the social scale, the quality decreasing as demand reaches a wider audience.

The dealers in the States are asked for the goods featured in the current trend-setting magazines. They, in turn, call on the British dealers and make ever-increasing demands for 'more of the same'.

Fashion buying is coupled with repetitive buying in the trade. If a dealer always does well with a particular item he will buy again — frequently, of course, paying a little more each time. Some dealers become specialists in particular, very narrow, groups of goods, not really because they have any particular knowledge but simply because they know that specific market and always do well in it.

PRICE BANDS:

These bands attempt to indicate the normal spread of prices for a particular piece or group of furniture. The shaded boxes highlighting the commonest price range. Like all price indicators, these bands should be treated with extreme caution as there will always be exceptions to every example.

The prices are not spaced equally along the band in many cases, as the spread of prices is not proportional.

Put yourself into the antique dealer's shoes, and ask yourself what should you look for in antique furniture.

You might be tempted to sum it all up in one word: 'profit'. You would almost certainly be totally wrong. Always assuming that you are not in the business purely to make a quick buck and also possess a modicum of taste and interest in antique furniture.

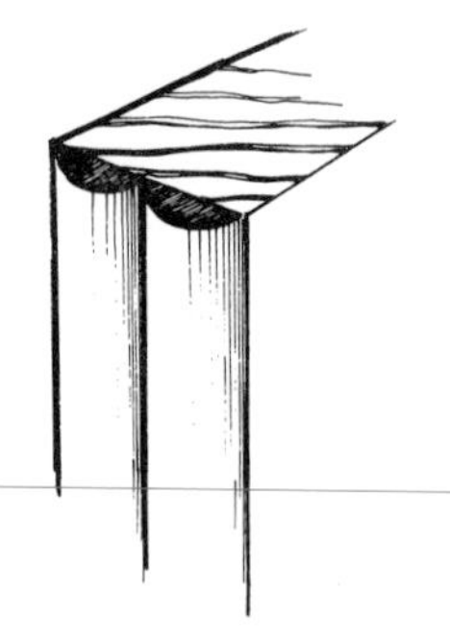

Reeding

So, let's walk into a sale room and have a look around . . . The chances are that you should be able to spot 'your lots' from fifty yards away. You will, almost certainly be looking for . . .

1 The general **'appeal'** of the piece — the overall **design, proportions.** Its obvious **quality.**

2 Next, you should look for **colour** and **patination.** A 'good' colour first and foremost. Either the original rich strong hues of mahogany and rosewood or the same woods faded-out to the colours of rich honey so coveted in the trade and by most knowledgeable collectors.

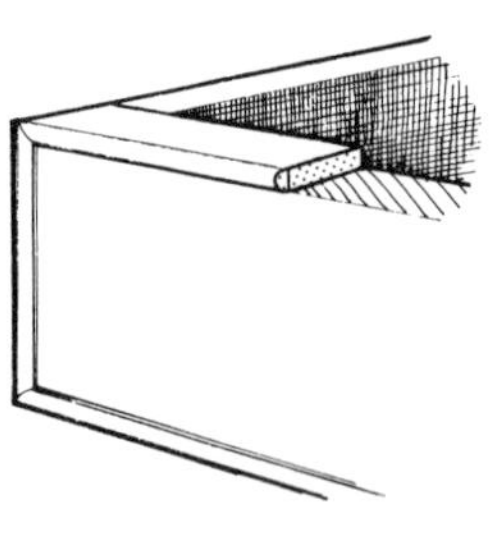

Cock beading

In many cases, colour can be created in the workshop — genuine patination is impossible to duplicate or fake. A dealer will often excuse the purchase of an otherwise 'lump' by praising its beautiful colour as if it excuses almost everything else . . . it does!

The **patination** is just as important as the colour — some would say even more so! It will be rich and deep showing all the signs of daily dusting, waxing and rubbing with lemon juice for the past two hundred years.

3 Thirdly, the general **condition. Originality** is the key word in this examination.

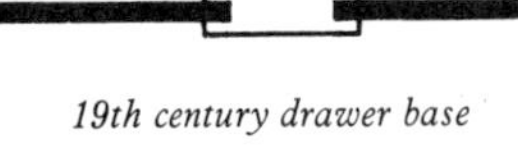

19th century drawer base

Out with the drawers, up and underneath to examine the feet, the back, sides, etc. Are all the legs and feet original? A good dealer will know where to look to see where damage is likely. Has it been less than expertly repaired? Are there any pink patches of the dreaded Honduras mahogany? Take a detailed and close look at all the areas where damage or weakness is likely to be expected.

Take special mental notes of all the dozens of little factors which go to make up the visual history of the piece.

18th century drawer base

Every piece of antique furniture is capable of expert restoration provided it is totally sympathetic. Twenty-five years ago a good dealer would not have considered buying anything that required restoration of any sort. Today, with the general shortage of stock, he may well consider buying anything of quality or with potential for restoration to its former condition.

A close examination of any drawers can often reveal a potted history of any piece of furniture. Removing a drawer is apparently the first thing that a dealer does when examining a piece. I say 'apparently' as he will have first considered the general condition, design, colour and patina of the piece before actually touching it. If it passes on all those criteria, the detailed examination follows.

This examination looks mainly at the **linings,** the drawer **construction,** the **dovetails,** the **handles,** the **runners** and the **locks.**

Drawer linings in 18th and 19th century English furniture are commonly made in oak or pine — mahogany being found only in pieces of very high quality. If other materials are found, especially teak or rosewood, the furniture was almost certainly made in the East to English order and design.

The experienced buyer will look first to see which way the **grain** runs in oak linings. Wood grain running from front to back indicates drawers made in the 17th or 18th century. In 19th century linings the grain runs from side to side. The actual drawer construction differs also between these centuries as you can see from our illustrations.

Pinned or nailed sides to drawer fronts rather than dovetails indicate construction either a) early English, b) Continental c) just poor.

The finer the **dovetail** — the better quality the construction. A gauge line down the depth of the dovetails almost certainly indicates hand rather than machine construction.

Nice little touches which can make a difference — like the original blue drawer lining paper still found intact. This should be preserved. After all, it cost the princely sum of one penny per drawer as an optional extra in the last quarter of the 18th century!

Examination of the **handles** can reveal further adventures in the life of the piece. If they are original (and not just of similar age) they will have been polished away to tissue paper thinness at the edges and bedded well into the wax surface. Do they show signs of continual polish? Are there any signs of original gilding on the handles, and have they achieved that wonderful green patina on their untouched undercut surfaces?

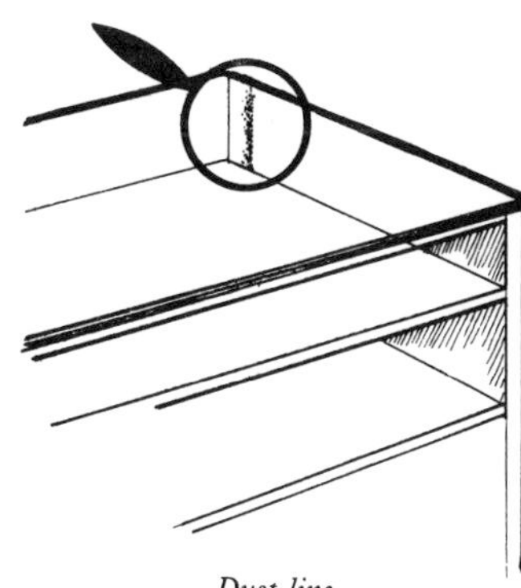

Dust line

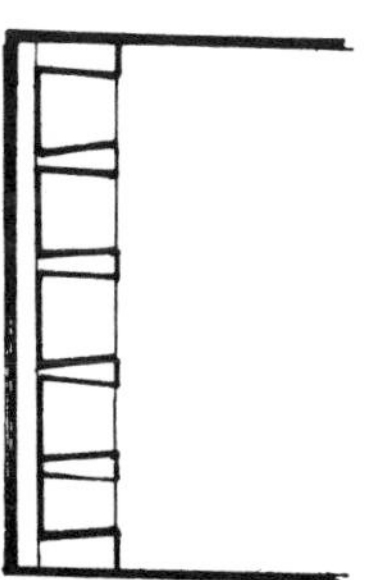

Dovetail joints with gauge line

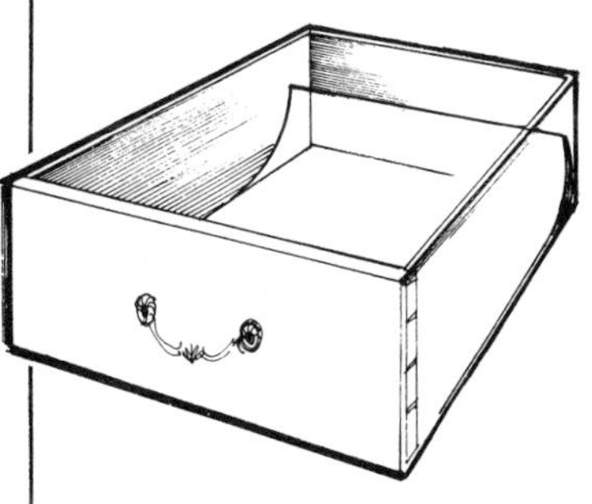

Drawer lining paper

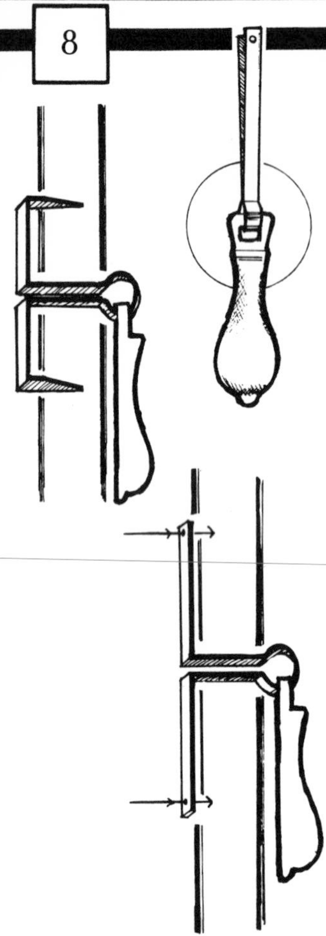

Peardrop handles with alternative fixings

Handle design can also assist to date the piece:

Pear-drop and plate rings	up to 1700
Engraved plates	1700-1720
Very plain plates	1720-1750
Swan drops	1750-1850
Rococo on very fine pieces	from 1750
Pressed brass plates	1800 onwards

Without being too dogmatic, the fussier the design, the later the manufacture. This 'rule' does not apply to rococco designs which were original only on the very highest quality pieces.

A quick look at the rear of the drawer front will show whether any holes exist from other handles. The commonest change is the addition of a large wooden knob in Victorian times with its huge wooden screw. If the Victorian addition is still in place, the original small twin holes will still be seen on either side. These were seldom disguised as the Victorians were only modernizing what to them was secondhand furniture. A quick check to see whether any rear hole matches up with a similar place on the front can be a strong clue as to whether the drawer front has been re-veneered.

It is perfectly permissible to find replaced drawer **runners.** They do become worn and were never intended to last the entire life of the piece. If they have been obviously replaced recently, it can lead the buyer on to look for other recent work or repair. If the drawer runners are in good condition you can apply a nice little test for quality. If the drawer can be easily pushed home with the light pressure of one finger on one corner only, the furniture was made by a master craftsman. Similarly, the drawer will almost certainly go in upside down! It will NOT, however, fit into any other drawer opening in the piece. Heavy use, especially with chests of drawers, can lead to damage to veneers on front rails. Damage or repair here can help to establish age.

Period lock

Victorian lock

The **locks, keys** and **escutcheons** can also play their part in the story . . . original locks always look well established and should not be disturbed. If you have a reason to remove one or more they can yield clues to dating. Many are marked with makers' names and sometimes, patent numbers or, in the case of Victorian examples, the diamond mark which can establish the actual year of manufacture. Georgian locks are frequently almost square in shape, later examples being more rectangular. Similarly, the key pins are set down lower than on later examples — just over one inch (25mm) is normal on 18th century cabinet locks.

When the (original) handles are thin pressed and embossed brass plates, you should expect to find inlaid ebony or satinwood diamond or shield shaped escutcheons. The design of the handles will not mirror the escutcheon shape, being usually round, oval or rectangular with cut corners.

Wear and tear can often be faked but there ARE signs . . . One giveaway is the sheer weight of the piece. Period English furniture made of so-called Cuban mahogany is incredibly dense and heavy. Later examples, made in Victorian times or later to Georgian designs were made in lighter weight mahogany or even in pine, stained and feathered to resemble more expensive mahogany. If the piece, chair, or whatever, is HEAVY, it's a good start.

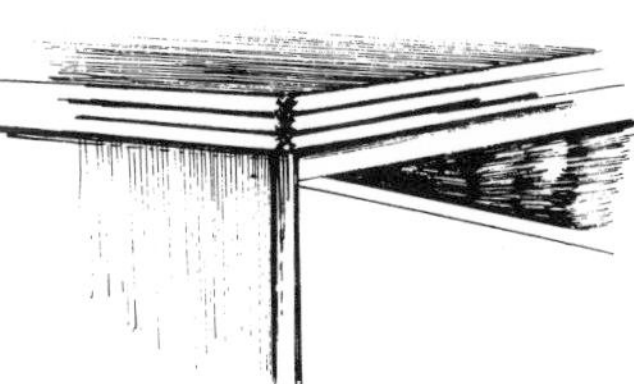

Wear and tear

FEET:

Understandably furniture **feet** do take the brunt of everyday wear and tear. Early furniture was frequently stood on bare stone-flagged floors or, at best, on uneven timber floors. Many dealers forgive replaced feet but invariably prefer the genuine article. Run your hand around the shaped edges of bracket feet — if these are really smooth the chances are that they are not original. Many restorers file and sand these underside edges to a smooth finish — originals were always left with saw marks in evidence.

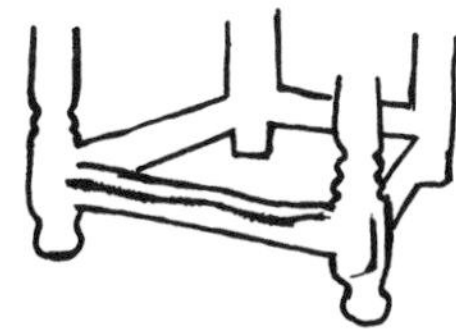

Worn stretchers

The same sentiments can also apply to original castors. Originality is a real plus.

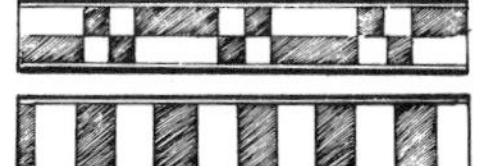

Bandings

WOODWORM

Woodworm always leaves its traces in genuine old wood and is frequently found in soft wood carcases of all old furniture and especially walnut. The grub does all the damage as he eats his way through the timber leaving a trail of tunnels in his wake. The flying insect phase is the only time the menace can spread to other furniture. They can be combated, in this stage, with special electric vapour machines, but the more usual remedy is commercial fumigation or branded liquid treatment, coloured wax filling any visible holes or, in especially bad cases, re-veneering.

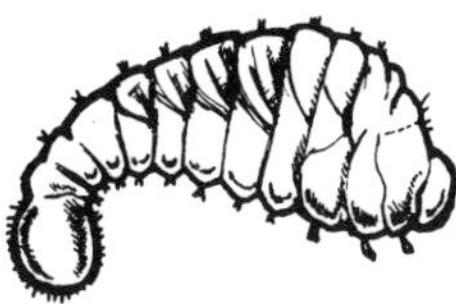

Woodworm grub

Woodworm seldom attacks mahogany, the only exception being any sapwood which was not cut away before manufacture, or through veneers as the insect escaped from the softwood carcase. Tracks and burrows will be found in the carcase under the veneer surface — if these are in the form of 'trenches' or open-topped burrows it could indicate that the wood has been planed (altered, shortened, etc.) and then reveneered.

Unless the damage caused by the worm has created basic difficulties which will need extensive restoration, woodwork traces can be tolerated and lived with. Many dealers will worry about the total lack of infestation signs rather than the opposite as a possible indication of authenticity or otherwise. Far better the traces of dead woodworm than none at all.

Flying stage

Identification Index

This index is to enable the buyer to identify a piece and the number refers to the page in this book where more information on that piece of furniture will be found.

Identification Index

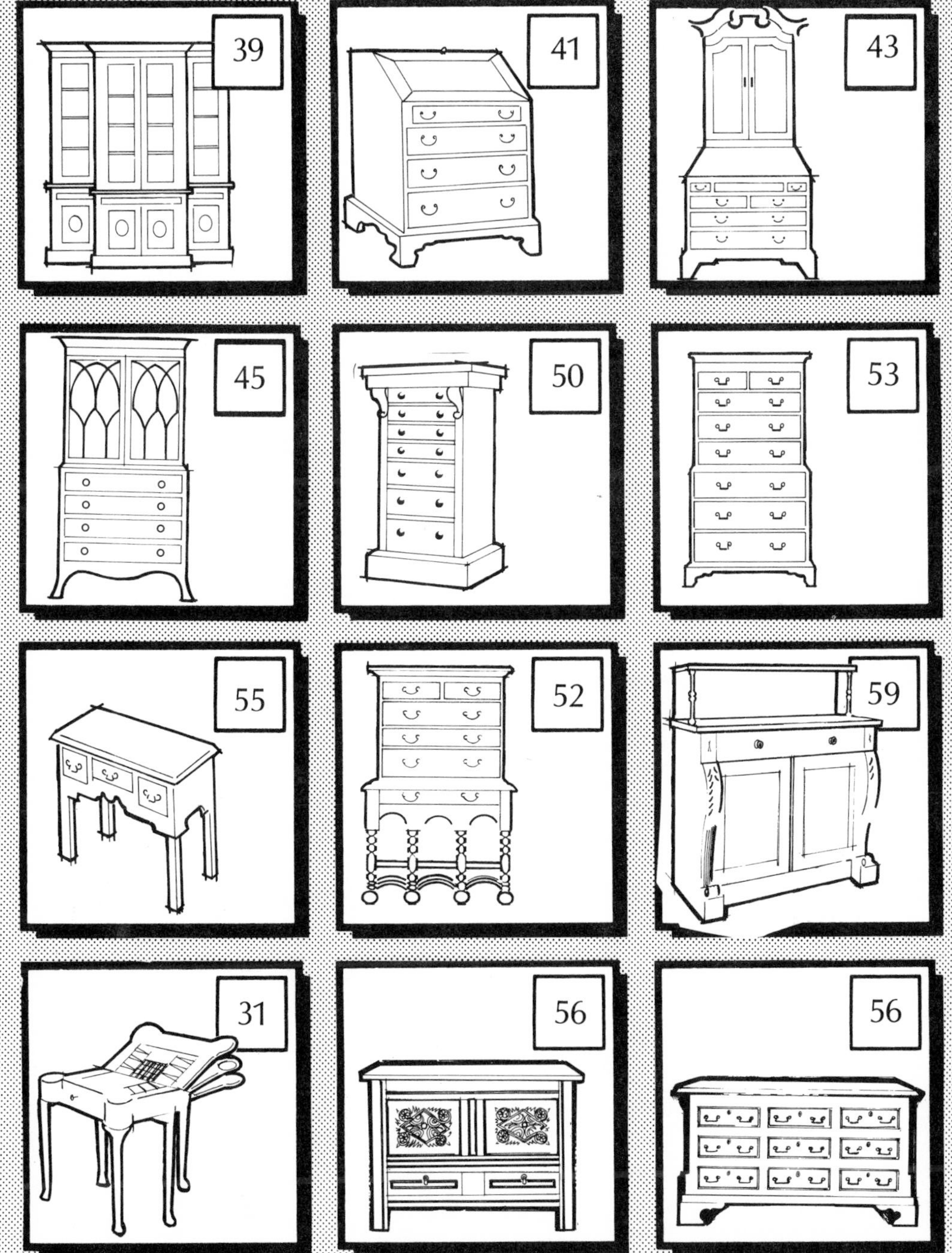

Identification Index

Identification Index

Identification Index

Identification Index

Selection of 18th century brass cabinet furniture patterns, 1750-1850.

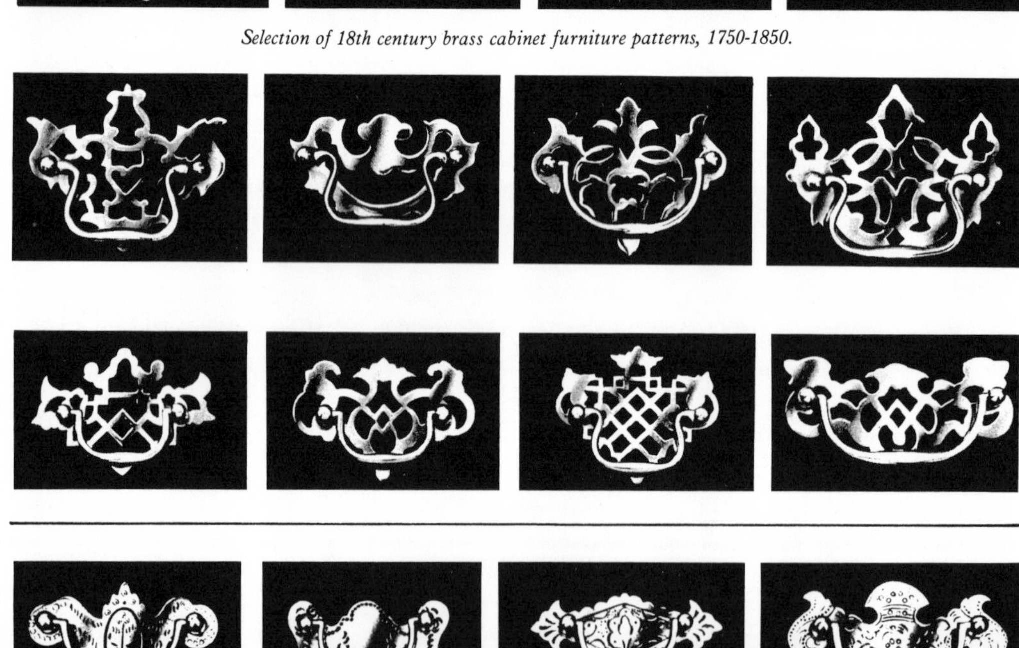

Earlier pattern, simple engraved back plates, circa 1700-1720.

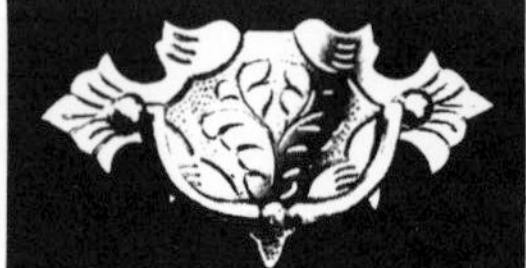

Illustrations of brassware courtesy of H. E. Savill of St. Martin's Lane, Scarborough, Yorkshire, England.

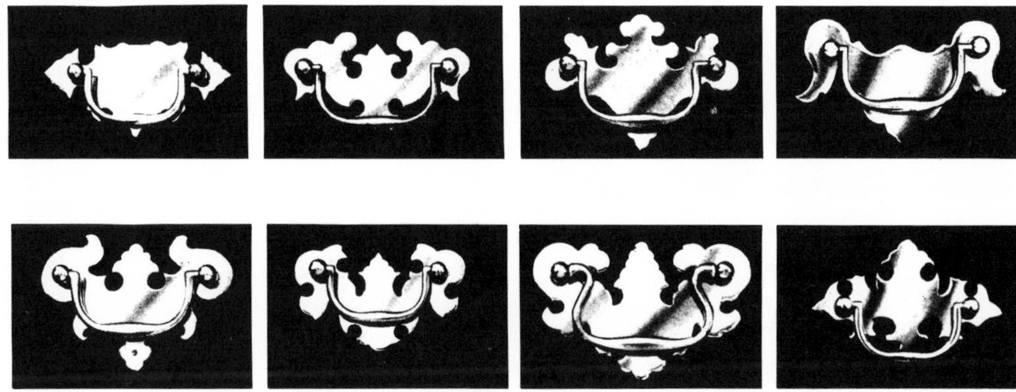

Selection of 18th century brass cabinet furniture patterns, 1750-1850.

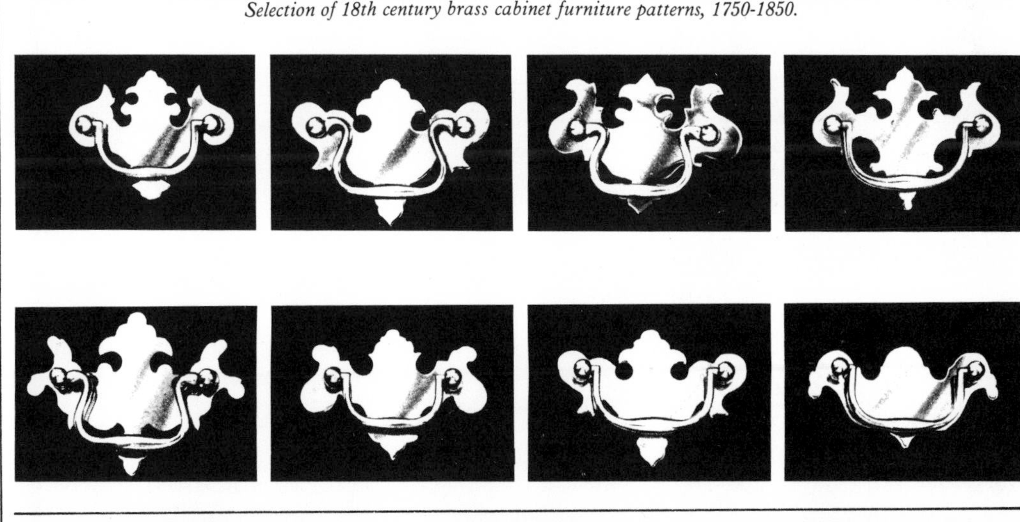

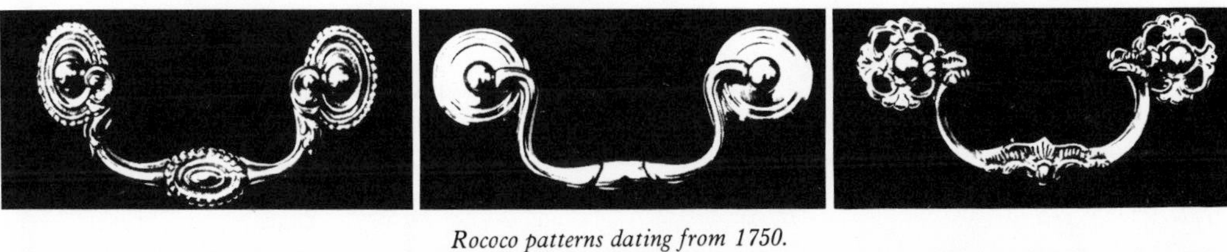

Rococo patterns dating from 1750.

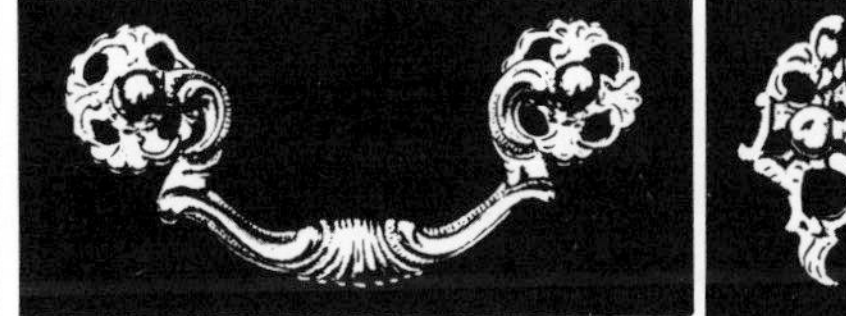

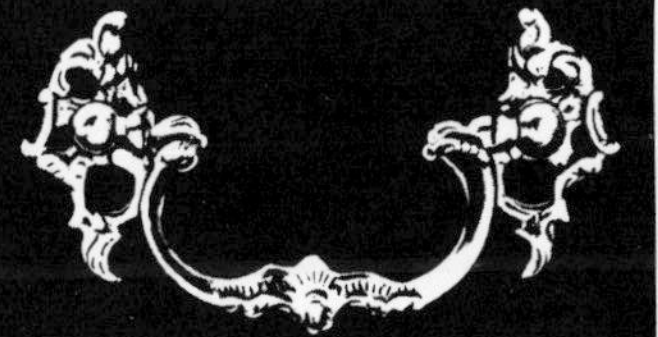

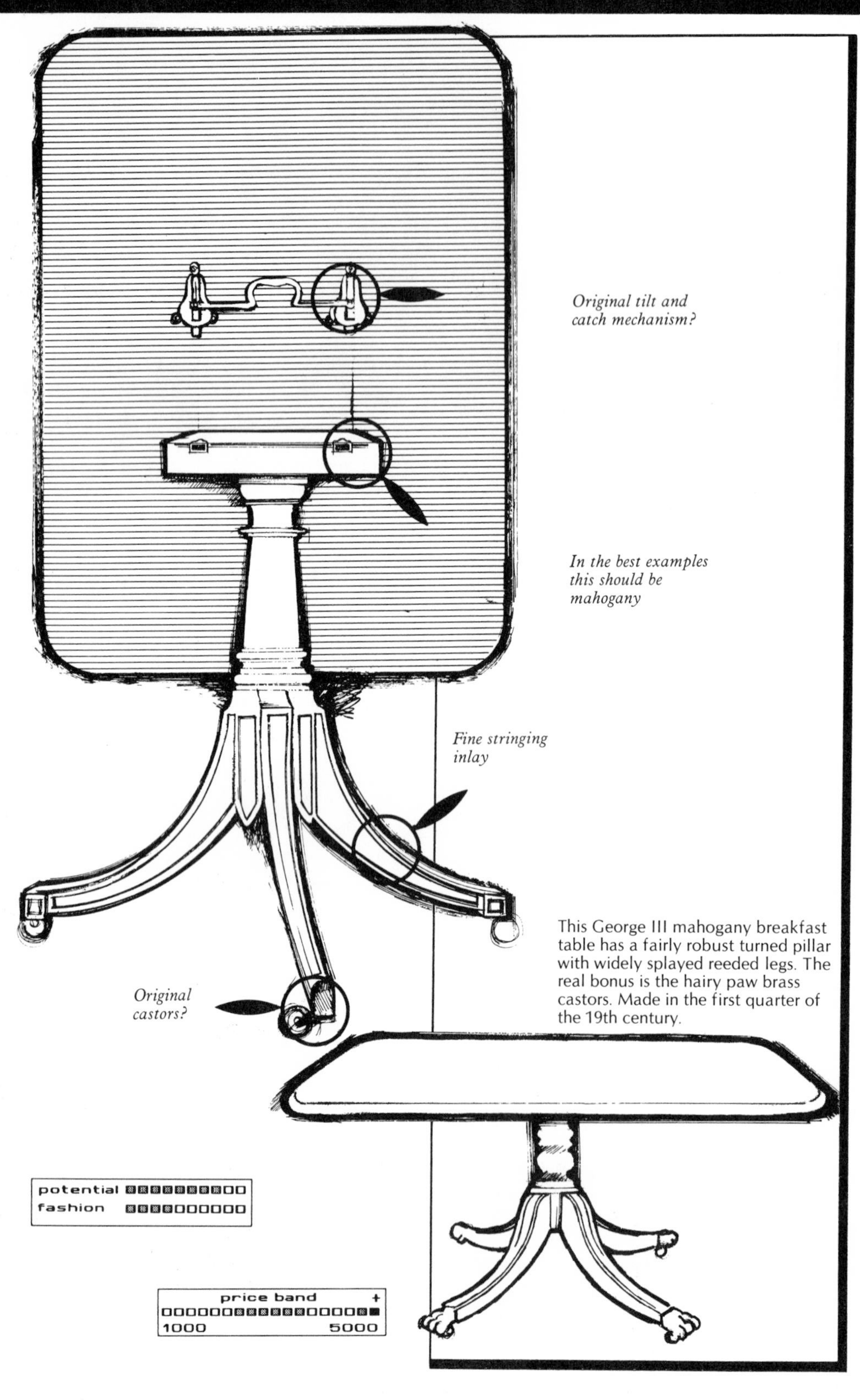

This George III mahogany breakfast table has a fairly robust turned pillar with widely splayed reeded legs. The real bonus is the hairy paw brass castors. Made in the first quarter of the 19th century.

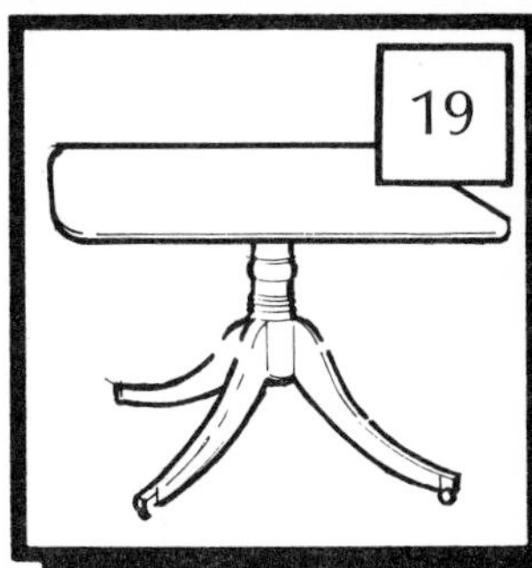

Breakfast Tables

Quick view: Essentially an elegant piece of high quality drawing room furniture.

Desirable woods: Well-figured mahogany or satinwood.

Shape: Oval, circular or rectangular — all have their particular attractions.

Restoration: No particular problems: usually a one piece top prior to veneering.

Fake?: Unlikely.

Configuration: Rectangular top with well-rounded corners, or oval with central pedestal splay legs and a tip-up top.

Decoration/inlays: Cross-banding in box, ebony, coramandel, kingwood (princess wood), or tulip wood.

Best period: 1780-1820.

Best size: The smaller the better!

Feet: Brass castors.

Features to look for: Must be of superb quality — it is not sufficient just for it to be a small dining table! Fine figuring on top is virtually essential in a good example.

Most valuable: The example in the large illustration opposite could well be the ideal Breakfast Table: small size, finely figured mahogany top with cross-banding in mahogany and coramandel and stringing in boxwood. The stem and feet are very elegant and also finely inlaid. The boxwood stringing on the legs runs down to the castors to accentuate the fine taper. Castors and all fittings are totally original and untouched.

In a word: A table for the connoisseur. This table would traditionally have found favour for an intimate breakfast in milady's bedroom.

Another early 19th century breakfast table. This example is the slightly more unusual circular shape. The pillar is turned and ends with four tapered splayed legs with brass paw castors. Much of the attraction of a table like this will depend upon the quality and matching of the veneers and crossbanding on the top.

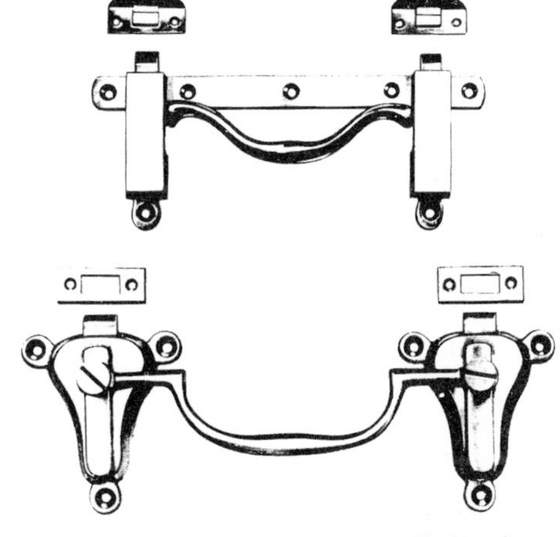

The tilt and catch mechanism usually found on breakfast tables.

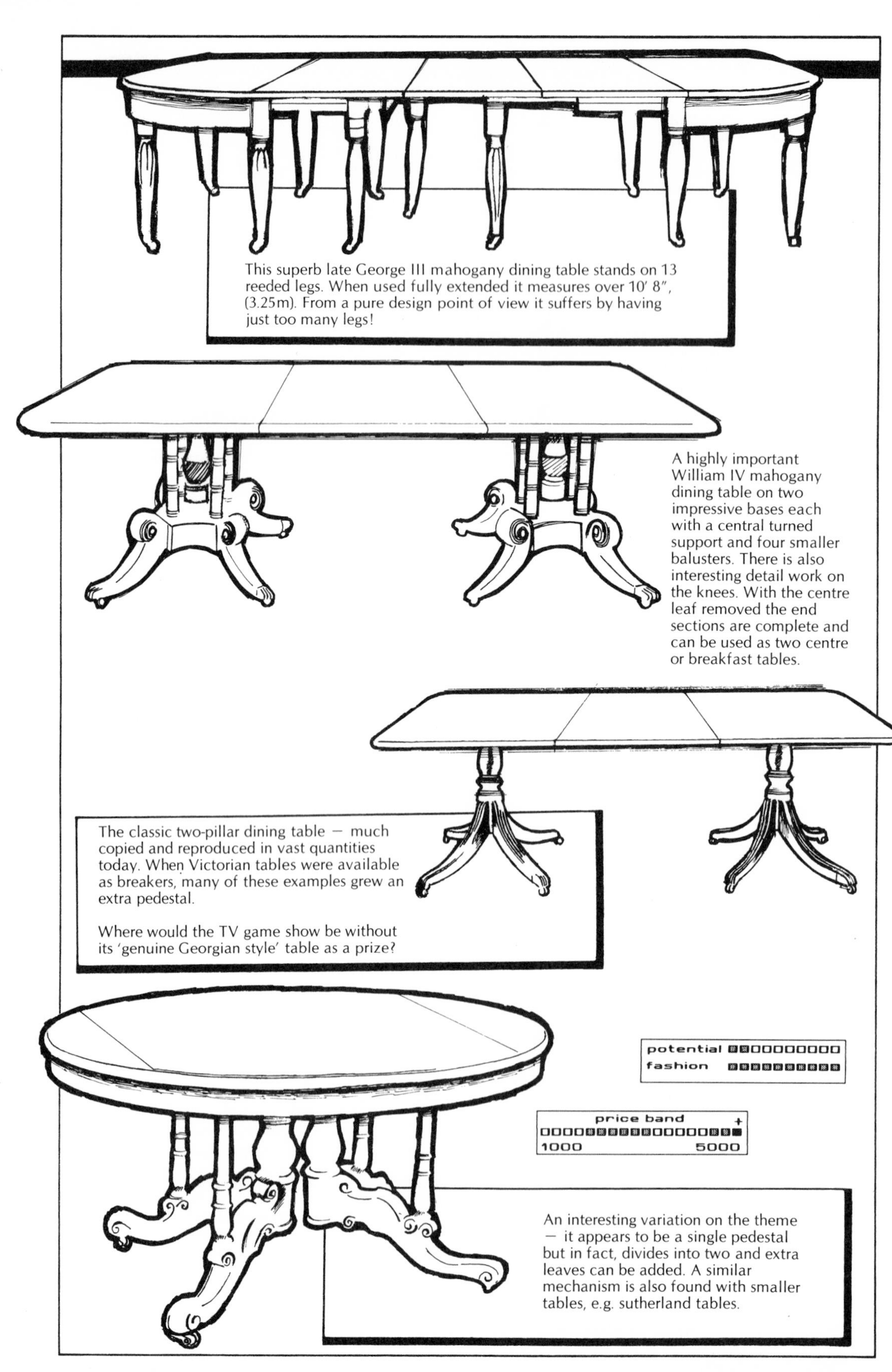

This superb late George III mahogany dining table stands on 13 reeded legs. When used fully extended it measures over 10′ 8″, (3.25m). From a pure design point of view it suffers by having just too many legs!

A highly important William IV mahogany dining table on two impressive bases each with a central turned support and four smaller balusters. There is also interesting detail work on the knees. With the centre leaf removed the end sections are complete and can be used as two centre or breakfast tables.

The classic two-pillar dining table — much copied and reproduced in vast quantities today. When Victorian tables were available as breakers, many of these examples grew an extra pedestal.

Where would the TV game show be without its 'genuine Georgian style' table as a prize?

An interesting variation on the theme — it appears to be a single pedestal but in fact, divides into two and extra leaves can be added. A similar mechanism is also found with smaller tables, e.g. sutherland tables.

Dining Tables

Desirable woods: Usually mahogany with cross-banding.

Shape: Many configurations, but usually a central rectangular section plus two rounded ends — where these can be used as complete side tables, they are referred to as 'D' ends.

Colour: Expect to find the extra leaves a very different (original unfaded) colour.

Restoration: No particular problem provided your restorer has the materials — extra leaves to replace missing examples can be very, very expensive.

Fake?: If in doubt, with a three or four pedestal table — as a last resort — weigh the pedestals — they should all be identical in weight!

Configuration: Most dining tables expand in some way, either with additional leaves (which can be stored in a special separate 'container') or semi-circular or triangular sections, as in the later so-called mechanical tables.

Decoration/inlays: Cross-banding plus carving on the base or legs.

Best period: 1750-1820.

Best size: The smaller sizes are more generally the most popular but the longest tables of quality will realize the biggest price. Most 18th century tables will be between 42″ and 48″ wide (106-121 cm); commonly the latter. If the 'period' table you are offered is only 36″ (91 cm) wide, beware. Many fakes were commonly made narrow to satisfy the demand from smaller homes.

Most valuable: Of the pedestal dining tables, the most valuable and therefore sought after are the three or four pillar examples. The vast majority of these however have been 'improved' in the recent past from more common two pillar examples. There was virtually a cottage industry adding extra pedestals during the 1950's and 60's when period and Victorian mahogany was available in large quantities. Since that time the extra pedestals have matured somewhat and are hard to distinguish.

In a word (or two): Short of eating off your knee — what alternative have you?

The oak drop-leaf dining table. Reproduced and faked in great numbers today and in the past. Look for especially small or especially large examples! If the table is capable of seating twelve people this is a bonus. Look also for a 'double gate' — that is to say, rather than one leg swinging up to support each flap, there would be two on each side.

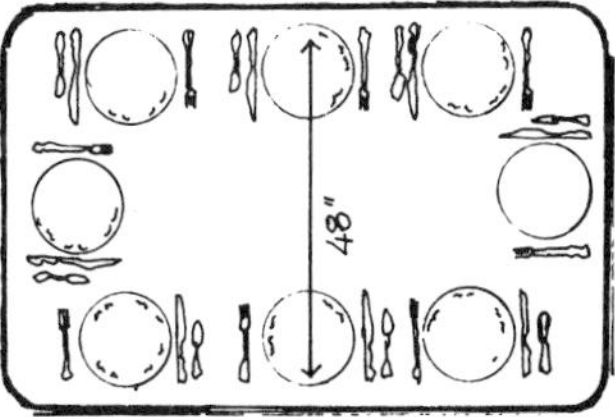

Period dining tables from the 18th century are usually about 48″ wide to allow for table decoration, etc., in the centre. Sheraton says "When they are but 3′ wide, being occupied on both sides, there is no space left in the centre for dishes." Beware of fashionably narrow twin pedestal dining tables about 36″ wide.

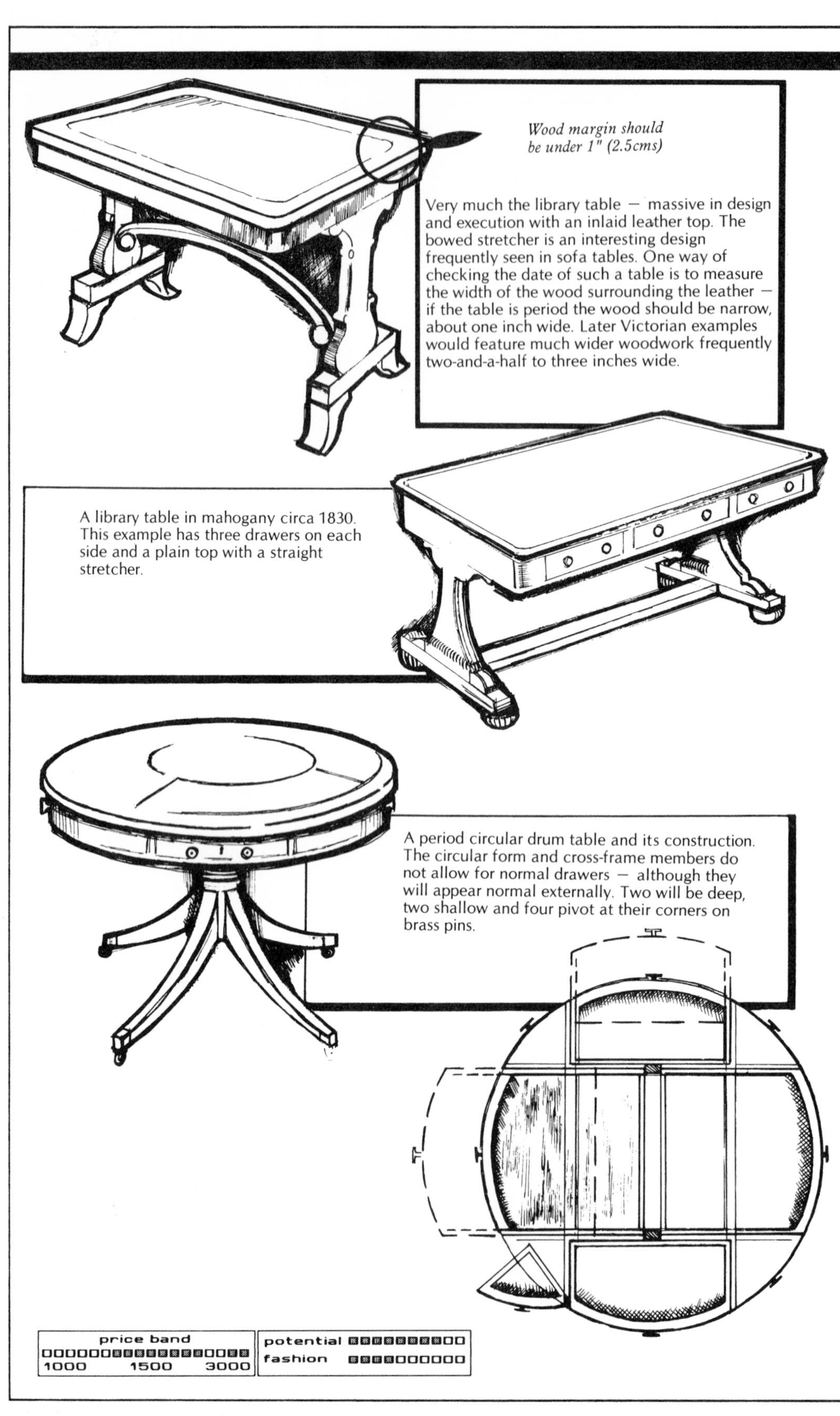

Very much the library table — massive in design and execution with an inlaid leather top. The bowed stretcher is an interesting design frequently seen in sofa tables. One way of checking the date of such a table is to measure the width of the wood surrounding the leather — if the table is period the wood should be narrow, about one inch wide. Later Victorian examples would feature much wider woodwork frequently two-and-a-half to three inches wide.

A library table in mahogany circa 1830. This example has three drawers on each side and a plain top with a straight stretcher.

A period circular drum table and its construction. The circular form and cross-frame members do not allow for normal drawers — although they will appear normal externally. Two will be deep, two shallow and four pivot at their corners on brass pins.

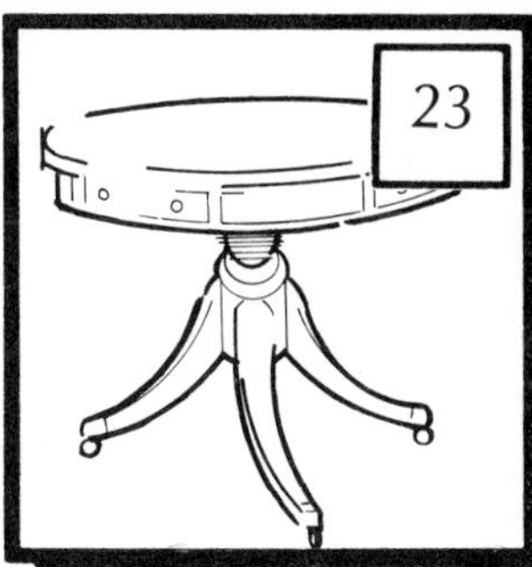

Library & Centre Tables

Quick view: A centre table or library table should look important, and possibly masculine. They usually feature a large circular or rectangular top on a very substantial base. Two especially interesting varieties are the **Rent table,** which has a deep circular top with numbered or labelled drawers on a heavy base, and the **Drum table,** which is similar but much finer and lighter, with a central pedestal and splay legs.

Restoration: Look for heavy wear around drawers. Pine cross-frames can shrink causing problems with cross-banding.

Fake?: Unlikely.

Decoration/inlays: Rent tables are usually in mahogany with cross-banding. Drum tables are also most common in mahogany; however fine examples are sometimes made in satinwood.

Best period: 1750-1840.

Best size: With rent tables, the larger are more important. Conversely a smaller, more elegant drum table would command a premium price.

Features to look for: Original leather work; legitimate provenance for a rent table — it's nice to know who the tenants paid their dues to! Wilfred Bull, the Essex dealer, offered a drum table in 1976 which featured small slotted brass plates inscribed 'Answered', 'Unanswered', 'Bills', 'Receipts' (c. 1765).

Interiors/drawers: The drawer configuration can be very interesting and is unique to these tables. Due to their circular construction eight normal drawers are impossible — the norm is to have only four, and the other four look identical but actually pivot from one front corner.

In a word (or two): The rent table is frequently not a visually attractive piece of furniture but always commands a high price today because of its rarity. There was, after all, only one in each large house.

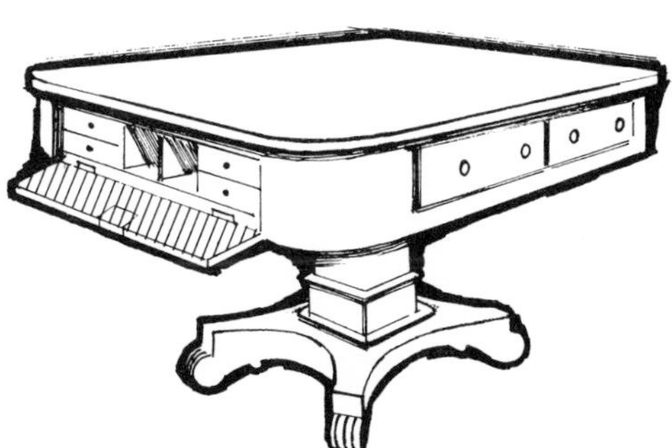

A very unusual mahogany George IV rent table sitting on a massive square section pedestal, on a relatively out-of-proportion platform base. The false drawer fronts drop down to reveal 'pigeon holes' and drawers with boxwood knobs.

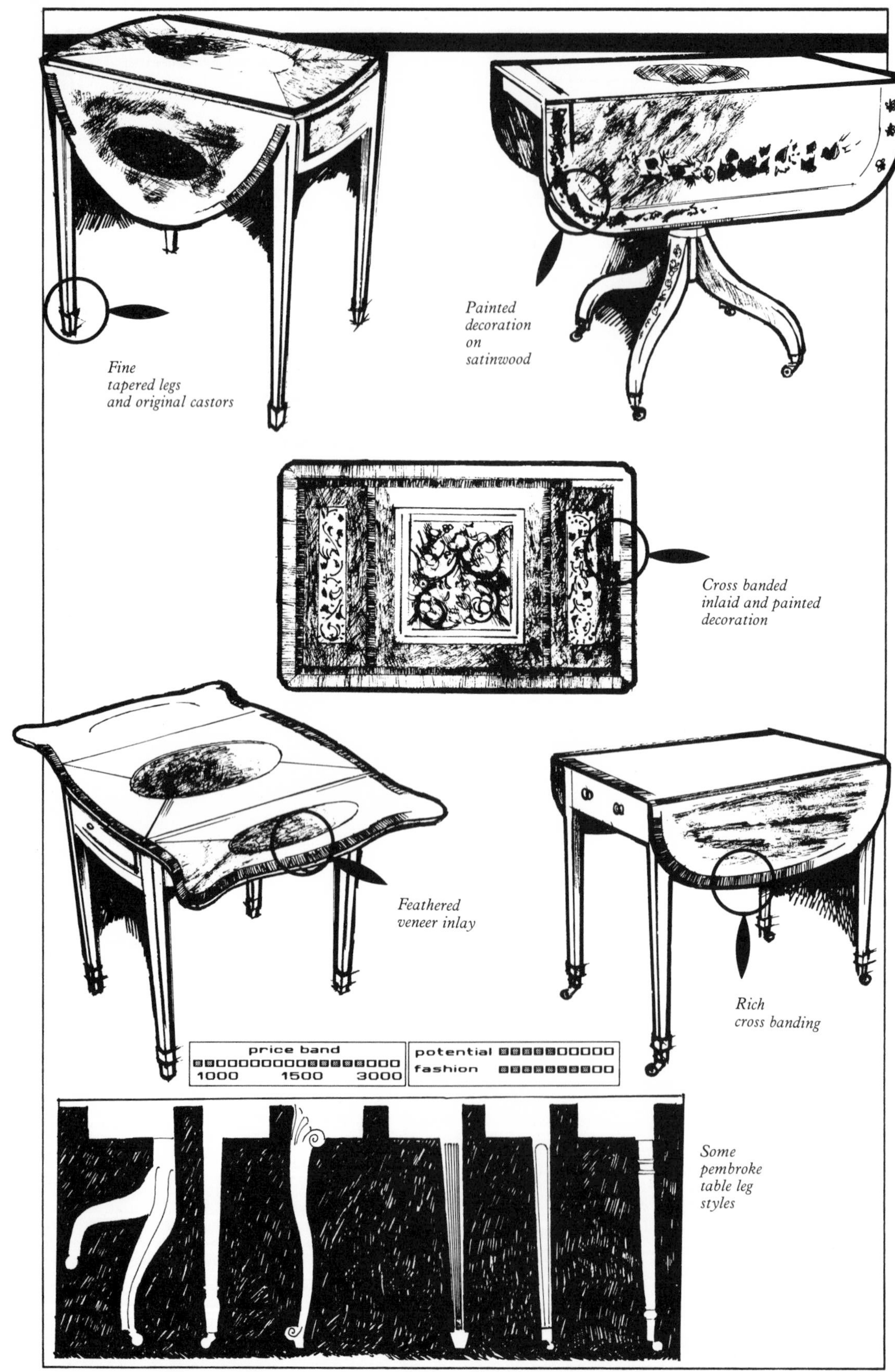
Fine
tapered legs
and original castors
Painted
decoration
on
satinwood
Cross banded
inlaid and painted
decoration
Feathered
veneer inlay
Rich
cross banding
price band
1000
1500
3000
potential
fashion
Some
pembroke
table leg
styles

Pembroke Tables

Quick view: A table, usually quite fine and small, with two leaves on both long sides of the top.

Desirable woods: Mahogany or satinwood.

Shape: Various, including circular, oval, square and rectangular and the so-called 'butterfly' pembroke which has leaves shaped rather like butterfly's wings.

Restoration: Look for Edwardian painted decoration on earlier, rather plain examples.

Fake?: The enormous prices commanded by all superior pembroke tables must attract the attention of the faker.

Configuration: Two leaves along long sides of the top, on a wide variety of supports.

Decoration/inlays: Decoration in every possible material and permutation is found, including cross-banding, marquetry, shaped veneer panels and hand painting, particularly on satinwood.

Best size: Small is beautiful!

Feet: Original castors?

Features to look for: Sheer quality of workmanship and design.

Interiors/drawers: Generally one drawer in one end, with a 'dummy' at the other.

Most Valuable: The so-called 'harlequin pembroke' which has a concealed, box-like compartment of drawers built into the top rising on counterweights.

In a word (or two): The consummate small high quality table — the delight of the purist. The pembroke is usually also an extremely useful size in the modern home. They can, however, vary from the very fine to the very ordinary.

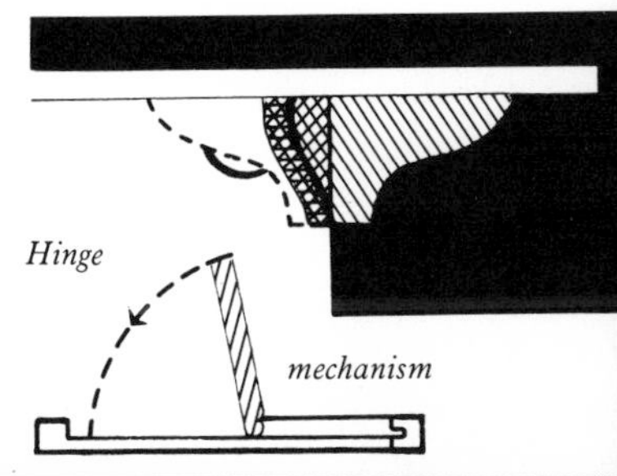

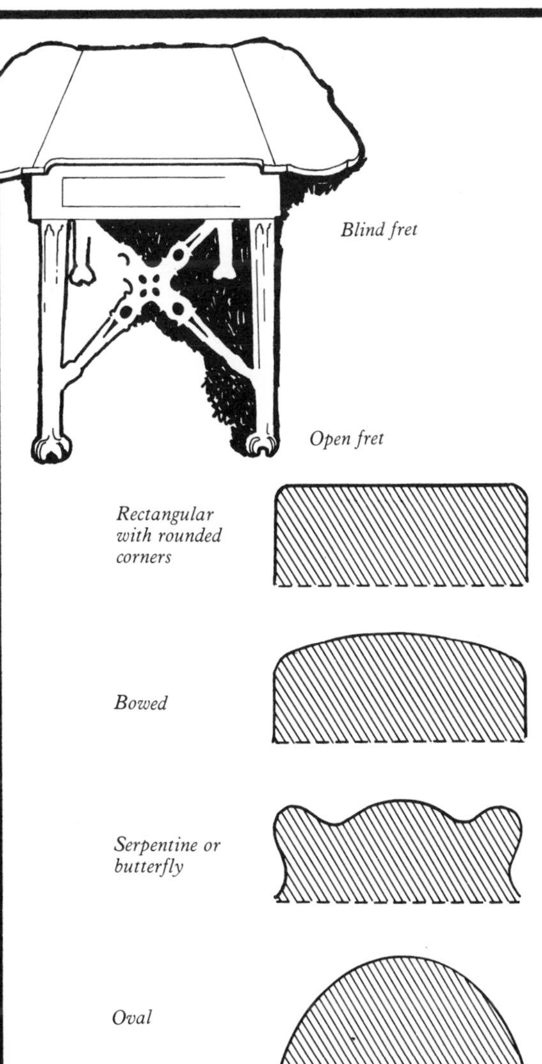

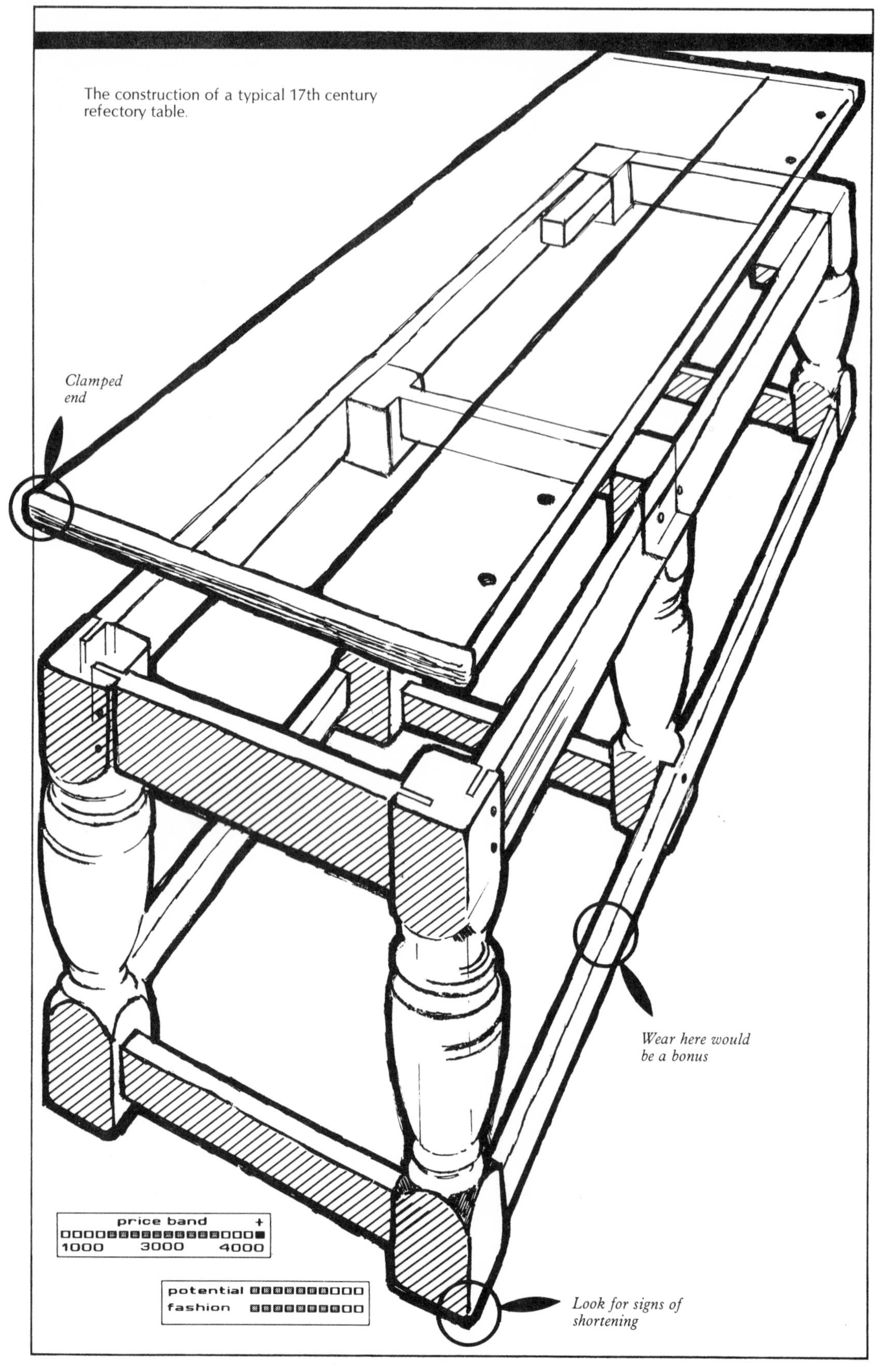

The construction of a typical 17th century refectory table.

Refectory Tables

Quick view: A long dining table which should show the signs that history has been actually created around it.

Best woods: Must be oak to be English! Fruitwood examples seen today are imported from France and Scandinavia; walnut examples have been imported in the past from Spain and Italy.

Restoration: Early oak should not be restored unless absolutely essential. Worm can be a problem with the sapwood in oak and very frequently in walnut.

Fake?: Highly likely and not only recently! Refectory tables were produced in England in large quantities by Dutch craftsmen at the beginning of the 20th century when they were very highly prized and priced.

Configuration: Top in three or four planks; decorated baluster legs and nicely worn stretchers or cross-rail — the construction all joined by pegs, not glue.

Colour: Colour is important. Look for the colour of the oak under the polish. If the oak is old it will be dark — if it's new it will be light, (the older the oak the darker and browner it gets.) New oak can be darkened by fuming with ammonia which makes it grey coloured.

Features to look for: Genuine wear. Wonderful patination — you can't fake this!

Most valuable: the bigger, longer and most original — the higher the price.

Oddities: Look for a hole in each corner of the top. This might indicate that the top was originally used on board a warship — it would have been slung from above to counter the rolling of the vessel.

In a word (or two): Not for the amateur if the price tag is high — take along a real expert in old oak.

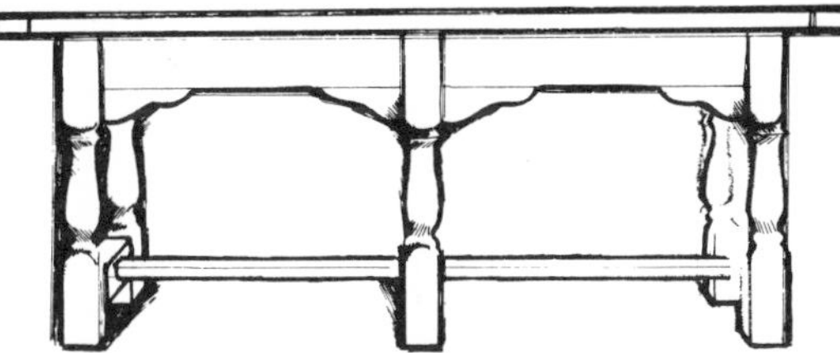

Simple 17th cent. refectory table with shaped apron sides, turned legs and single stretcher.

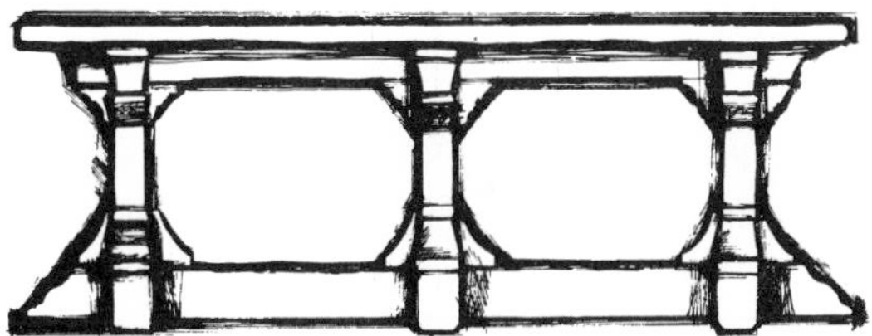

A dramatic late 17th century oak refectory table with a three plank top. The six-legged supporting frame is in the Gothic style. Circa 1680.

A simpler, although classic, 17th century oak refectory table. The oak three plank top has clamped ends. Four turned legs and plain frame and stretchers, circa 1680.

A refectory table made in oak in the late 17th century with carved frieze on four baluster turned legs.

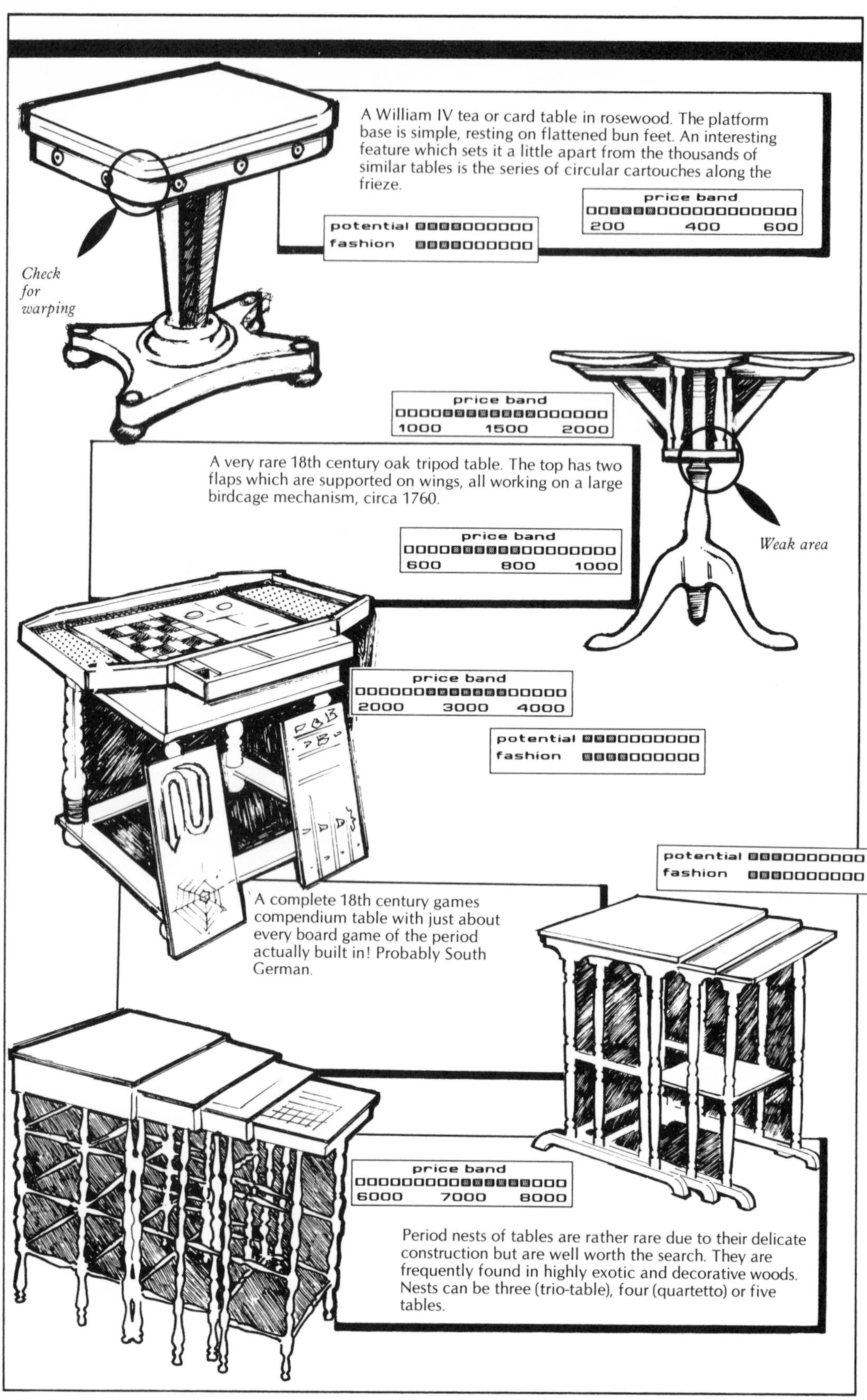

A William IV tea or card table in rosewood. The platform base is simple, resting on flattened bun feet. An interesting feature which sets it a little apart from the thousands of similar tables is the series of circular cartouches along the frieze.

A very rare 18th century oak tripod table. The top has two flaps which are supported on wings, all working on a large birdcage mechanism, circa 1760.

A complete 18th century games compendium table with just about every board game of the period actually built in! Probably South German.

Period nests of tables are rather rare due to their delicate construction but are well worth the search. They are frequently found in highly exotic and decorative woods. Nests can be three (trio-table), four (quartetto) or five tables.

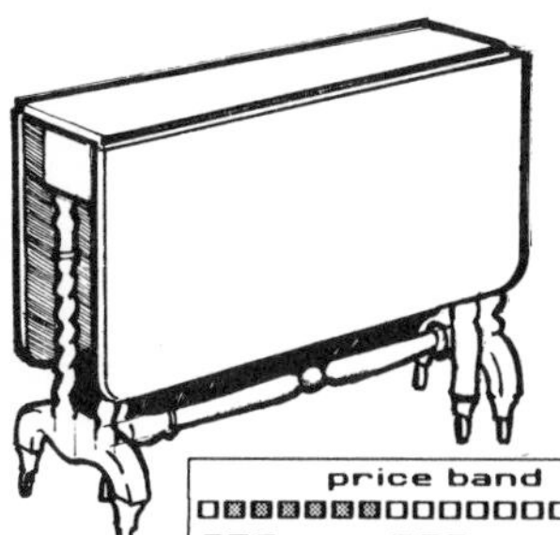

The sutherland table is the most useful of small tables. It s proportionally large leaves fold down into a very small area and take up very little room. Despite these obvious advantages it is not highly valued. Mostly in mahogany. Usually Victorian.

price band		
□■■■■■■□□□□□□□□□□□		
250	500	750

potential	■■■■■■■□□□
fashion	■■■□□□□□□□

A Miscellany of Tables

price band		
□□■■■■■□□□□□□□□□□□		
2000	2500	3000

A William and Mary side table in oak with especially fine turned baluster legs and curved X stretchers, circa 1680.

potential	■■■■□□□□□□
fashion	■■■■■■■□□□

Original bun feet?

A highly important William and Mary side table in oyster-veneered olivewood.

price band		
□□□□■■■■■□□□□□□□□□		
3000	3500	4000

potential	■■■■■□□□□□
fashion	■■■■■■■□□□

Look for thick knife-cut veneers

A small (only 28″ long) William and Mary walnut side table with a fold-over flap top supported by a rare gate-leg action, circa 1690.

price band		
□□□□□□□□□□■■■■■■□□		
6000	8000	10000

potential	■■■□□□□□□□
fashion	■■■■■■■□□□

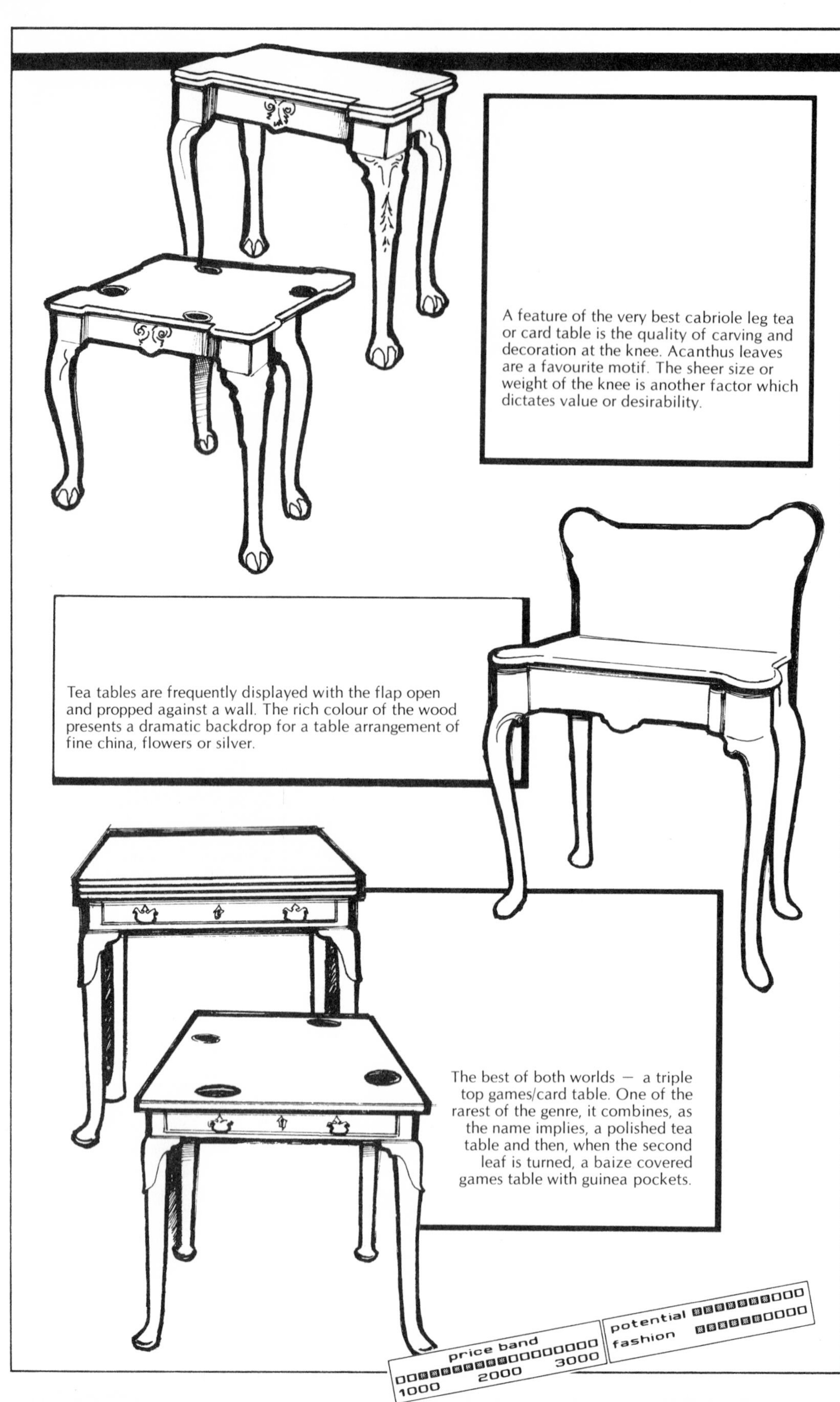

A feature of the very best cabriole leg tea or card table is the quality of carving and decoration at the knee. Acanthus leaves are a favourite motif. The sheer size or weight of the knee is another factor which dictates value or desirability.

Tea tables are frequently displayed with the flap open and propped against a wall. The rich colour of the wood presents a dramatic backdrop for a table arrangement of fine china, flowers or silver.

The best of both worlds — a triple top games/card table. One of the rarest of the genre, it combines, as the name implies, a polished tea table and then, when the second leaf is turned, a baize covered games table with guinea pockets.

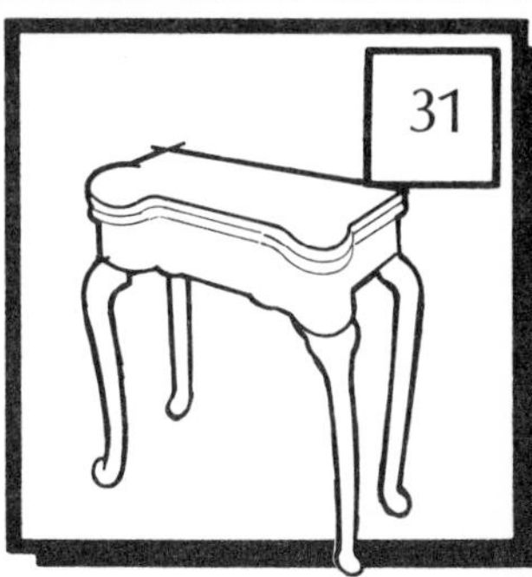

Card & Tea Tables

Desirable woods: Mahogany and Rosewood, plus exotic woods,

Shape: Rectangular or half-round (demi-lune).

Hinges: The hinge on the pivoting leg is known in the trade as a 'finger' or 'knuckle joint' hinge.

Fake?: Unlikely.

Decoration/inlays: Brass inlays in some fine Regency rosewood examples.

Best period: 1775-1820.

Construction, restoration: Biggest problem is the completely missing leaf. In oval tables frames are laminated to give strength then shaped — these can sometimes crack. Bridle joints at top of legs are weak points and crack away from frame. Satinwood legs are made in beech and then veneered. Mahogany examples were usually solid — although not always. Twisted tops can also be a problem due to cracking and warping of pine frame. Pivot legs in beech are liable to have been enjoyed by wood worm! The fine tapered legs ending in spade feet, inlaid with box to exaggerate taper, are delicate and may have been damaged and poorly repaired in the past.

Features to look for: Fine figured veneers, cross-banding or inlaid decoration. Guinea pockets and candle slides on card tables would be a plus. Expect to find the top of a tea table, when opened, a much darker and un-faded colour.

Potential: Fine bases with damaged or missing tops have been known to grow into sofa tables!

Most valuable: Finer varieties sometimes found in pairs. The most valuable are, perhaps, satinwood examples with fan inlays or painted decoration.

Oddities: 'Triple tops' — a rare variety with, as the name suggests, three folding tops (games/card/tea) are the tops!

In a word (or two): Can vary from the superb to the virtual rubbish. Most card and tea tables have been well used and may well have suffered as a consequence.

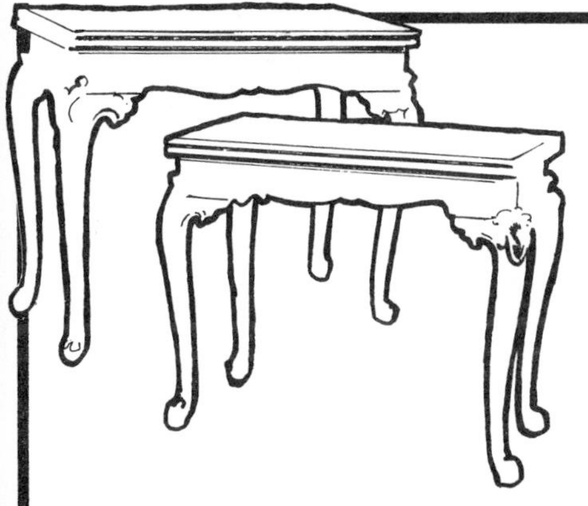

The best card or tea tables were made in matched pairs. If these survive together to the present day, they will represent an added value well in excess of double the individual price.

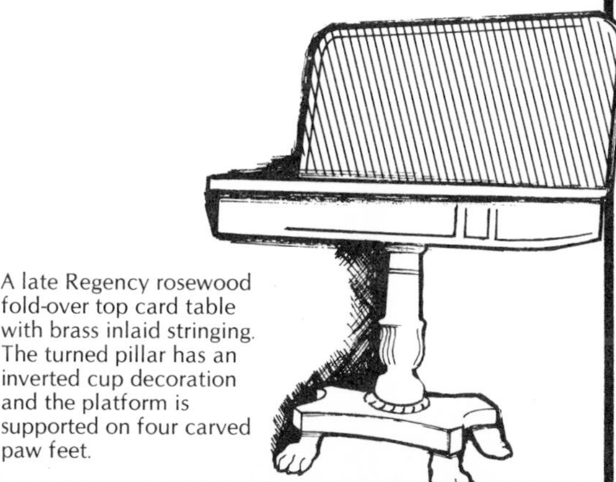

A late Regency rosewood fold-over top card table with brass inlaid stringing. The turned pillar has an inverted cup decoration and the platform is supported on four carved paw feet.

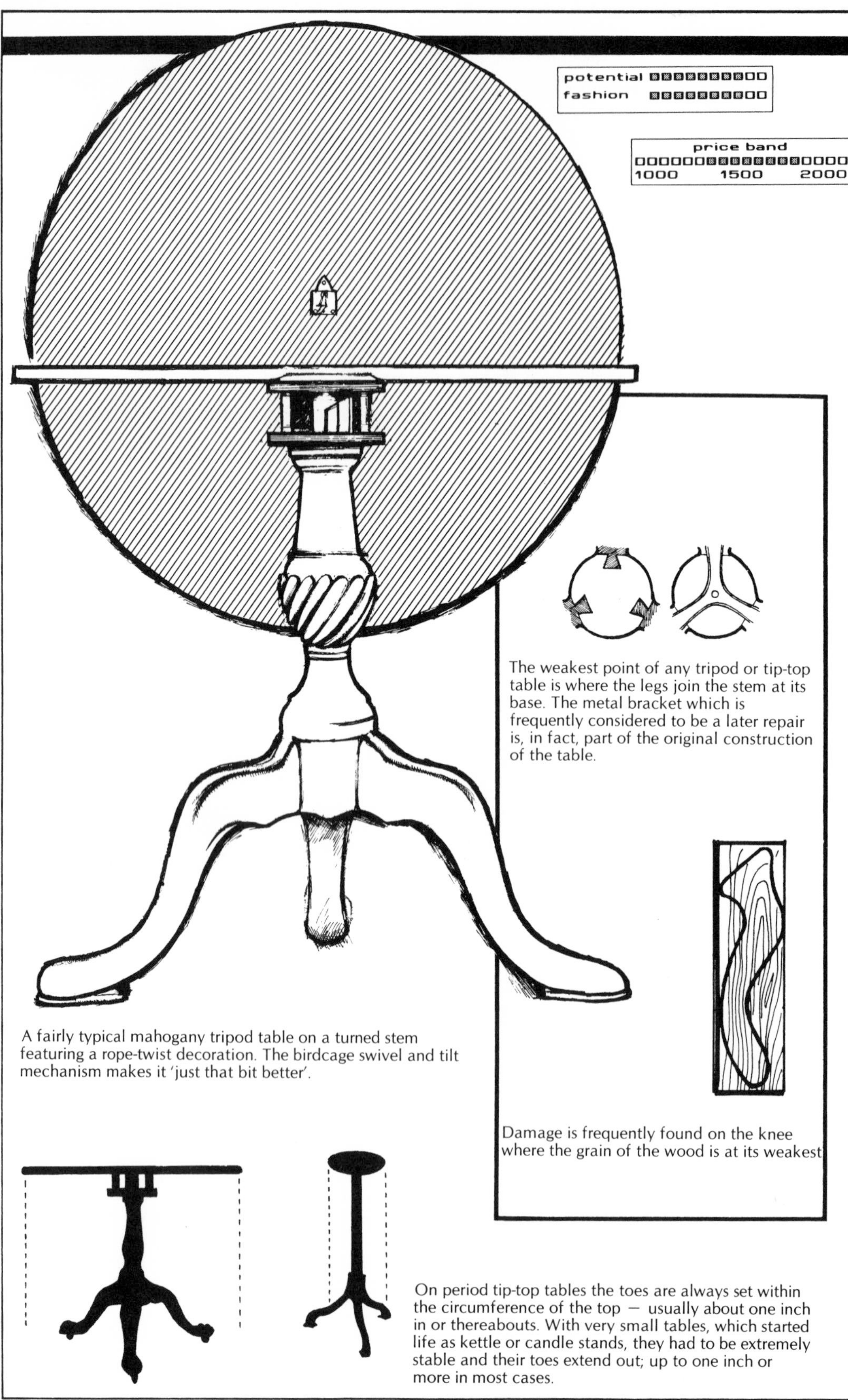

The weakest point of any tripod or tip-top table is where the legs join the stem at its base. The metal bracket which is frequently considered to be a later repair is, in fact, part of the original construction of the table.

A fairly typical mahogany tripod table on a turned stem featuring a rope-twist decoration. The birdcage swivel and tilt mechanism makes it 'just that bit better'.

Damage is frequently found on the knee where the grain of the wood is at its weakest

On period tip-top tables the toes are always set within the circumference of the top — usually about one inch in or thereabouts. With very small tables, which started life as kettle or candle stands, they had to be extremely stable and their toes extend out; up to one inch or more in most cases.

Tripod Tables

Quick view: Circular tip-up, stem and three splay feet.

Desirable woods: Oak tables are perhaps the commonest 'country' tables, but heavy cuban mahogany may well be the most desirable — although fruitwood or yew examples would certainly be well contested at auction.

Restoration: Main problem areas:
a) at the foot of stem the legs may have broken away at their dove-tail joints into the stem. This area may have been strengthened by a tri-form metal plate. This plate was almost certainly fitted as part of the original construction and not, as commonly thought, a later repair addition.
b) break at the swan neck portion of the leg, just above the foot, where the grain of the wood is at its weakest point — this is especially difficult to restore.

Fake?: Many pie-crust top tripod tables are fakes. The stem may be genuine but the top may have been re-worked from an older example, the carved 'pie-crust' added. This carved or dished top should have been made from a solid piece — look to see if extra wood has been added to allow this carving to take place latter. The more important of the genuine Chippendale designs were enthusiastically copied in the later quarter of the 19th century and these will now be quite patinated and used, and will be very difficult to detect; always look for traces of indentation or wear where the block at the head of the stem meets the top.

Best stem: The simple and classic 'Cannon Barrel' which looks, as you might suppose, like a cannon barrel, or the carved baluster.

Best top: Dished, pie-crust, galleried with fret work or finely turned spindles; plain.

Features to look for: Birdcage mechanism on swivel — tip-up top tables. This desirable feature consists of two platforms, divided by four short turned pillars, joined to the stem by a wooden wedge. On the best quality tables the four birdcage pillars should mirror the design of the main stem.

Most valuable: A genuine pie-crust or supper table.

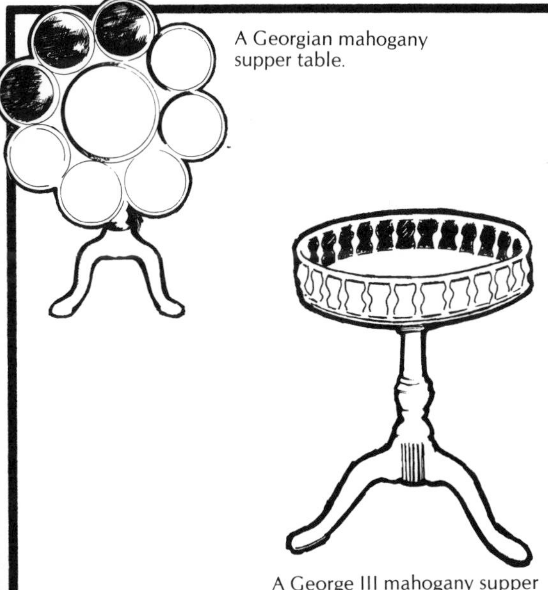

A Georgian mahogany supper table.

A George III mahogany supper table with a turned-pillar gallery on a rope-twist stem with three splayed legs.

Detail of the birdcage mechanism which allows the top to turn and swivel. Some authorities contend that the pillars in the birdcage should be a mirror image of the main table stem.

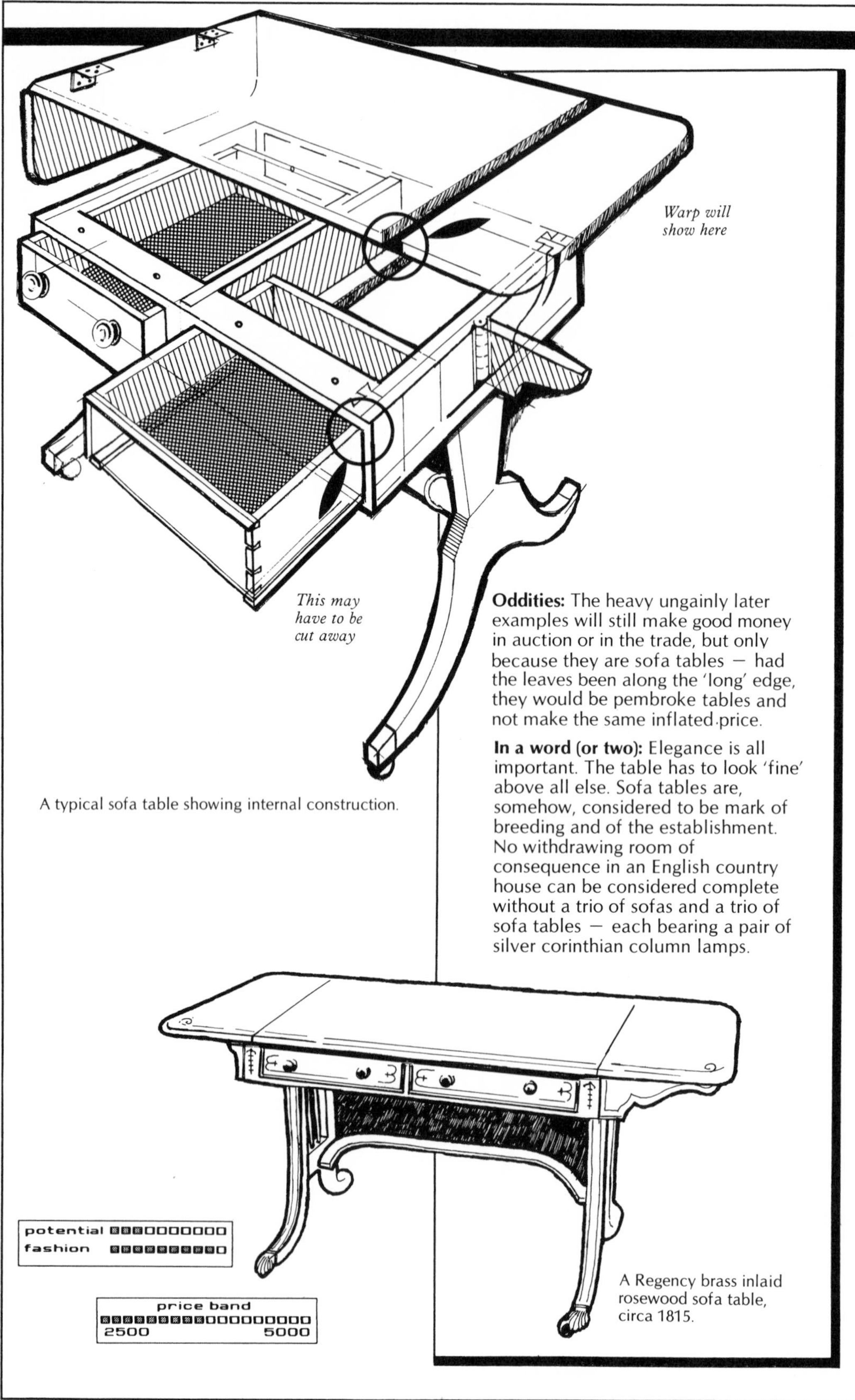

A typical sofa table showing internal construction.

Oddities: The heavy ungainly later examples will still make good money in auction or in the trade, but only because they are sofa tables — had the leaves been along the 'long' edge, they would be pembroke tables and not make the same inflated price.

In a word (or two): Elegance is all important. The table has to look 'fine' above all else. Sofa tables are, somehow, considered to be mark of breeding and of the establishment. No withdrawing room of consequence in an English country house can be considered complete without a trio of sofas and a trio of sofa tables — each bearing a pair of silver corinthian column lamps.

A Regency brass inlaid rosewood sofa table, circa 1815.

Sofa Tables

Quick view: A table specifically designed to stand behind a sofa. Consists of a base, top and drop-leaves at either end. Compared to other tables of the same period, of similar construction, size, etc., the sofa table is one of the highest valued.

Best woods: Mahogany and (later) rosewood plus a whole host of really exotic woods.

Shape: The top is always the same basic shape.

Restoration: Problems can arise with tops. The basic top construction is usually in three or four pieces of timber with veneers. If the frame timber was unseasoned* it will create shrinkage which splits the veneer. The biggest difficulty arises when this shrinkage causes the leaves to splay outwards from their normal horizontal position. This shrinkage can be caused by central heating or just standing the table in direct sunlight. The fault is difficult to correct as it means shaving away timber from the frame — not always possible if there is decoration, brass inlay, etc., present.

Fake?: Very possible because of this table's high value.

Configuration: The sofa table is derived from the pembroke table — which differs in having its two leaves on the long sides of the top.

Decoration/inays: Inlays of almost every colour and complexity are found in these tables. Brass inlays are common (usually in Regency rosewood examples) and very desirable.

Best period: 1780-1820: the age of English elegance.

Best size: Look for a relatively narrow top — later examples sometimes tended to be rather broad of beam and heavy, and are less prized.

Features to look for: Fine workmanship, fine woods, fine inlays and stringing, — above all fine design.

Interiors/drawers: Usually two opening, two false. Some examples have built-in writing surfaces or compartments.

Most valuable: Probably a sofa table in a really exotic wood — zebra wood, perhaps.

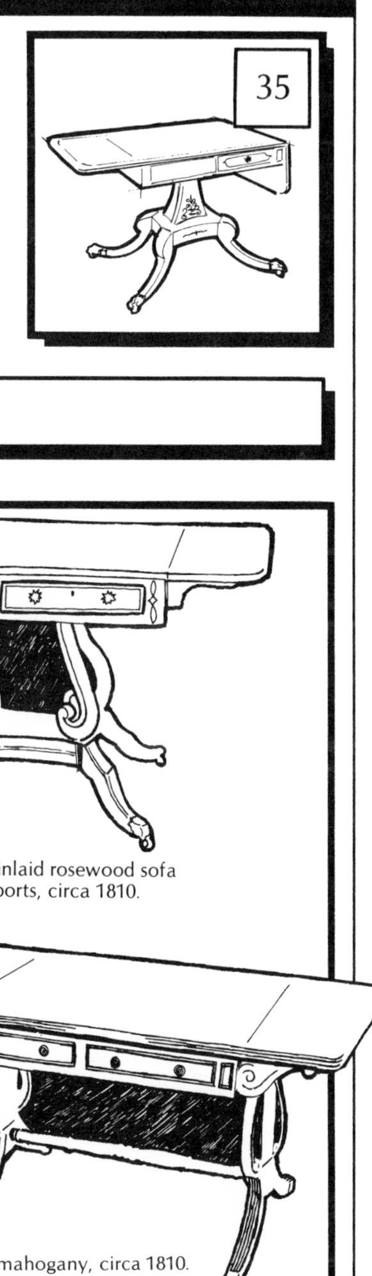

A Regency brass inlaid rosewood sofa table on lyre supports, circa 1810.

A Regency sofa table in mahogany, circa 1810.

Regency sofa table in mahogany with an elaborate and interesting pedestal.

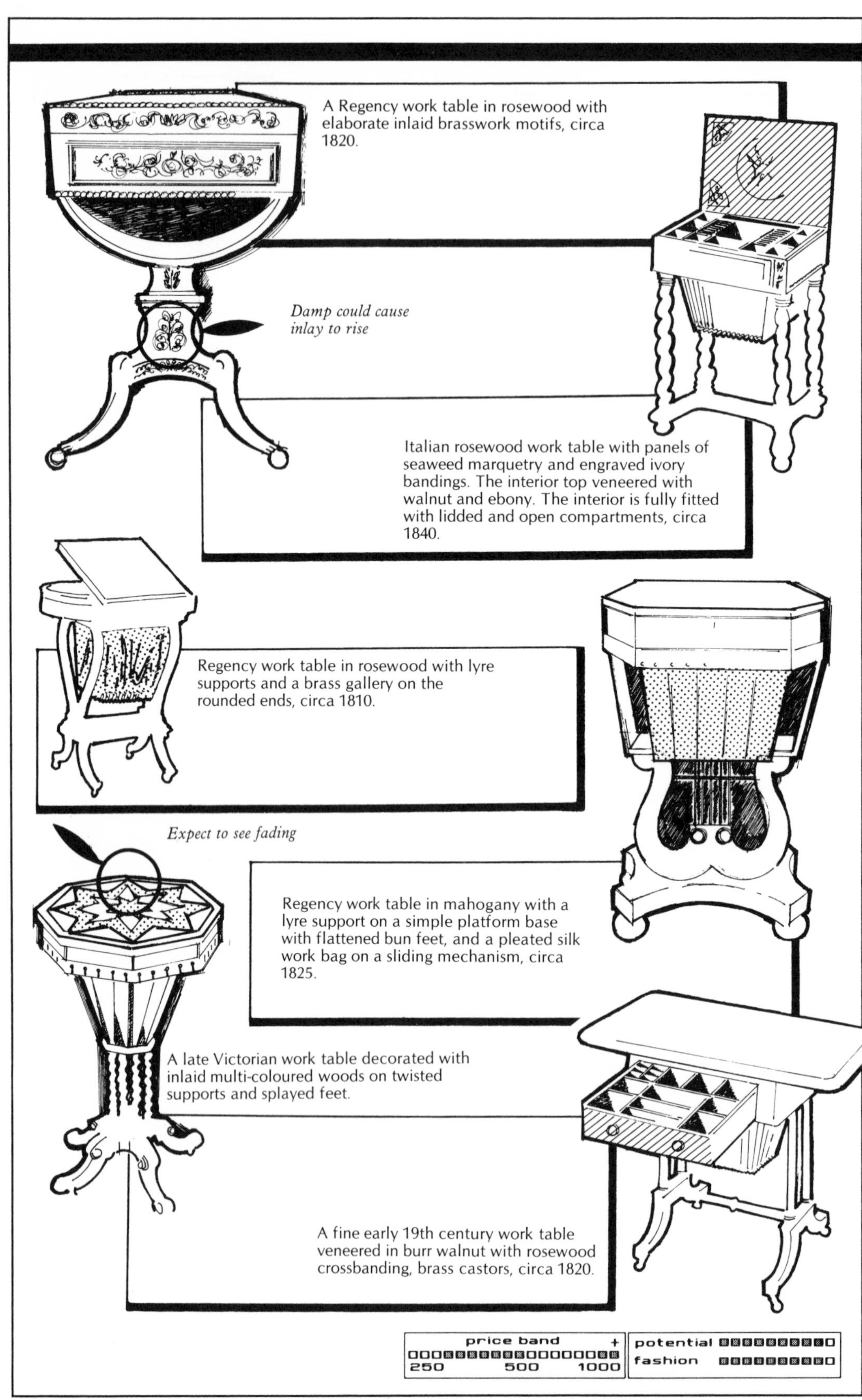

A Regency work table in rosewood with elaborate inlaid brasswork motifs, circa 1820.

Damp could cause inlay to rise

Italian rosewood work table with panels of seaweed marquetry and engraved ivory bandings. The interior top veneered with walnut and ebony. The interior is fully fitted with lidded and open compartments, circa 1840.

Regency work table in rosewood with lyre supports and a brass gallery on the rounded ends, circa 1810.

Expect to see fading

Regency work table in mahogany with a lyre support on a simple platform base with flattened bun feet, and a pleated silk work bag on a sliding mechanism, circa 1825.

A late Victorian work table decorated with inlaid multi-coloured woods on twisted supports and splayed feet.

A fine early 19th century work table veneered in burr walnut with rosewood crossbanding, brass castors, circa 1820.

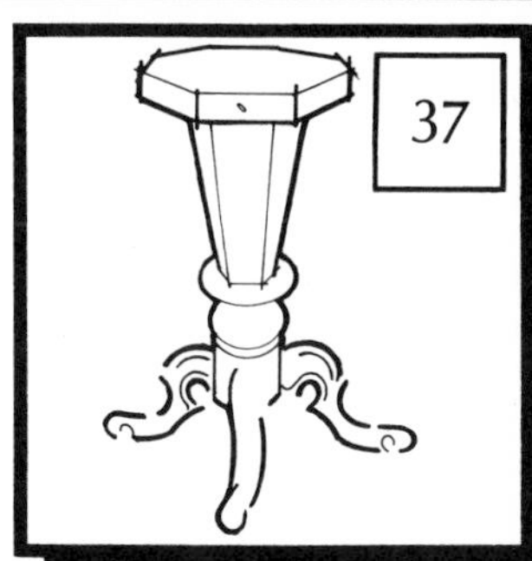

Work & Sewing Tables

Quick view: A box designed to hold needlework materials, supported on legs or a shaped support.

Shape: Very varied, the drawings illustrate only a tiny selection.

Restoration: The original fabric work bag will have seen fairly regular use over the years and may be badly worn — especially the inner lining, as opposed to the outer decorative bag. Replacement fabric would be acceptable — provided it is of the highest quality and in correct or sympathetic material — e.g. not synthetic. No special problems should be encountered with the timber areas. Brass-inlaid Regency examples could present a problem and call for specialist assistance.

Fake?: Not likely.

Decoration/inlays: Wide variety, ranging from simple stringing to elaborate marquetry and inlaid panels.

Best period: 1800-1820.

Best size: Size is not a factor compared to quality, however a good big one would probably command a higher price than a smaller example.

Features to look for: Extra, perhaps 'secret', features would be a bonus.

Interiors/drawers: Original silk bag in good condition would be a plus.

Most valuable: Classic design, interesting interior and elaborate inlays. Exotic materials. Original fabrics.

Oddities: Perhaps an example which also contains a games compendium or other novelty feature, secret drawers, slides, etc., would be considered a bonus and command a premium price.

In a word (or two): Should be a classic example of design and workmanship and a miniature of the larger, more important pieces of furniture being designed and produced in the same period. An ideal candidate for inclusion in an antiques fair. The poor Victorian examples are pretty horrible — the best work tables are classic examples of the cabinetmaker's art.

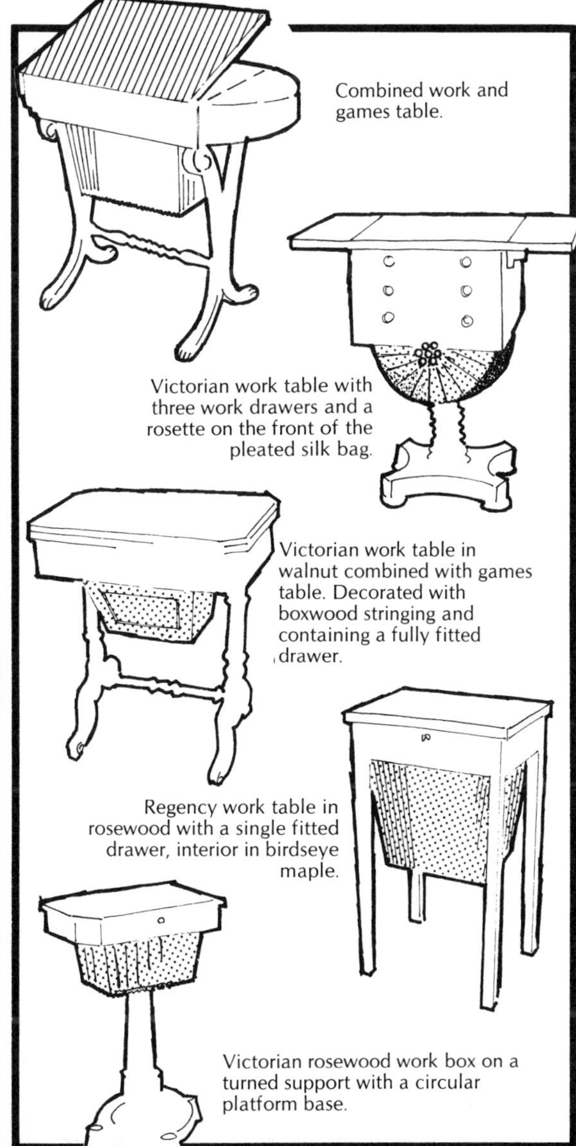

Combined work and games table.

Victorian work table with three work drawers and a rosette on the front of the pleated silk bag.

Victorian work table in walnut combined with games table. Decorated with boxwood stringing and containing a fully fitted drawer.

Regency work table in rosewood with a single fitted drawer, interior in birdseye maple.

Victorian rosewood work box on a turned support with a circular platform base.

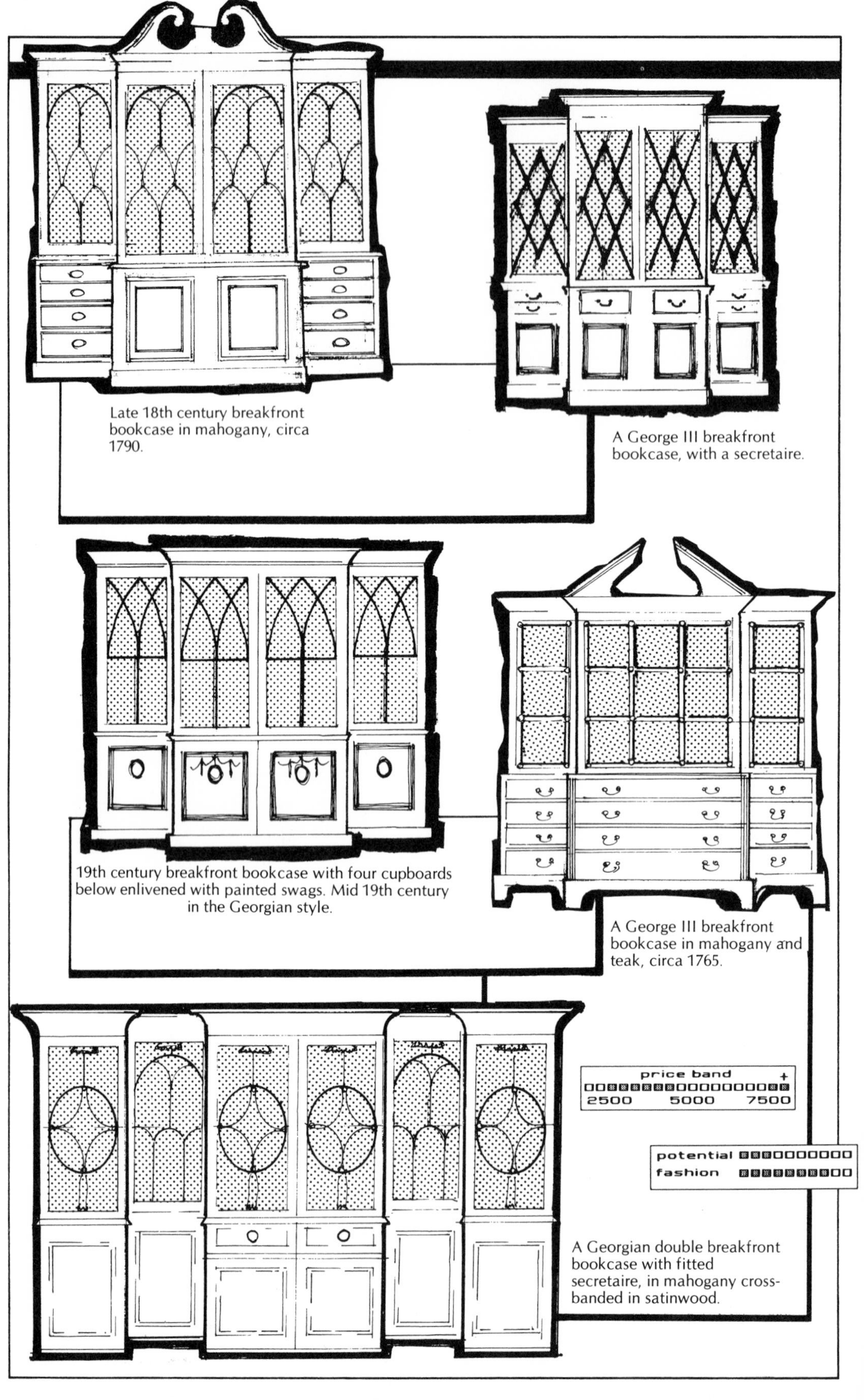

Late 18th century breakfront bookcase in mahogany, circa 1790.

A George III breakfront bookcase, with a secretaire.

19th century breakfront bookcase with four cupboards below enlivened with painted swags. Mid 19th century in the Georgian style.

A George III breakfront bookcase in mahogany and teak, circa 1765.

A Georgian double breakfront bookcase with fitted secretaire, in mahogany cross-banded in satinwood.

Quick view: In many dealers'and antique enthusiasts' eyes, the most desirable piece of large English furniture — always chosen to be illustrated in sale catalogues and in dealers' advertisements.

Best woods: Mahogany and satinwood, walnut in Victorian examples.

Shape: Several different 'breakfront' configurations — see the diagrams.

Restoration: No particular difficulties — period glass should always be used however.

Fake?: Main area for 'fake' would be an example altered from either a Georgian or Victorian breakfront wardrobe — the main addition being glazed doors and possibly a more impressive pediment, plus brass period-style handles. Unlikely to be a total fake, (see 'Improving Furniture'). With glazed-door examples, check to see if the astragals have been set actually into the door frame — this is always a sign of quality.

Configuration: Glazed cupboards above, either blind or glazed cupboards, drawers or secretaires below. A very rare example would contain a bureau or bureaux.

Decoration/inlays: The degree of style and quality of carving and astragals all contribute to extra value.

Best period: 1770-1820.

Best size: All sizes are highly desirable. In many dealers' eyes the larger the better. Up to 18' or 20' wide would be most sought-after.

Feet: Bracket or ogee, or a platform plinth on late examples.

Interiors/drawers: When secretaires are included in the configuration, quality of interiors would make a further contribution to value. Shelves in genuine 18th century bookcases were always set into grooves. Shelves supported by wooded pegs or wedges date from the first quarter of the 19th century.

Most valuable: Satinwood with fitted pair of bureaux.

In a word (or two): Don't be discouraged by the high prices in the sale rooms — 'breakfronts' can still be found in the strangest places.

Breakfront Bookcases

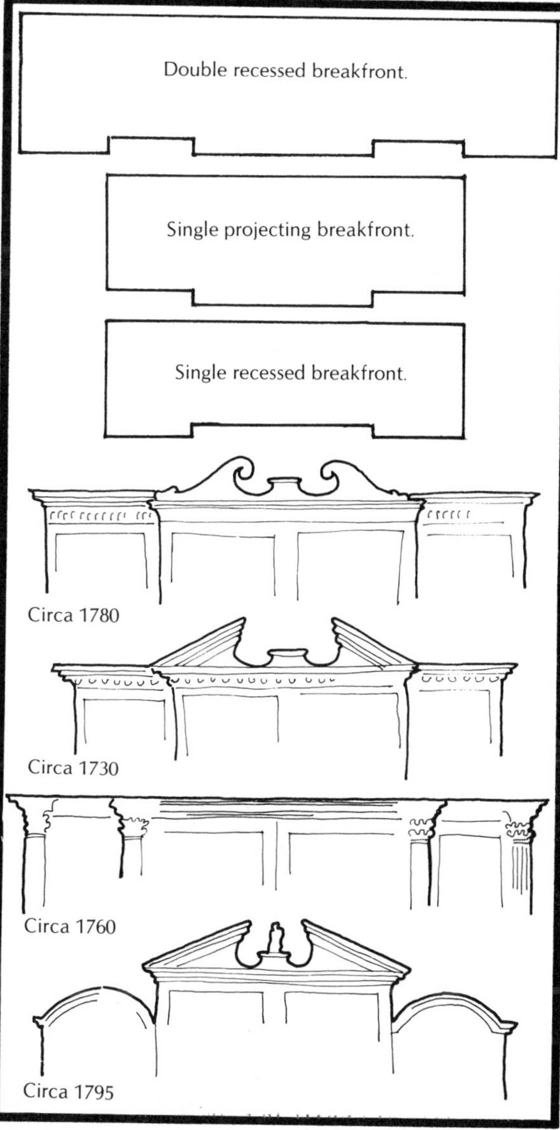

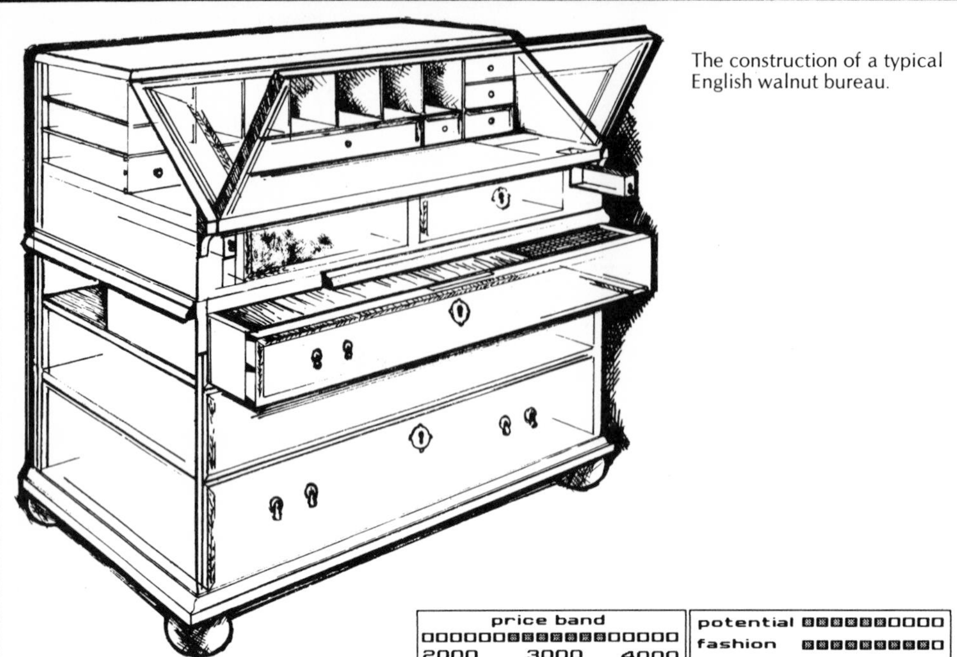

The construction of a typical English walnut bureau.

price band			potential	■■■■■■□□□□
□□□□□□■■■■■■■□□□□□□			fashion	■■■■■■■■■□
2000	3000	4000		

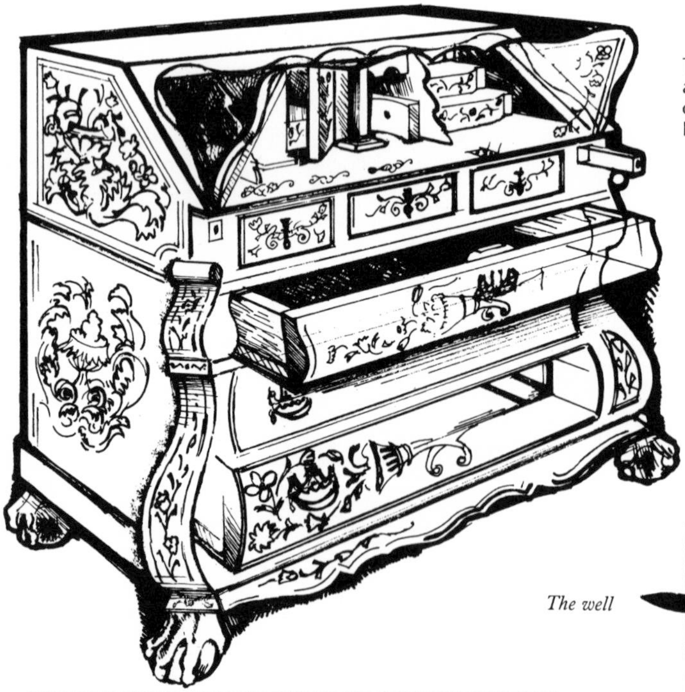

The more massive construction of a continental marquetry bureau of the same period as the above English example.

price band			potential	■■■■■□□□□□
□□□□■■■■■■■■□□□□□□□			fashion	■■■■■■□□□□
2000	4000	6000		

The well

An early English walnut bureau showing the position of the well in place of the top drawer.

Bureaux

Desirable woods: Mahogany, walnut or oak, (less frequently satinwood or fruitwoods).

Size: The smaller the better — under 36″ (1m), especially with walnut examples.

Restoration: Two major potential dangers to look for . . . a twisted fall front (caused by the lock being 'cut in' when the bureau was made). This will always cause warping over the years even when the veneer is on solid mahogany. A bureau must have a flat fall-front — a bent or twisted fall can't be satisfactorarily straightened. Expect also to find damage or repair to the area into which the lock bolt shoots — this timber is very thin and the bureau may have been forcibly opened in the past. Bureau sides are also frequently split.

Veneer on pine bracket feet can also cause problems. Feet were frequently cut to make the writing surface lower! Never buy a bureau from someone of small stature!

Beware: Heavy carved oak bureaux have invariably had the attentions of a Victorian enthusiast.

Feet: Bun feet on walnut and oak, bracket or ogee feet on mahogany. If considering a walnut example with bracket feet, remove the bottom drawer and look for the tell-tale dowel or dowel hole in the frame or bottom board — the remains of the earlier bun foot.

Fake?: Highly unlikely unless in walnut. If the top of a mahogany bureau is especially wide, say between 11″ to 12″ (30cm), it may well have been made originally with a bookcase.

Features to look for: Secret drawers and compartments. Early oak and walnut bureaux frequently had a compartment known as a **well,** which was entered through an internal slide and replaced the top drawer. Later examples had four long drawers, or two short and three long.

Interiors/drawers: A nicely 'stepped' interior is a big bonus.

Most valuable: Small, walnut, about 2′ 6″ wide (80cm).

Oddities: English design, but of Indian manufacture, in padook — just try and lift one!

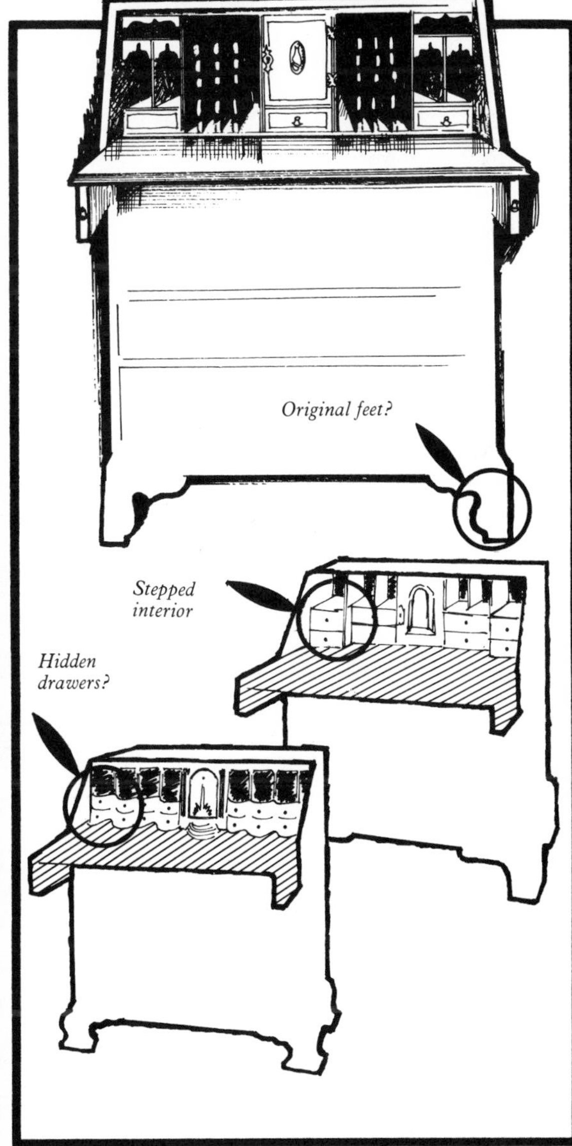

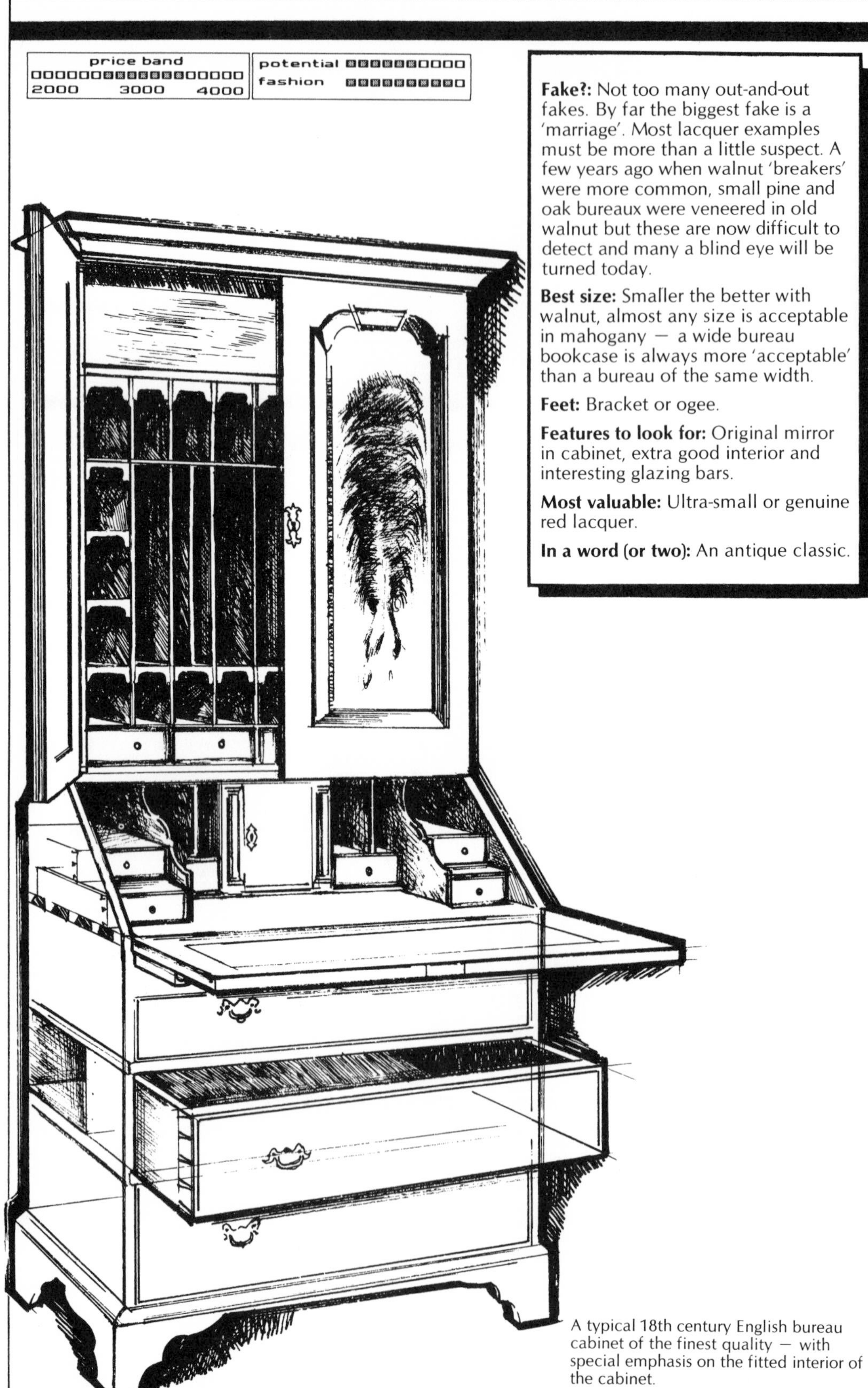

Fake?: Not too many out-and-out fakes. By far the biggest fake is a 'marriage'. Most lacquer examples must be more than a little suspect. A few years ago when walnut 'breakers' were more common, small pine and oak bureaux were veneered in old walnut but these are now difficult to detect and many a blind eye will be turned today.

Best size: Smaller the better with walnut, almost any size is acceptable in mahogany — a wide bureau bookcase is always more 'acceptable' than a bureau of the same width.

Feet: Bracket or ogee.

Features to look for: Original mirror in cabinet, extra good interior and interesting glazing bars.

Most valuable: Ultra-small or genuine red lacquer.

In a word (or two): An antique classic.

A typical 18th century English bureau cabinet of the finest quality — with special emphasis on the fitted interior of the cabinet.

Bureau Cabinets

Quick view: In the eyes of many dealers, the créme de la créme of English antique furniture.

Desirable woods: Walnut or mahogany.

Restoration: Assuming always that sufficient suitable materials are available, restoration problems will probably be confined to the fall of the bureau. Most of the work to be attempted in this area was inherited from the day the lock was originally cut in. This cutting-in of the lock causes the timber to warp which is almost impossible to rectify. It does not respond to clamping, etc. Twisting even occurs when the veneer is on solid mahogany. Suffice it to say that a flat fall would be a big plus factor when choosing a bureau cabinet. However, as most examples have this particular family failing, it can be forgiven and should not influence you against investing in an otherwise attractive piece. The lock also causes damage to the thin area where the lock bolt shoots. There are very few bureaux which have not sustained accidental or deliberate damage to this part. Expect to see signs of repair here.

The veneer on pine bracket feet can also cause problems as they take the brunt of day-to-day use. Many have also been cut down to make the writing surface lower.

If you have to replace glass in the bookcase portion, do try and use period glass. Old print and picture frames are a common source.

Mirror: When the cabinet has mirrored doors, original mirror glass should always be sought. Look for a tell-tale blue/grey appearance to the glass — the mirror effect was achieved by applying mercury to the rear of the glass and this gives it its typical colouration. Old glass is also thin — place a coin or a pencil tip against the front of the mirror and 'read' its thickness. As a test, take a piece of modern mirror to a museum and compare its thickness with a genuine old mirror.

Configuration: Standard bureau base with cabinet above, either blind doors with fitted interiors or glazed with bookshelves.

Best period: 1750-1800.

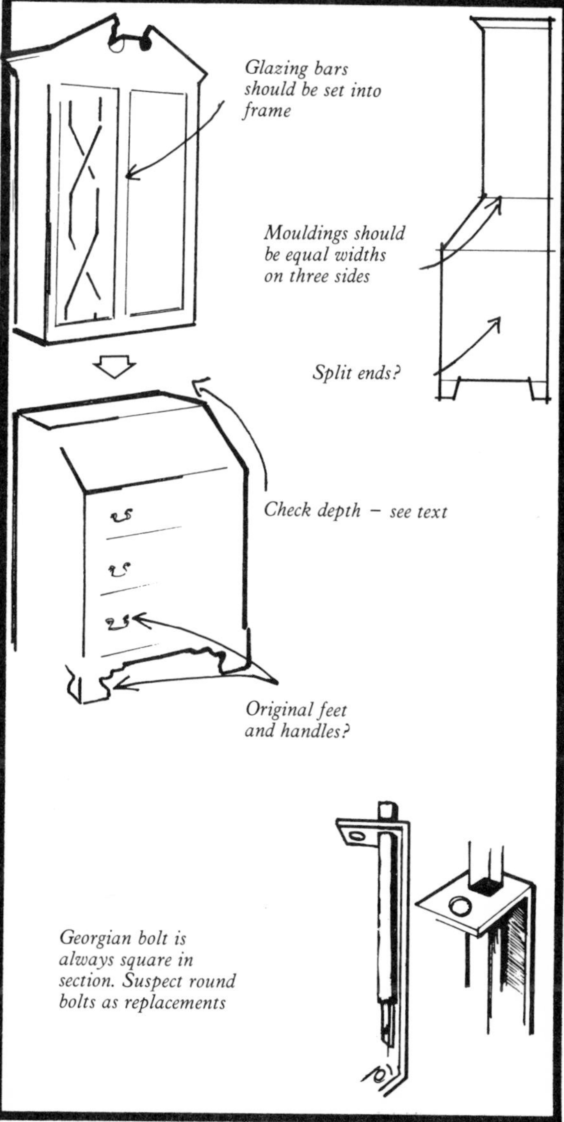

Georgian bolt is always square in section. Suspect round bolts as replacements

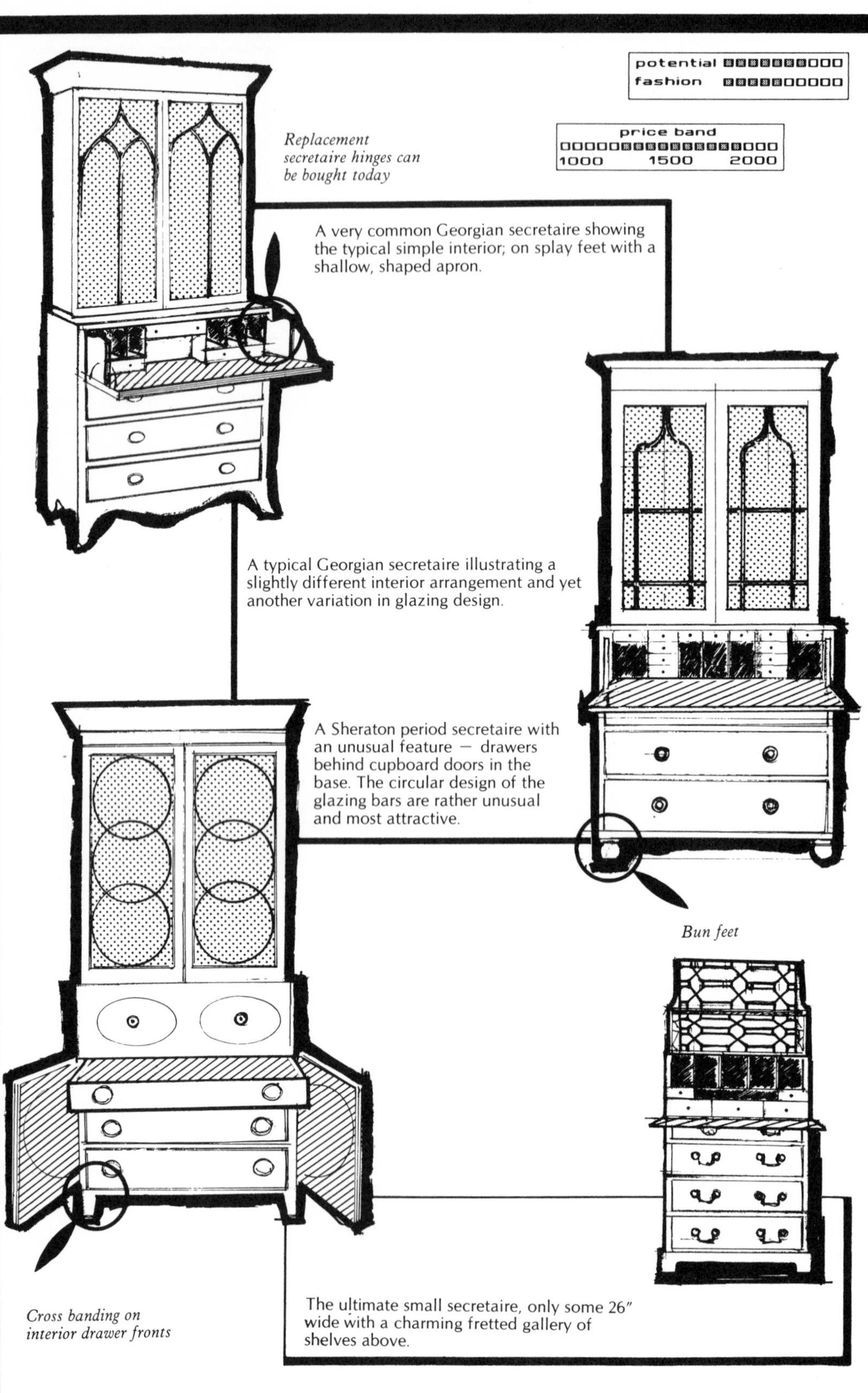

Replacement secretaire hinges can be bought today

A very common Georgian secretaire showing the typical simple interior; on splay feet with a shallow, shaped apron.

A typical Georgian secretaire illustrating a slightly different interior arrangement and yet another variation in glazing design.

A Sheraton period secretaire with an unusual feature — drawers behind cupboard doors in the base. The circular design of the glazing bars are rather unusual and most attractive.

Bun feet

Cross banding on interior drawer fronts

The ultimate small secretaire, only some 26″ wide with a charming fretted gallery of shelves above.

Secretaire Bookcases

Quick view: Although the same general configuration as the bureau bookcase, a more 'refined' example is sought here. More inlays and decoration and dramatic glazing design, etc. Unless this refinement is present, the secretaire can be a little flat and massive.

Desirable woods: Mahogany and satinwood, never oak or walnut.

Handles: Swan drop handles or pressed brass plate handles.

Restoration: No particular problems — replacement brass secretaire hinges are readily available.

Fake?: Unlikely if not a marriage. We have had a total fake, small size, nicely glazed bookcases, good interior — unfortunately all in early walnut veneer! No such animal exists.

Configuration: Secretaire below, bookcase or cabinet above, open fretted shelves on some early (usually small) examples.

Decoration/inlays: Inlaid decoration on fall.

Best period: 1790-1850.

Best size: The majority are large — in the region of 48 inches wide (120cm). Very tiny (under 2'6", 76cm) examples are rare and expensive. They frequently have wonderful fretted gallery shelves above.

Feet: Bracket or splay.

Interiors/drawers: The rule is plain fronted with a series of plain drawers and shaped pigeon holes with a central door — maybe with a star inlay.

Most valuable: Value can be greatly influenced by design and quality of glazing bars — much more important than with a Bureau Bookcase. A nice marquetry example would be nice.

In a Word (or two): If your taste is for later furniture, they can hold a copious quantity of stocks and bonds in tasteful elegance.

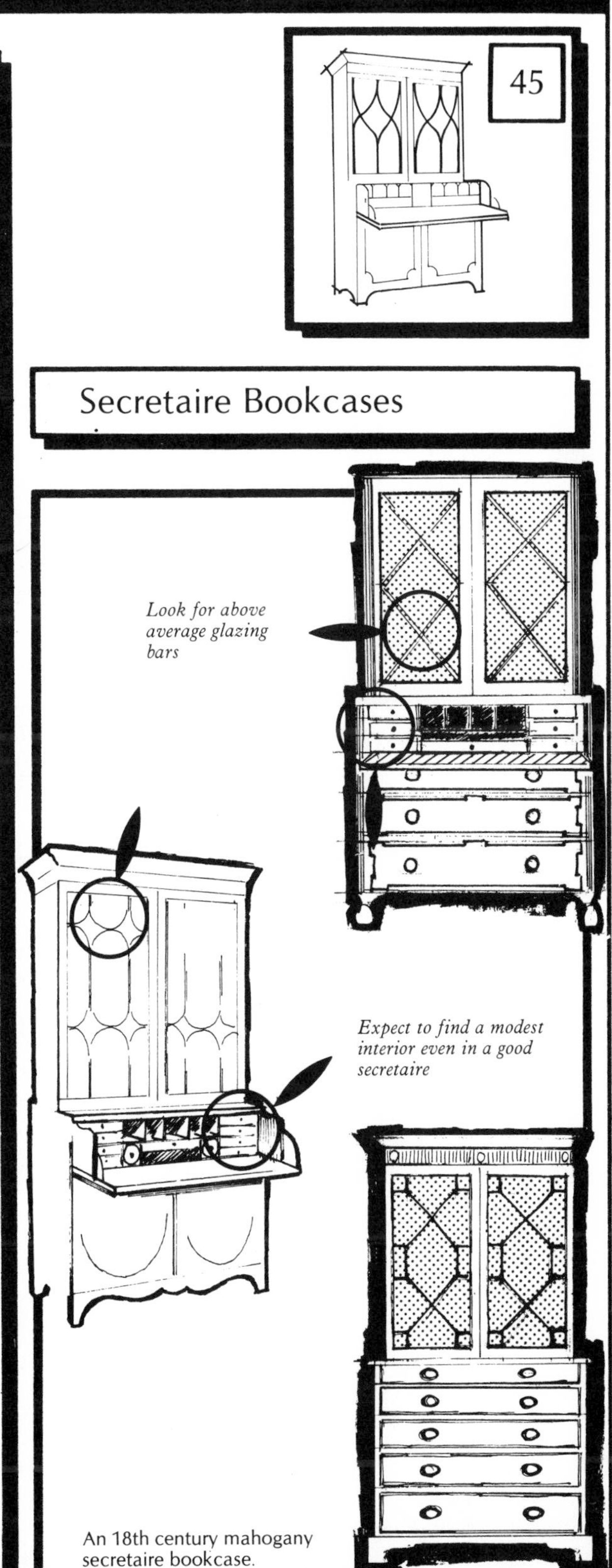

An 18th century mahogany secretaire bookcase.

Pine Finds

PINE FURNITURE — the affordable antiques — are treated here with a slightly different format and headings.

Paint: Why was it painted in the first (or second) place? Does the paint hide a terrible secret? Many pieces have certainly been painted for a good reason; a very bad repair job in the past, an unsuccessful earlier stripping attempt using a blow torch turning the nice little chest into a burnt offering. Scorch marks of a misplaced iron, perhaps. Perhaps the whole piece has been painted with red lead paint which is almost impossible to remove. Water based emulsion paints or lacquers can also cause problems unless high temperatures are employed.

Frequently pieces of furniture which have failed to strip successfully have been repainted and dropped back into an auction.

Paint is not all bad however. It's the action of the paint on the timber over the years that gives a successful stripped piece its lovely colour. On the other hand the paint may be totally original and even bear traces of stencil decoration. You should certainly think twice about stripping this!

Today, most pine furniture is stripped using either hot (90-100°C) or cold caustic soda. The hot method is to be preferred as it is very much faster in operation and nothing is worse for glue and joints than prolonged soaking in cold caustic. After the short hot dip, it should be well washed with a steam gun and the whole process can be finished in less than one hour.

Caustic may 'bleed' white crystals for some time afterwards if it has not been sufficiently washed. This can usually be cured by liberal washing-down with common vinegar. After stripping and thorough drying, all joints should be checked and re-glued as required and the whole piece sanded and wax polished. One big plus — you are not likely to suffer from woodworm after caustic stripping!

Although still very reasonable in price, old pine has increased in value and demand to the extent that reproduction furniture is now manufactured in vast quantities, ostensibly from old timber.

This cottage industry thrives in Newark in Nottinghamshire but genuine old pine is seldom in evidence in the workshops.

Furniture can be stripped using the very best method — strips or shards of freshly cut glass dragged across the surface. The cutting edge being continually re-cut to keep it sharp. This method gives a smooth finish which should not even need sanding and is to be highly recommended. A fine finish can also be obtained by using a special tool — tempered steel file, bent over and then sharpened to a cutting edge. This is almost as good as glass and a great deal safer to use. Some dealers favour a rough finish using triangular scrapping tools, however this is very much an acquired taste.

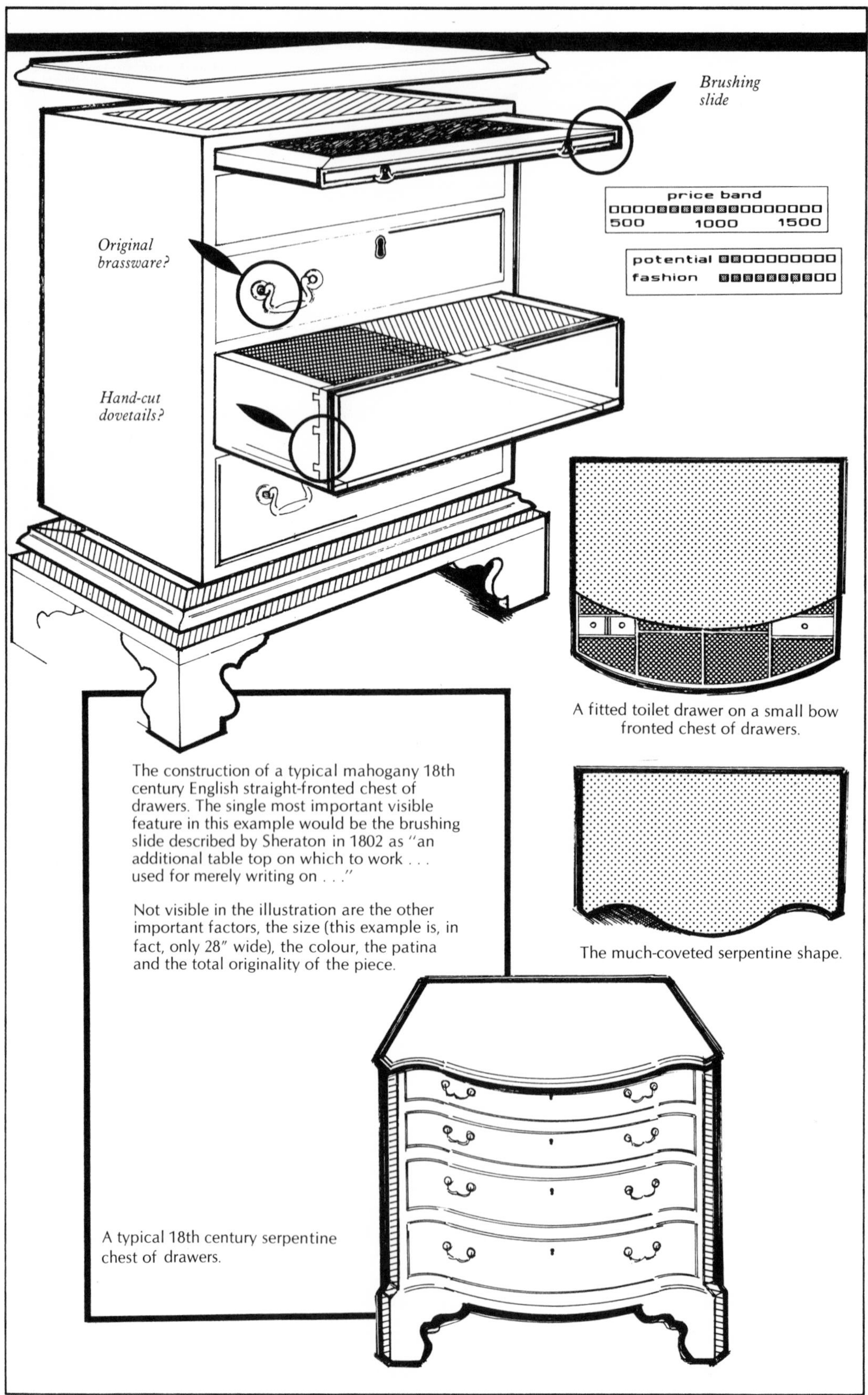

A fitted toilet drawer on a small bow fronted chest of drawers.

The much-coveted serpentine shape.

The construction of a typical mahogany 18th century English straight-fronted chest of drawers. The single most important visible feature in this example would be the brushing slide described by Sheraton in 1802 as "an additional table top on which to work . . . used for merely writing on . . ."

Not visible in the illustration are the other important factors, the size (this example is, in fact, only 28″ wide), the colour, the patina and the total originality of the piece.

A typical 18th century serpentine chest of drawers.

Georgian Chests

Quick view: The piece of furniture which can frequently sum up all that is best in honest 18th century English craftsmanship.

Shape: Straight-fronted, bow-fronted or serpentine.

Handles: Should be original — see chart.

Restoration: Allowable if well done.

Fake?: Not likely to be a total fake — a 'cut down' from a larger chest is very possible. Look to see if the drawers are out of proportion to the whole front. Less common today, as large Georgian chests make good money in their own right.

Configuration: Best layout is two short drawers and three long below.

Decoration/inlays: Cross-banded or quartered top could be considered a plus feature.

Best period: 1750-1800.

Best size: With straight-fronted, under 36″ (1m) wide without doubt; with serpentine, any size — they are usually 40 to 48″ (100-120cm) wide.

Feet: Depending on configuration, bracket with straight-fronted, ogee with serpentine and splayed with bow-fronted.

Features to look for: Brushing slide would be a very big plus. Nicely chamfered or blind fretted ends would be almost essential on serpentine chests.

Potential: Don't change a thing if original. Added Victorian wooden knobs can be changed back to brass. Drawers can benefit from the addition of cock-beading if plain-fronted.

Interiors/drawers: Serpentine chests should have fitted top drawer for toilet accessories. Straight and bow fronted should have cock-beaded drawer fronts.

Most valuable: Serpentine, of any size followed by a small (under 36″, 1m) straight-fronted chest with brushing slide, in a rich brown colour.

Oddities: Triangular, corner-shaped chests, frequently bow-fronted as well!

In a word (or two): Every home should have one! A steady, popular and very useful item not easily influenced by trends or fashions.

A bow-fronted chest of drawers with a fitted top drawer — rather a rare feature but much to be desired, and could well be a later addition.

A straight-fronted chest of drawers with a fitted top drawer featuring lidded compartments and a hinged mirror.

Batchelor Chests

Short description: An early 18th century chest of drawers designed specifically for a gentleman's dressing room.

Best woods or materials: Well-figured walnut, veneered onto an oak frame; veneered or plain oak sides.

Shape: Square, masculine and chunky.

Handles: Ring-pulls or plain, simple, plate handles.

Restoration: No particular problems here if suitable period walnut veneer is available – the only difficulty might arise when earlier work is uncovered and ethical issues are raised. Should the restorer tell the owner that his highly expensive purchase is made up out of bits and pieces?

Fake?: Highly possible. Batchelor chests have always commanded a premium price and were made in large quantities when genuine period walnut was available from breakers or, more usually, walnut chests on chests considered unfashionable and much less desirable by the trade.

Configuration: A chest of four drawers with a fold-over top supported by a pair of slides, providing extra top surface for writing or, today, for toilet accessories.

Decoration/inlays: Cross-banding on drawer fronts and top; top also quartererd. Especially nice examples could feature chamfered or pillared ends.

Best period: Queen Anne period, about 1720.

Best size: Small, under 30″ wide and correspondingly shallow. Batchelor chests also tend to be low in height – usually about 30-31″.

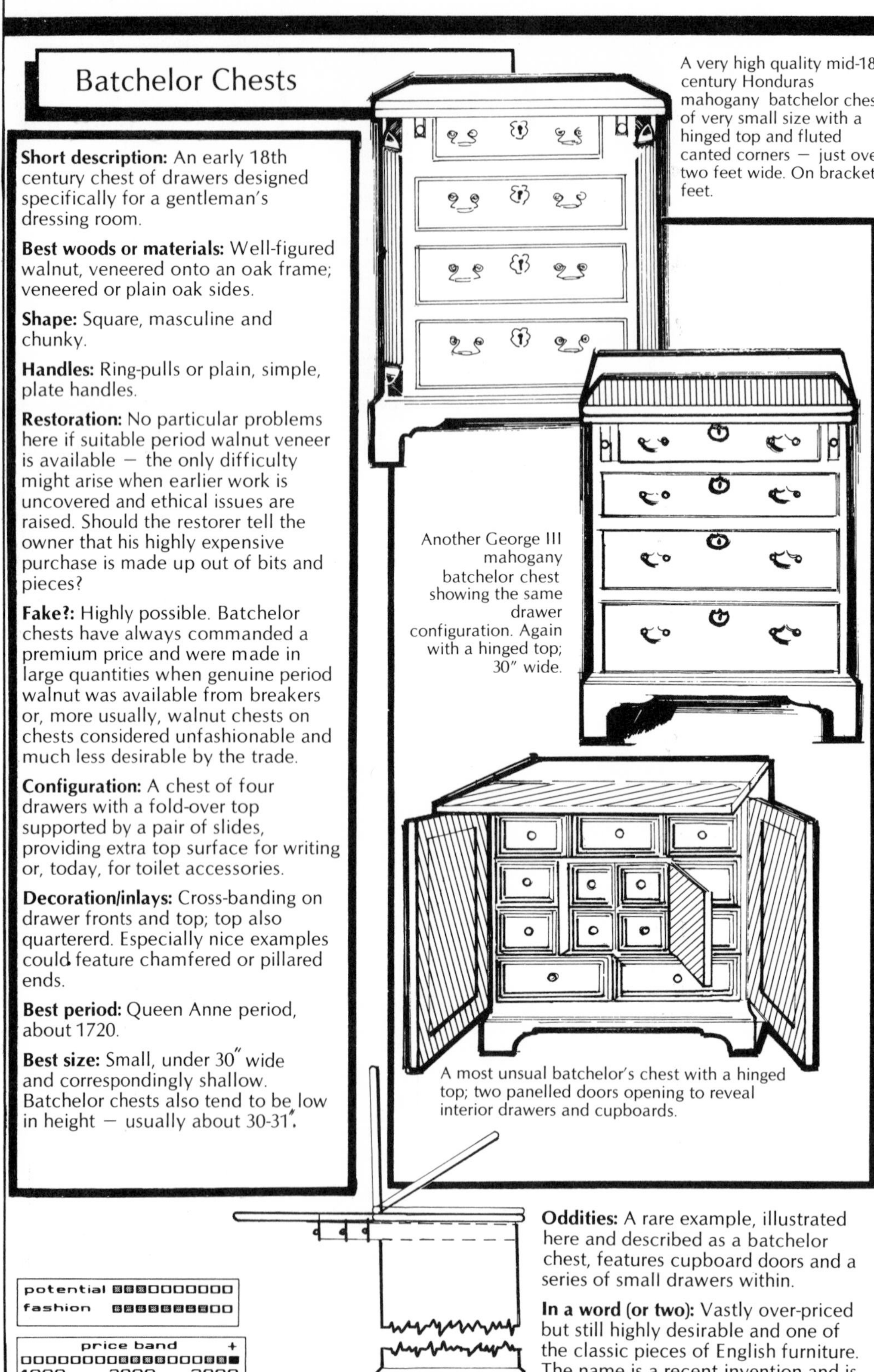

A very high quality mid-18th century Honduras mahogany batchelor chest of very small size with a hinged top and fluted canted corners – just over two feet wide. On bracket feet.

Another George III mahogany batchelor chest showing the same drawer configuration. Again with a hinged top; 30″ wide.

A most unsual batchelor's chest with a hinged top; two panelled doors opening to reveal interior drawers and cupboards.

Oddities: A rare example, illustrated here and described as a batchelor chest, features cupboard doors and a series of small drawers within.

In a word (or two): Vastly over-priced but still highly desirable and one of the classic pieces of English furniture. The name is a recent invention and is not found in trade descriptions or invoices of the period.

potential
fashion

price band +
1000 2000 3000

Wellington Chests

Quick view: A tall, narrow chest of drawers, the drawers all 'locked' together by hinged flaps either side.

Best woods: Mahogany veneer or walnut.

Handles: Brass or wooden knobs.

Fake?: Very unlikely.

Decoration/inlays: Inlaid stringing in boxwood, etc., quality of carving may vary considerably.

Best size: Very little variation in size.

Feet: Usually a plinth, rather than feet.

Features to look for: Original lock fitted.

Interiors/drawers: Drawers may be fitted as collectors' cabinet.

Oddities: Fitted with secretaire drawer.

In a word (or two): Well worth considering if you collect anything that will fit in the.drawers — coins, butterflies, pot lids, etc., — the list is endless.

The wellington chest is very much a product of the Victorian era — when 'collecting' was the fashionable occupation for both ladies and gentlemen. No gentleman's residence was complete without a room set aside for his 'cabinet of curios' where sea shells, butterflies and mineral specimens could be displayed 'to advantage'. It was the age of science and discovery and the wellington chest sums it all up in one piece of furniture.

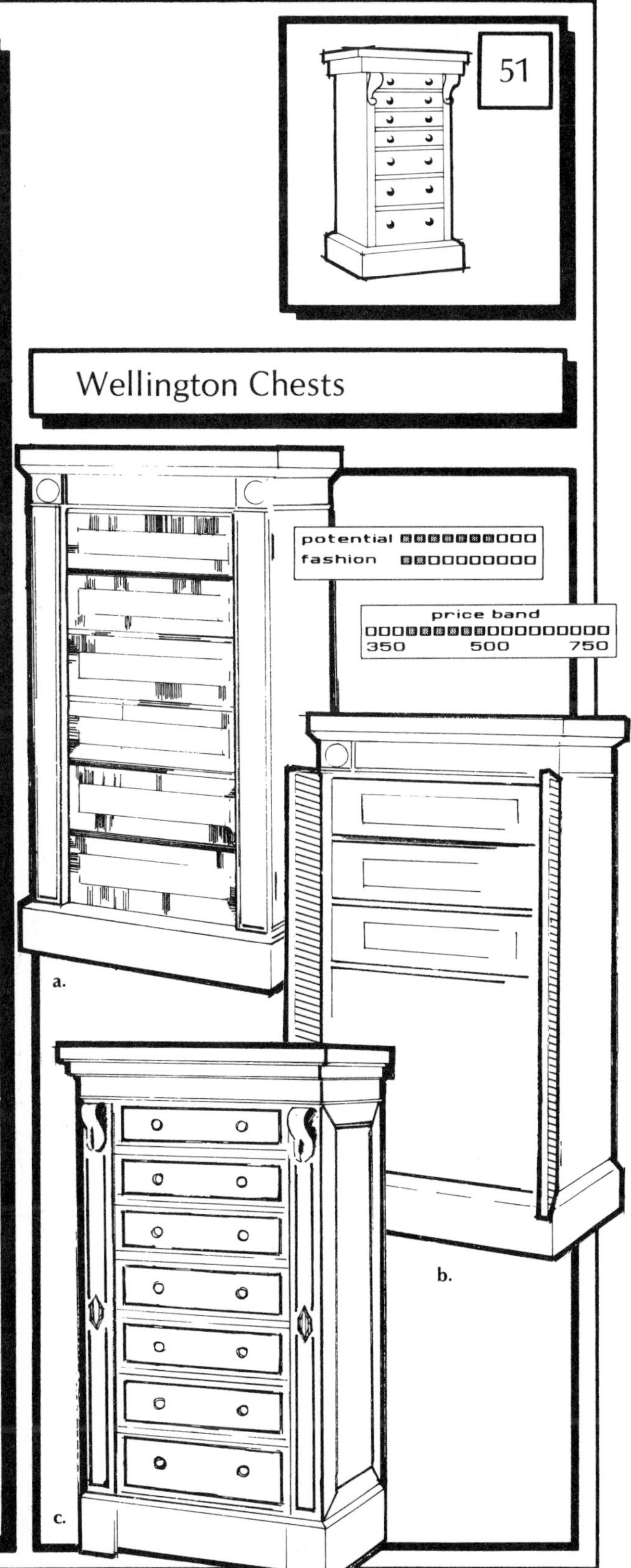

a. A Victorian rosewood and brass inlaid wellington chest, circa 1870.

b. How the hinged panels work!

c. A fine satinwood wellington chest with cross-banding and stringing in various woods, mid 19th century.

52

price band
2000 2500 3000

Chests-on-Stands

A fine William and Mary chest-on-stand made in Virginian walnut.

Early 18th century oak chest-on-stand.

potential
fashion

Quick view: Basically a chest of drawers on a stand.

Best woods: Oak or walnut, never mahogany.

Restoration: Stands/feet: Check damage to feet or even total replacement. Stands should be made of oak, pine or beech, the legs turned out of solid wood and on bun feet. Oak will be solid which would have had a better chance of survival and could, therefore, be original.

Fake?: The stand is frequently of later manufacture, a marriage or even totally 'wrong'. The original walnut stands were often eagerly devoured by wood-worm working from the feet up.

Configuration: Upper chest, three long and two or three short drawers; the stand on turned legs with 'interesting' stretchers, plus two or three drawers; shaped apron.

Decoration/inlays: Oyster veneered examples are especially attractive and highly prized.

Best period: William and Mary.

Best size: Unimportant.

Features to look for: Shaped apron on stand and quality of construction, turning, and detail and design of stretchers.

Drawers: Good cross-banding on walnut drawer fronts.

Most valuable: Walnut would make the highest price; oak examples are, however, rarer.

In a word (or two): Rare and highly desirable, especially if totally original.

17th century

Chests-on-Chests

Desirable woods: Walnut or mahogany.

Shape: The basic shape is one straight-fronted chest upon another.

Restoration: Permitted and no problem.

Fake?: Unlikely to be total fake — they were much rather the raw material of the earlier faker and restorer who could make two much more saleable chests from one piece; were frequently considered large and ugly.

Configuration: In the lower half, four long drawers; in the upper, three long and two or three short drawers.

Decoration/inlays: Look for fine detail in freize, dentil mouldings and chamfered ends.

Best size: Small, under 3′6″ (1 m) wide.

Feet: Basically bracket or ogee.

Features to look for: In walnut there is a popular fallacy that the sides of the best examples should also be walnut veneered. Oak and pine sides, simulated to resemble walnut are quite correct. In mahogany examples look for a brushing slide or secretaire in lower half and finely carved detail work. Look for handles which line up right through top and bottom, however don't dismiss the piece if they don't! The handles may well have been replaced in a different position. Check the original positions by looking for holes in the drawer fronts. Check also the figuring of the veneers top and bottom — they should match right through, as should the back boards and the carcase frame.

Interiors/drawers: Secretaire fitted would be bonus.

Most valuable: Small walnut example of excellent faded honey colour followed by a mahogany piece fitted with a secretaire.

In a word (or two): Two chests in one!

price band
1000 3000 4000

potential
fashion

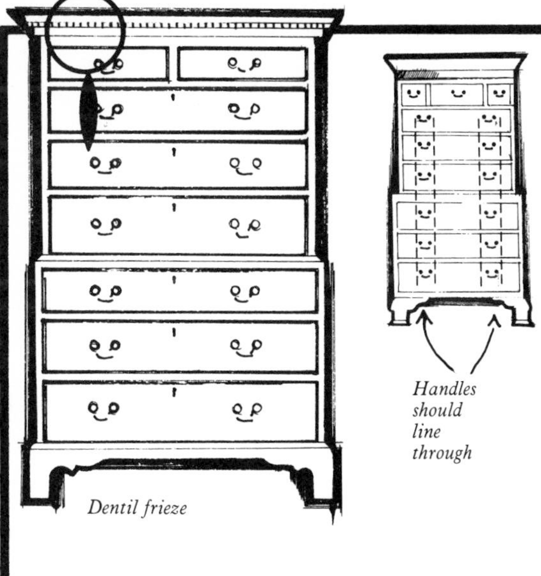

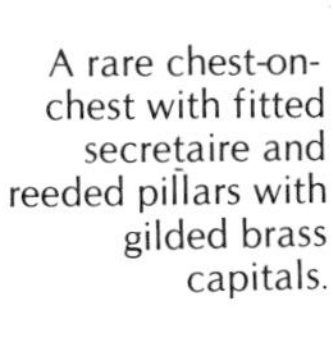

A rare chest-on-chest with fitted secretaire and reeded pillars with gilded brass capitals.

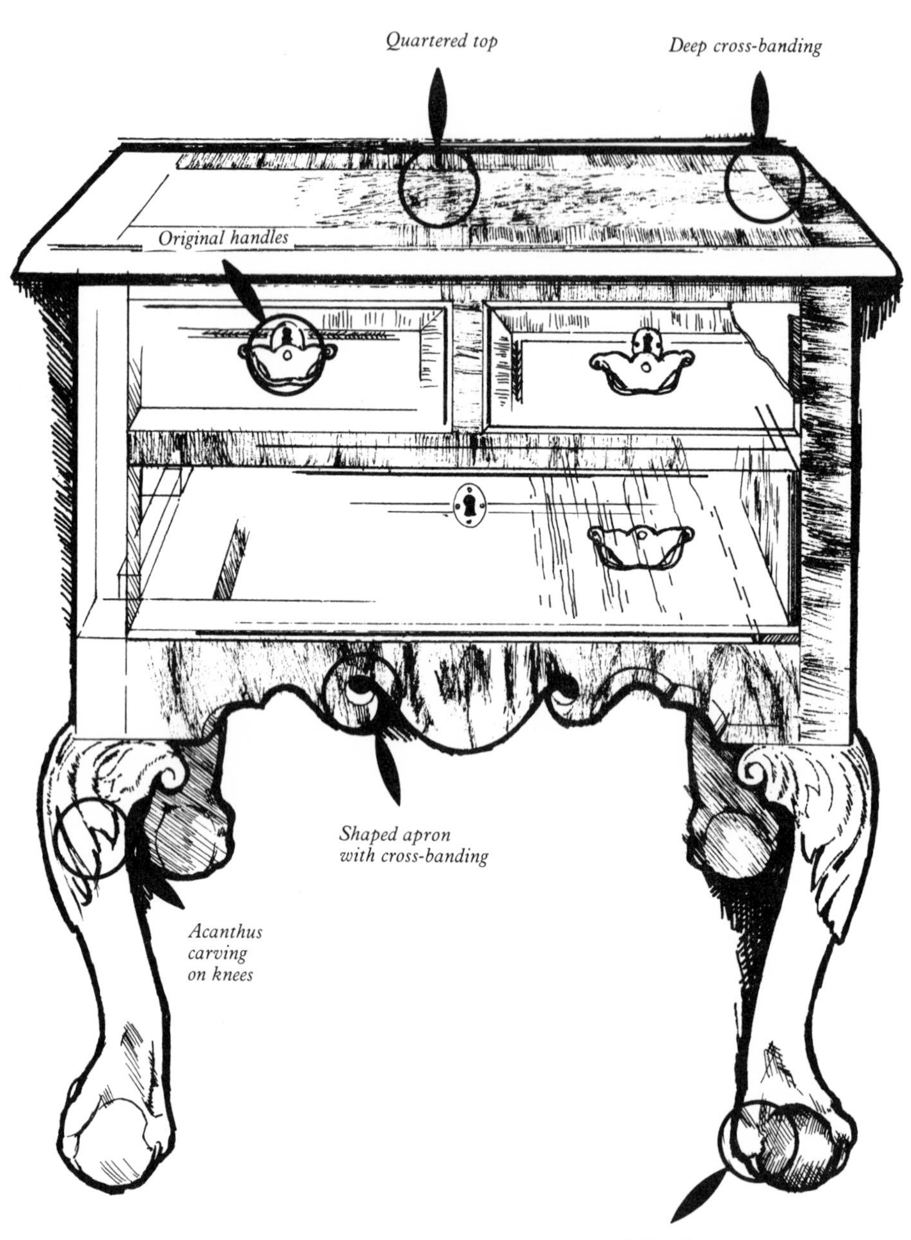

price band			potential	fashion
2000	3000	4000		

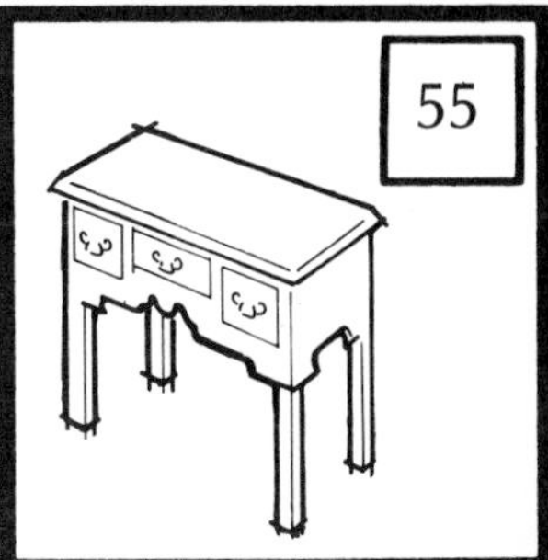

Low Boys

Configuration: Central drawer and two side drawers, slightly stepped down — see illustrations to the right.

Desirable woods: Walnut or mahogany veneer on a basic simple pine frame. Also rare examples in various fruitwoods. Oak examples with walnut cross-banding.

Best period: Early 18th century — I believe I would be correct in saying that low boys were only made in the 18th century. There is a wide variation in treatment and quality between London and provincial examples, although the basic style and configuration is the same; London manufacture being, as ever, the superior article.

Best size: About 30″ wide, 31″ high (75cm × 75cm).

Fake?: Unlikely. I rather doubt that they were ever sufficiently popular to attract the attentions of the Victorian copyist — a fate enjoyed by most other examples of Georgian furniture.

Legs: Solid; walnut, mahogany or oak — never veneered.

Beware: Woodworm damage to walnut or pine. If a solid walnut leg is badly affected this could present a considerable restoration problem — the least of which will be finding a suitably large piece of seasoned wood.

Top: Quartered veneer; each quarter of the top matching in towards the centre, with extra wide cross-banding, especially found in walnut examples.

Feet: Usually a pad foot, sometimes a trowel foot. The very best examples will have a ball and claw foot — as in the example opposite.

Drawers: Almost always three drawers in slightly different configurations — the best drawer fronts should be cross- and feather-banded.

Features to look for: Crisp, deep carving on knees; interesting feathering and good matching of veneers.

In a word (or two): A very nice, useful, and really quite rare piece of English furniture. Probably originally made as a dressing table. If you see a house sale advertised which features a low boy it may be well worth a view. I have seldom found a low boy in anywhere other than an interesting house.

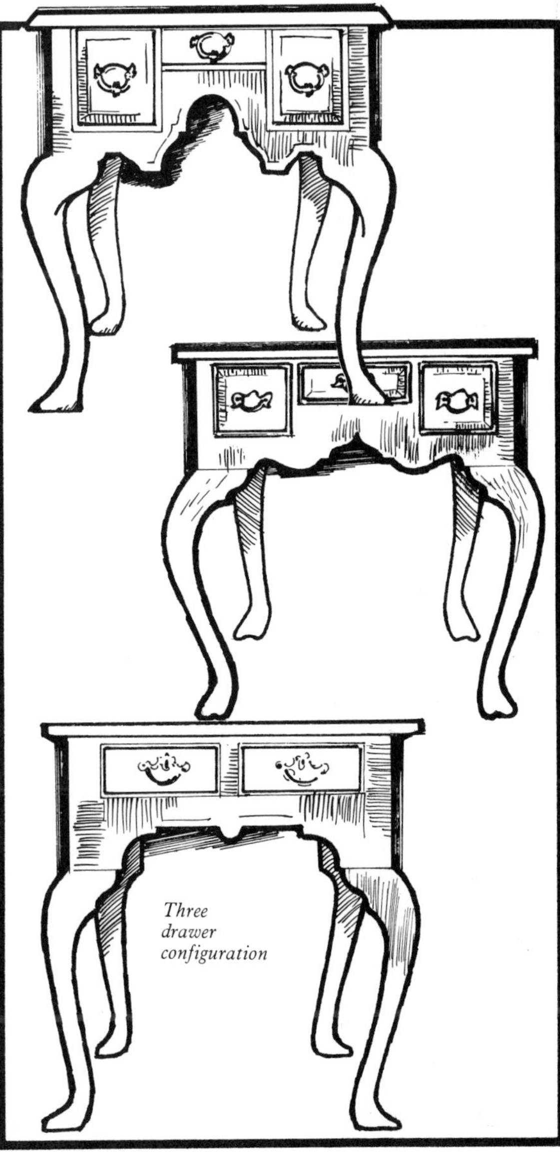

Three drawer configuration

Mule & Marriage Chests

Holly and bog-oak decoration

False!

Short description: A mule chest is basically a kist or coffer pretending to be something else! It looks, for all the world, like an extended oak chest of drawers with perhaps four rows of three drawers each. The marriage chest is another kist or coffer, this time with two drawers at the base.

Handles: In both examples swan-neck handles will be found. The interesting thing about mule chests is that all the dummy drawers are complete with a full complement of handles and even escutcheons!

Restoration: No particular restoration problems.

Configuration: Mule chests: nine or twelve drawer fronts with only the bottom row being genuine drawers. Lifting top lid. Marriage chest: a kist with two drawers in the base.

Decoration/inlays: Mule chests would have a plain top perhaps with walnut cross-banding, repeated again on all the drawer fronts.

Best period: 1730 to 1830.

Best size: Most mule chests are in the region of 5′ 6″ long, (165cm).

Colour: Mule or marriage chests — golden oak.

Feet: In both cases short bracket or ogee feet.

Features to look for: Quartered, rounded or fluted pillars would be an attractive feature on a mule chest.

Potential: Today many dealers find mule chests useful fodder for a quick and easy conversion to a dresser. The genuine drawer fronts (and hopefully original brasses) are there already. All they need are drawer linings and some work.

Interiors/drawers: Oak-lined drawers in both cases. Lidded candle box frequently in marriage chest.

Most valuable: Examples of marriage chests with marquetry panelled fronts, sometimes with castle scenes.

In a word (or two): Two interesting pieces of English country furniture. However the mule chest especially with a domed top is not particularly useful, as little or nothing will stand on it! With flat top it should be more useful than a normal kist but they generally tend to be bland and unattractive.

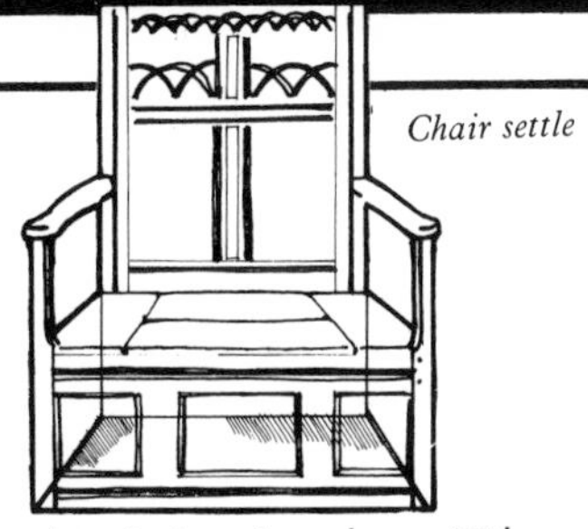
Chair settle

Settles

Short description: In oak, an 17th or 18th century seat for three. In pine the sofa equivalent for a country cottage or hostelry.

Best woods: Oak or pine, occasionally fruitwood.

Shape: In earlier versions, a rectangular frame on square or carbriole legs, sometimes with a slightly shaped apron. Pine settles can be either straight or bow (curve) backed.

Restoration: No particular problem areas. In early versions with an upholstered squab seat, care should be taken to replace string or twine 'springing' with the correct pattern. This pattern varies according to the county of origin.

Fake?: Highly unlikely with earlier oak patterns. Whilst not 'fakes' in the terms of this Guide, many pine settles offered today may have started their career as pews in a church or chapel. These may look rather 'churchy' with totally straight backs and seats and, perhaps, triangular panelled ends. They will also be even more uncomfortable than other settles. Pitch pine was widely used in pew construction in English and Welsh chapels during the 18th century and if your settle is made from this material the chances are that it had a religious start in life.

Best size: I cannot imagine a 'best size' for a settle. Unless you are committed to a country kitchen and use a pine settle en suite with a pine table as a breakfast area; the oak settle must surely find a home only as a decorative piece in a very large house.

Legs: Square section or cabriole.

Features to look for: Nicely panelled backs, maybe cross-banded in walnut or fruitwoods in early 19th century pieces; acanthus carving on the knees of cabriole legs. In pine versions, perhaps a seat wide enough to sit on would be a good place to start!

In a word: Uncomfortable!

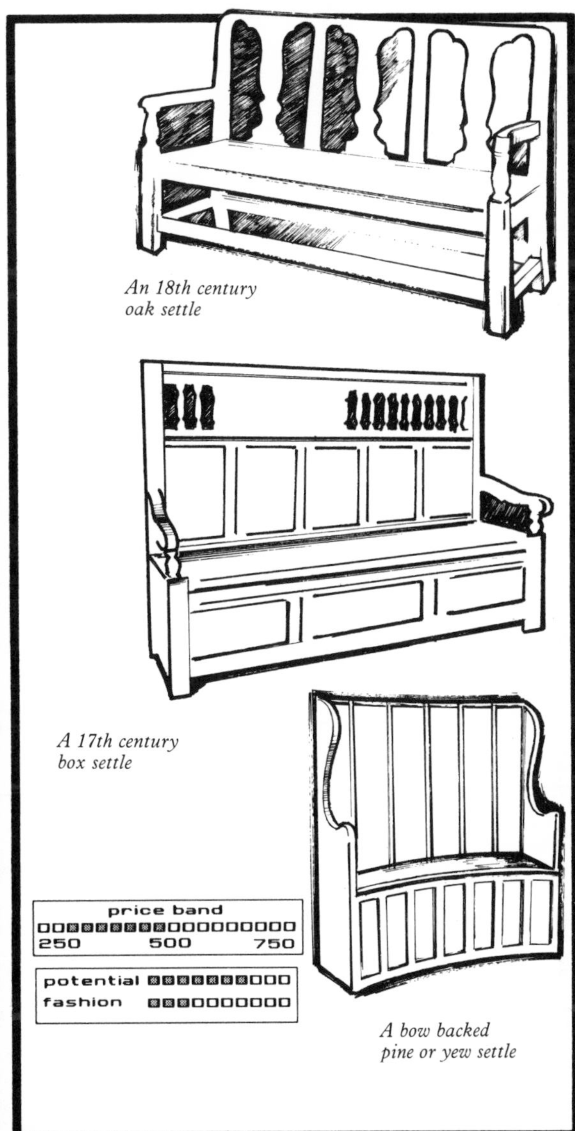
An 18th century oak settle

A 17th century box settle

A bow backed pine or yew settle

price band
250 500 750

potential
fashion

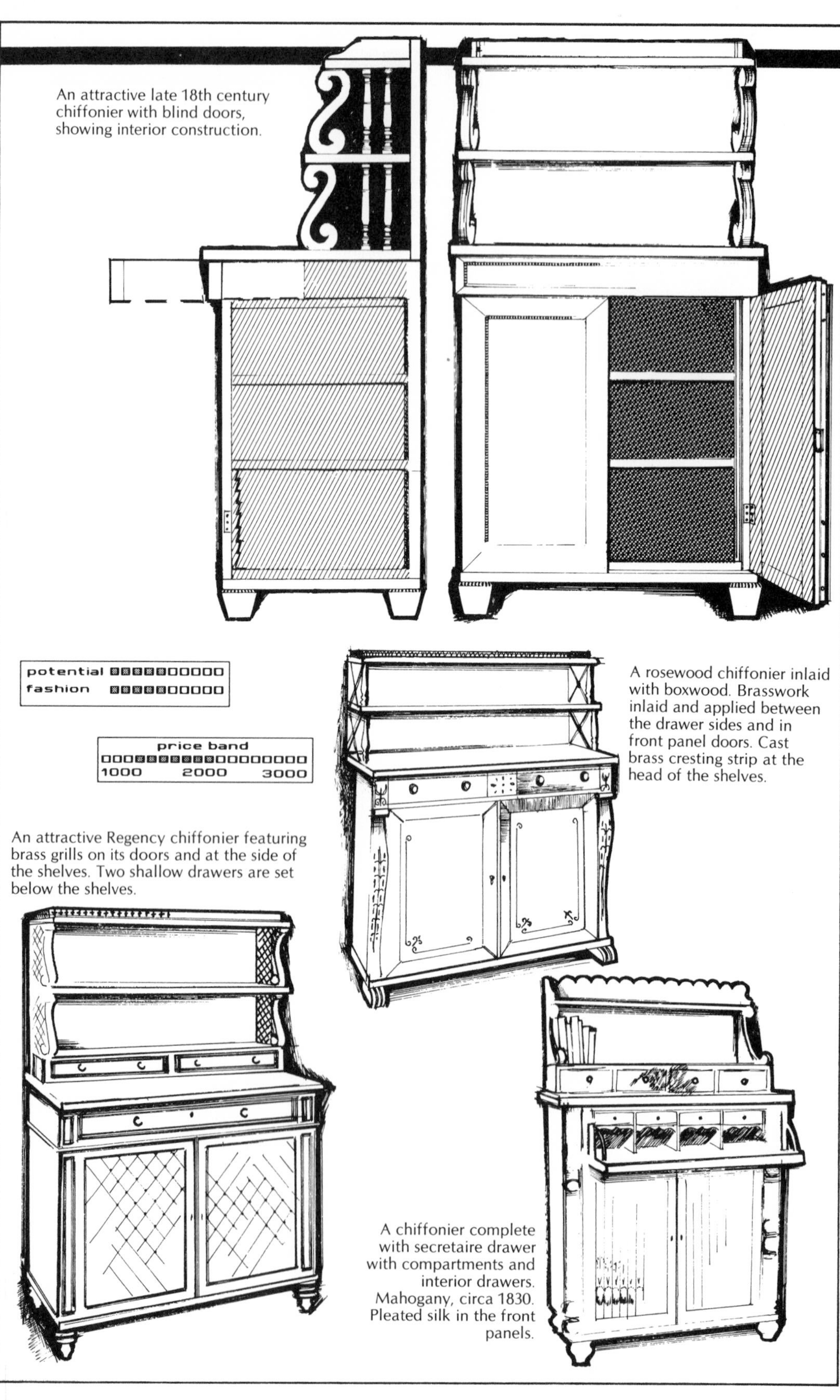

An attractive late 18th century chiffonier with blind doors, showing interior construction.

A rosewood chiffonier inlaid with boxwood. Brasswork inlaid and applied between the drawer sides and in front panel doors. Cast brass cresting strip at the head of the shelves.

An attractive Regency chiffonier featuring brass grills on its doors and at the side of the shelves. Two shallow drawers are set below the shelves.

A chiffonier complete with secretaire drawer with compartments and interior drawers. Mahogany, circa 1830. Pleated silk in the front panels.

Chiffoniers

Quick view: Twin door cupboard, with drawer above, surmounted by galleried shelves in varying designs. Victorian examples are often shaped with mirror backs.

Best wood: Mainly mahogany or veneered rosewood.

Shape: Georgian and Regency chiffoniers are, in the main, rather well designed and can be termed 'classic'. Usually straight fronted, some breakfront. Victorian examples, however, are frequently heavy and lacking in any refinement.

Restoration: No particular difficulties — all materials are readily available. Cast brass items can be matched by lost wax process.

Fake?: Unlikely to be total fake, although may have been considerably 'improved'. Brass grills may not be original — if grills ever were!

Configuration: Usually two cupboard doors, one drawer and two shelves above.

Decoration/inlays: Brass inlay on rosewood examples.

Best period: 1780-1820: Regency examples are the most elaborate.

Best size: Small, under 3′ (1 m) wide.

Colour: Look for good figuring on mahogany blind door panels.

Feet: Early examples might have decorated and carved turned feet; later squat spade feet. In Regency chiffoniers the feet were very much an extension of the side columns and could end in paw feet. Victorian chiffoniers usuallly boast platform bases.

Features to look for: Secretaire fitted in drawer.

Potential: A plain chiffonier can offer a good deal of scope for improvement with fresh pleated silks, brass grills and galleries, etc. Victorian examples are best shipped abroad for a substantial profit.

Interiors/drawers: Fitted secretaires in rare examples. The norm is a single drawer and one shelf in the lower cabinet.

In a word (or two): A very useful, frequently decorative antique; possibly under-rated.

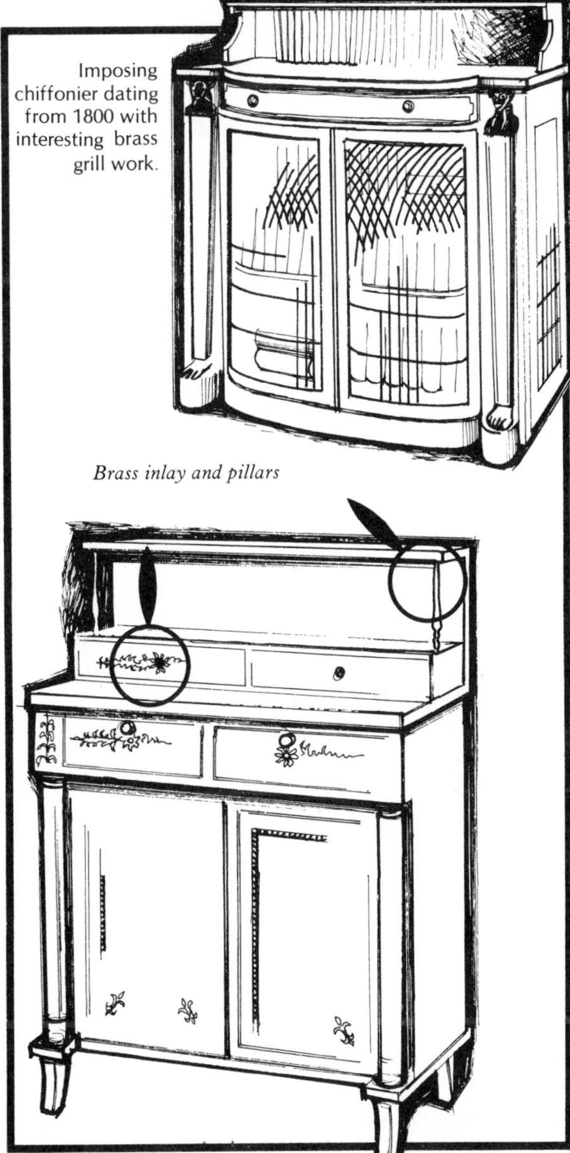

Imposing chiffonier dating from 1800 with interesting brass grill work.

Brass inlay and pillars

Georgian design, circa 1780.

Georgian design, circa 1770.

A late Georgian design in mahogany, circa 1810.

Victorian design in mahogany, circa 1840.

Regency design in rosewood, circa 1830.

Regency design in rosewood, circa 1820, lyre motifs.

Regency design in mahogany, circa 1810.

A rare and most attractive George III supper canterbury showing the original purpose of the canterbury as an elbow height bottle holder.

Canterburys

Quick view: An open-topped container, usually on four legs with a single drawer below, popularly supposed to hold Georgian or Victorian music. Research indicates that early canterburys were designed to hold bottles, cutlery, etc., for an informal supper. There are early references to 'supper canterburys' which featured a tray top or galleried superstructure.

Desirable woods: Most period canterburys are found in mahogany or rosewood and the vast majority of those made in Victorian times are in finely figured walnut.

Shape: The plainer, the earlier; elaborate versions are always Victorian.

Restoration: No particular problem areas.

Fake?: Highly unlikely in last five years or so, as most competent restorers would be more gainfully employed on more substantial work. However, certainly faked in considerable numbers in the last quarter of the 19th century and in the 1920's.

Decoration/inlays: Stringing or inlays in some Victorian examples and ormolu mounts on rare Regency rosewood.

Best period: Victorian walnut may well be the most saleable from a trade viewpoint.

Features to look for: Especially fine carving and work on Victorian examples. Finely turned spindles and details on 18th century pieces.

Most valuable: Victorian walnut canterbury/whatnot, or authenticated examples by the leading designers; Thomas Hope, George Smith, Gillows, all of whom made beautiful canterburys.

In a word (or two): One of those odd pieces where the later ornate examples will make a higher price than the classic Georgian design.

price band
500 750 1000

potential
fashion

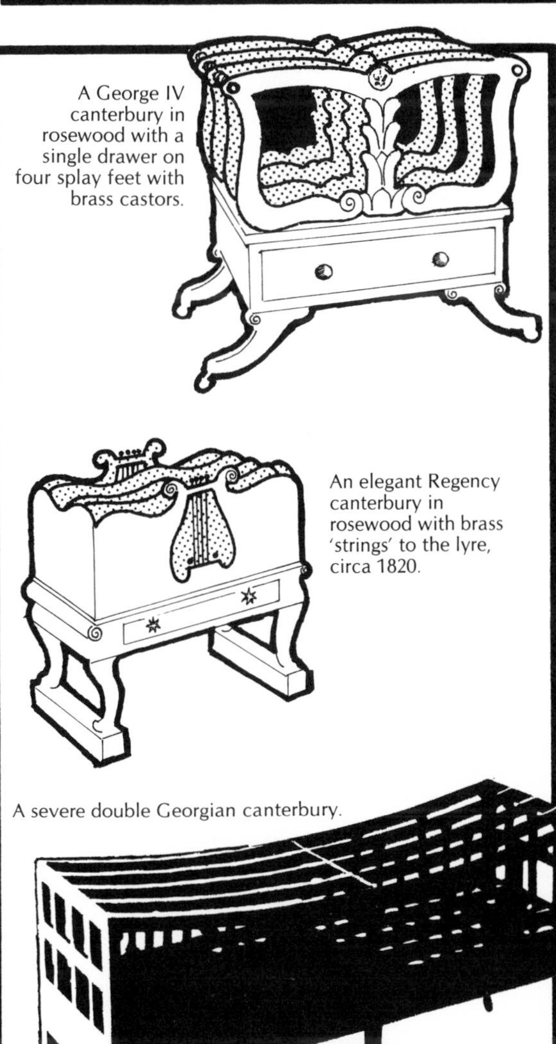

A George IV canterbury in rosewood with a single drawer on four splay feet with brass castors.

An elegant Regency canterbury in rosewood with brass 'strings' to the lyre, circa 1820.

A severe double Georgian canterbury.

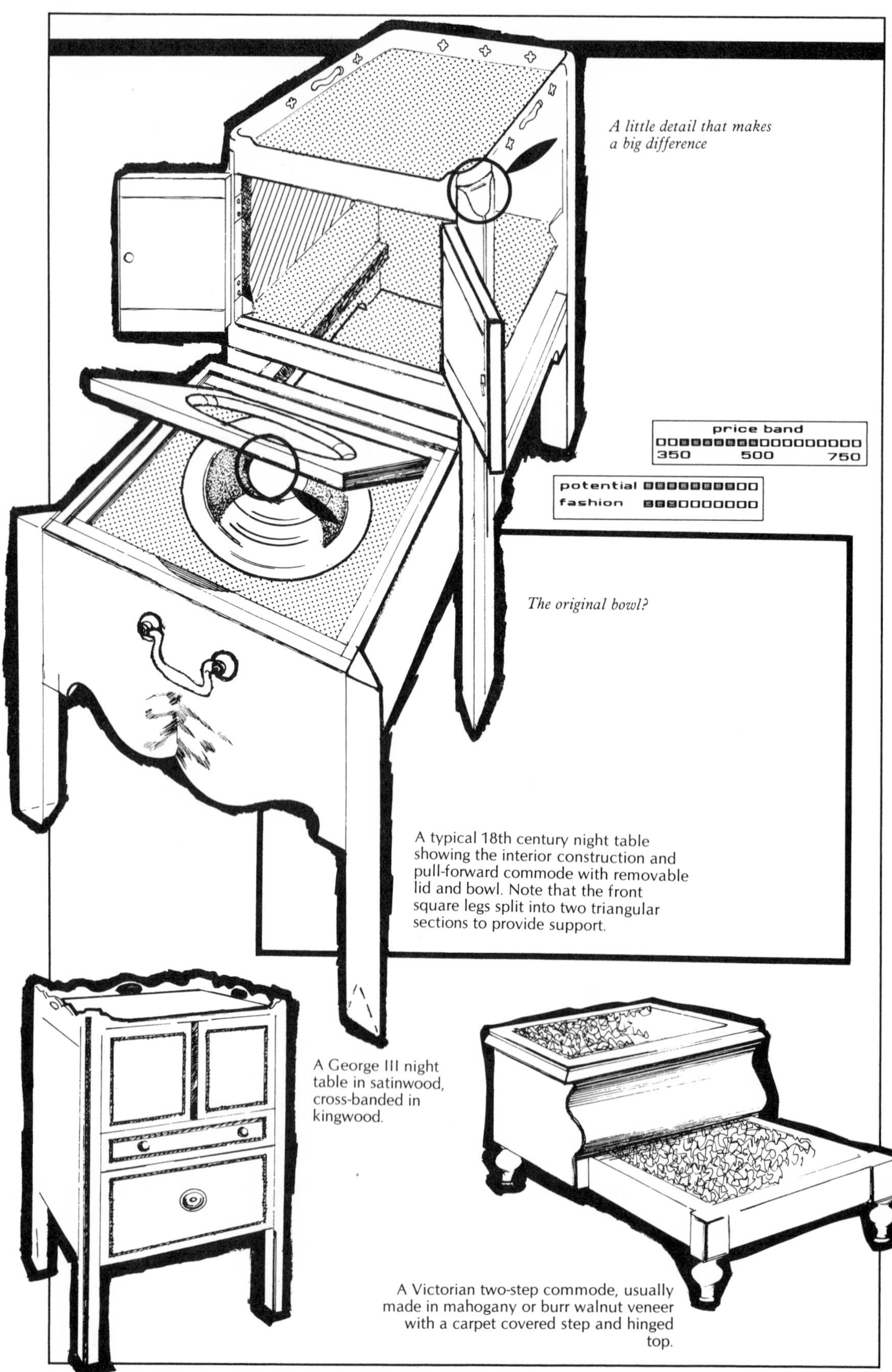

A typical 18th century night table showing the interior construction and pull-forward commode with removable lid and bowl. Note that the front square legs split into two triangular sections to provide support.

A George III night table in satinwood, cross-banded in kingwood.

A Victorian two-step commode, usually made in mahogany or burr walnut veneer with a carpet covered step and hinged top.

Commodes

Quick view: Georgian, Victorian and Edwardian period pieces designed to hold and hide chamber pots.

Desirable woods: Mahogany is the norm; satinwood the highly priced exception.

Shape: Various — see illustrations for some examples.

Restoration: Should present no particular problem. Tambour fronts can be time consuming to repair.

Fake?: Unlikely.

Configuration, Georgian: Tray top, cupboard below and pull-forward 'seat' with bowl (and cover). Some commodes were frequently made to resemble small chests of drawers, with false drawer fronts to disguise their true vocation. The **Victorian** mahogany versions make ideal fodder for today's 'improver' — see Improving Furniture. Some late Georgian and Victorian commodes double as steps used to climb into the high beds of the period.

Decoration/inlays: Cross-banding and finely carved detail.

Best period: Georgian examples command the highest prices.

Best size: The 'usual' size for the Georgian night table illustrated in the large drawing opposite is about 22″ (55cm) wide.

Features to look for: Originality, unchanged condition, fine detail in period examples. Tambour front would be desirable extra feature. Carrying handles are found on some 18th century night tables.

Potential: Victorian and Edwardian commodes or 'pot cupboards' make ideal export material and are simply converted to drinks cabinets.

Interiors/drawers: In period examples. the porcelain bowl should be present.

In a word (or two): An affordable small piece of social English history usable in many guises in the modern home.

price band
150 200 250

potential

fashion

A three-step commode frequently converted into a drinks cabinet.

A Victorian fluted circular pot cupboard with built-in wash basin. Usually in mahogany veneer or walnut.

Look for inlaid decorative panels. These may be considerably older than the carcase
price band
1000 3000 4000
potential
fashion
Dowel fixings do not indicate true age
Quality of carving is important. The deeper and more undercut the better!
Beware light coloured oak
Expect to find wear. If not – suspect!

Oak Cupboards

Desirable woods: Always in oak, pegged or morticed and tenoned together, seldom dovetails; drawers pinned together, panels slotted into grooves.

Shape, configuration: Basic shape of two or three large cupboards, surrounded by a pair of drawers and further pair of cupboards set back with a platform in front. If a third open-fronted compartment is added to the top, it is termed a 'Welsh tridarn'.

Restoration: How much more 'work' can they stand?

Fake?: Very, very likely. Made in huge quantities at the beginning of the 20th century — frequently by Dutch craftsmen working in England in old oak which was imported by the boat load.

Decoration/inlays: Profuse carving and (infrequently) marquetry inlays.

Best period: 17th century.

Best size: Small, under 5′ (1.5m) wide.

In a word (or two): A dramatic, substantial, and frequently handsome piece which you should enjoy even though it may not be as old as you might perhaps wish it to be.

THE FOOD HUTCH, a rare and highly desirable variety of oak cupboard. Usually found today as a small standing cupboard with a combination of blind doors and open baluster-turned doors. They were originally intended for the storage of foodstuffs. Wall-hanging versions were found in churches when they contained bread to be given free to parishioners and supplied by local benefactors.

THE BUFFET (or more correctly court cupboard) consists of a series of two or three very substantial open shelves separated by massive carved baluster supports. Genuine early English examples are very rare — the vast majority on offer were made in the early 20th century.

A Jacobean period carved oak food hutch, circa 1680.

An early 17th century oak food hutch.

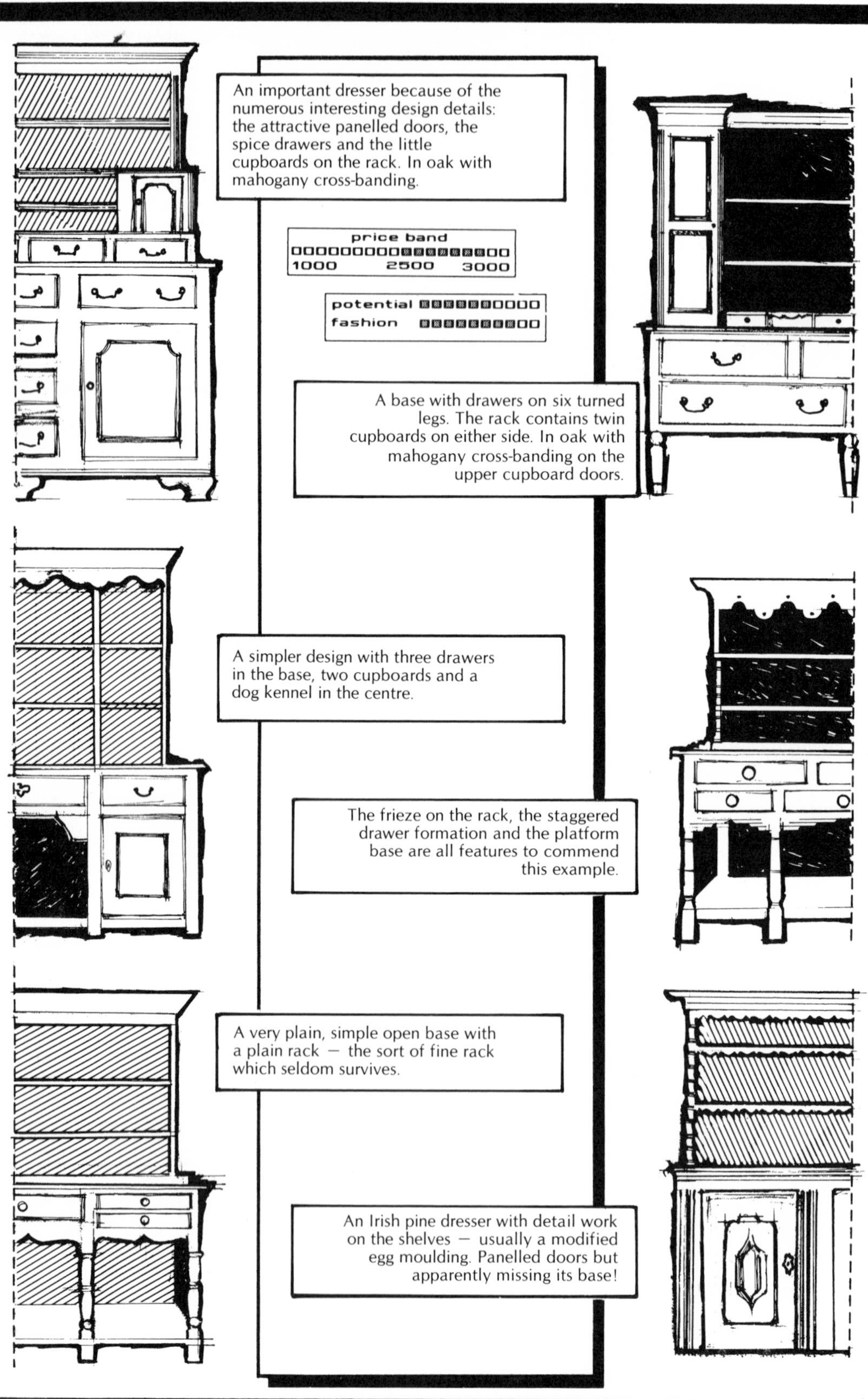
An important dresser because of the numerous interesting design details: the attractive panelled doors, the spice drawers and the little cupboards on the rack. In oak with mahogany cross-banding.
price band
1000 2500 3000
potential
fashion
A base with drawers on six turned legs. The rack contains twin cupboards on either side. In oak with mahogany cross-banding on the upper cupboard doors.
A simpler design with three drawers in the base, two cupboards and a dog kennel in the centre.
The frieze on the rack, the staggered drawer formation and the platform base are all features to commend this example.
A very plain, simple open base with a plain rack — the sort of fine rack which seldom survives.
An Irish pine dresser with detail work on the shelves — usually a modified egg moulding. Panelled doors but apparently missing its base!

Dressers

Quick view: A useful kitchen cupboard now promoted to the ranks of highly desirable antique. There is a story that dresser bases were given as wedding presents and the rack followed five years later, on the wooden anniversary. A lovely story and maybe even true; it would help to explain why so many bases and racks do not match perfectly.

Desirable woods: Oak, pine, some fruitwoods — although not common.

Restoration: Pine is the most difficult to match successfully.

Fake?: Not likely, although marriage of base and new rack very possible.

Configuration: Base can be either cupboards or drawers, or a mixture of both — some examples include a dog kennel or a chicken coop!

Decoration/inlay: Some mahogany cross-banded oak drawer fronts.

Racks: Seldom original — mainly because they are of fairly flimsy construction and will have suffered considerable damage. Many were fixed to the wall and would suffer even more damage when moved.

Best size: 5′ to 6′ (1.5-2m) wide — show extreme caution with very small dressers.

Colour: Rich warm colour with good patination.

Features to look for: Spice drawers in rack. Original and/or elaborate rack — it's fair to say that the more elaborate the rack is, and the more decorative the friezes, cupboards, drawers — the higher the price.

Most valuable: In oak; good colour, deep patination and original complicated rack and frieze.

In a word (or two): Dressers are very much 'kitchen furniture' and have only recently been promoted to the realms of desirable dining room or even living room furniture.

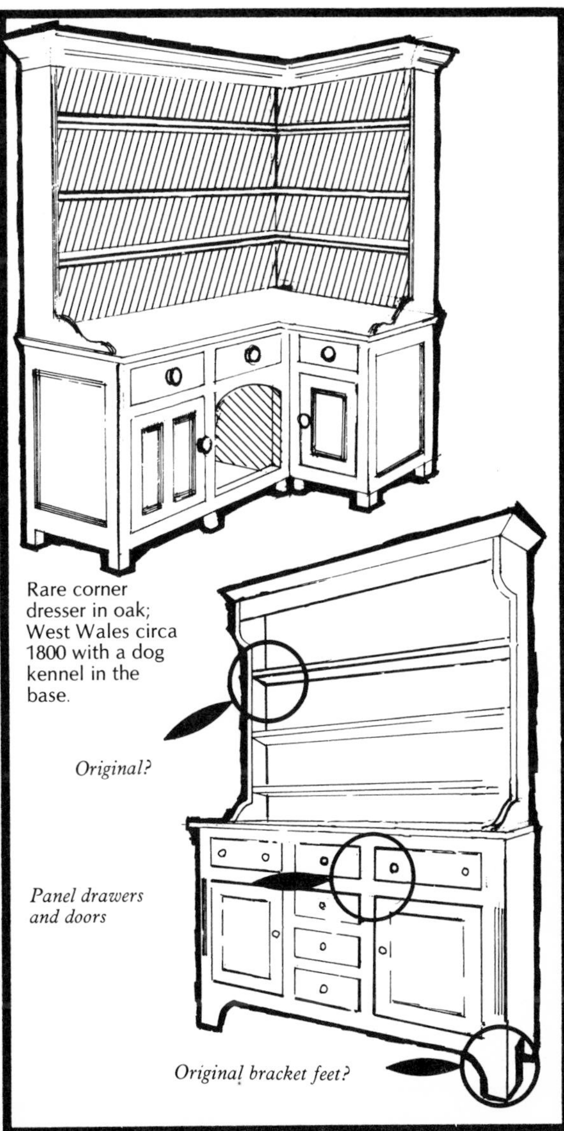

Rare corner dresser in oak; West Wales circa 1800 with a dog kennel in the base.

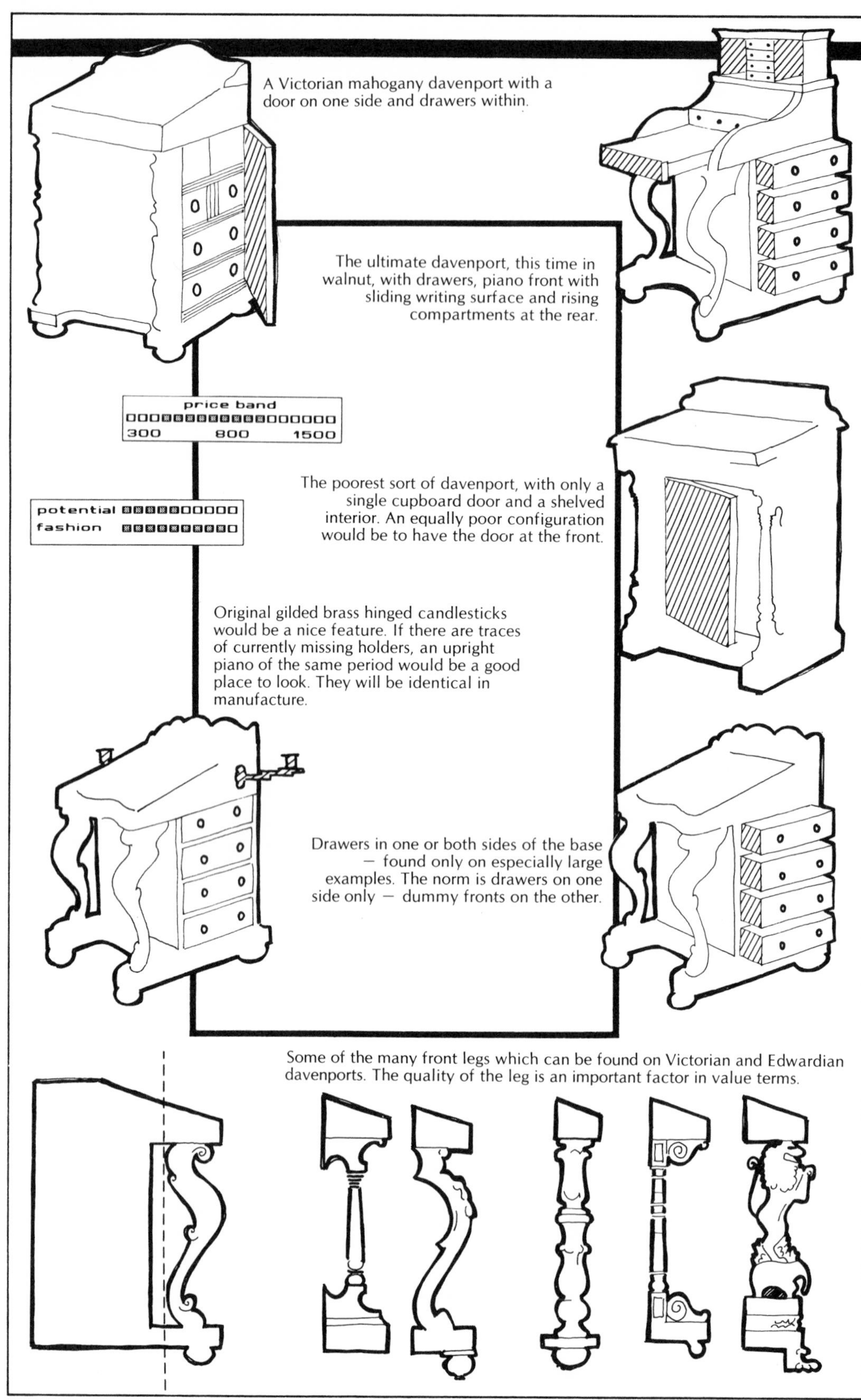

A Victorian mahogany davenport with a door on one side and drawers within.

The ultimate davenport, this time in walnut, with drawers, piano front with sliding writing surface and rising compartments at the rear.

The poorest sort of davenport, with only a single cupboard door and a shelved interior. An equally poor configuration would be to have the door at the front.

Original gilded brass hinged candlesticks would be a nice feature. If there are traces of currently missing holders, an upright piano of the same period would be a good place to look. They will be identical in manufacture.

Drawers in one or both sides of the base — found only on especially large examples. The norm is drawers on one side only — dummy fronts on the other.

Some of the many front legs which can be found on Victorian and Edwardian davenports. The quality of the leg is an important factor in value terms.

Davenports

Quick view: A frequently charming small desk, the writing surface supported by two front legs, the base containing a series of drawers or cupboards.

Desirable woods: Georgian examples in mahogany or exotic woods. Victorian davenports tend to epitomize the design and technical inventiveness of that period.

Handles: Relatively unimportant.

Restoration: The weights and rise and fall mechanism on mechanical davenports can present problems for the restorer.

Fake?: Unlikely.

Configuration: Various permutations; some have a rising section for writing materials together with a hinged 'piano' front. The qualities of front legs, the combination of drawers and side or front cupboards or, rarely, cupboard door over drawers are all present.

Decoration/inlays: In the Georgian examples, little decoration other than a brass gallery. With Victorian or Edwardian, as much carving or inlays as possible.

Best period: For the purist, the plain Regency example.

Best size: Small, under 20" (50cm) wide.

Features to look for: Mechanical features; candle slides.

Potential: Should not require 'improvement' other than replacement of brass gallery.

Interiors/drawers: Interiors and drawers usually of simple construction.

Most valuable: Either a period example in an exotic wood or a heavy carved walnut mid-Victorian example. However, do take care not to over-value late Victorian or Edwardian with poor quality walnut veneers, shallow (or 'mean') carving on the knees, and cupboard in front of base.

In a word (or two): Not the most 'useful' of desks but an attractive and highly rated piece.

A Georgian (or Victorian copy) showing the sliding writing compartment which allows it to be used slightly less uncomfortably. Davenports are not really for using! This example in mahogany also has a side writing slide to provide more working surface.

price band			potential ■■■■■■■□□□
□□□□□■■■■■■□□□□□□□			fashion ■■■■■■■□□□
1000	1500	2000	

This period mahogany example has the typical sliding top but contains tiny drawers in the side for ink wells and the like.

price band		
2500	3500	6000

potential

fashion

Most partners' or large pedestal desk are 'important' if they have any semblance of age or quality.

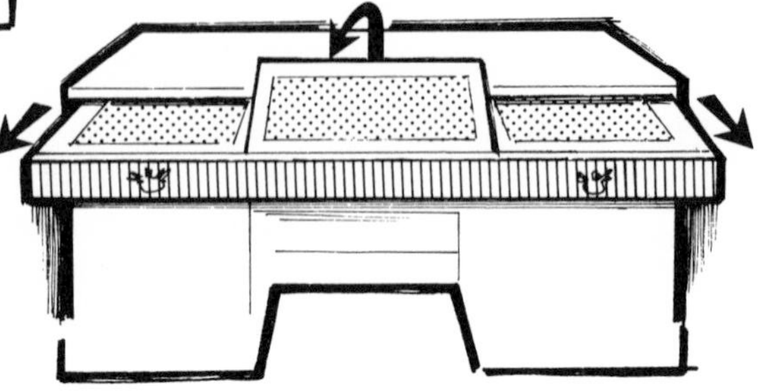

In this example the entire top drawer pulls forward to provide a vast area of extra work surface. The side leather-topped sections then slide backwards to expose compartments; the central section hinges upwards as a writing or reading stand.

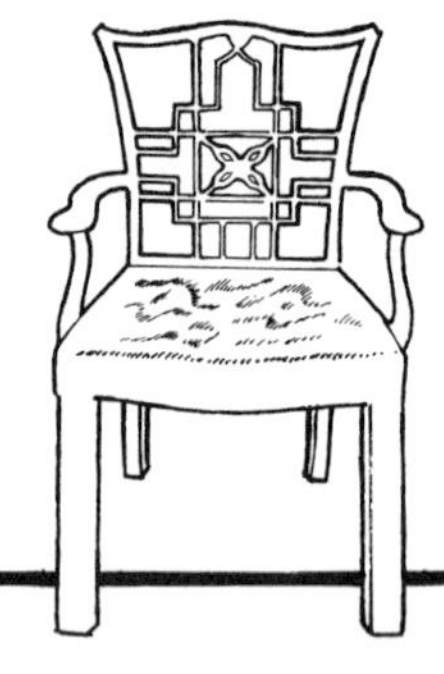

Odd elbow or carver chairs make excellent desk chairs!

price band		
250	500	750

potential

fashion

ROLL & CYLINDER TOP DESKS

Quick view: The roll-top desk was found in every small business office the world over. Now very much in favour in the United States.

Desirable woods: Roll top — oak; cylinder — mahogany.

Restoration: Specialist restorers have large stocks of spare parts.

Fake?: Very unlikely; too expensive to reproduce.

Configuration: Desk section with roll opening mechanism, busy interior with numerous pigeon holes, pencil holders, twin (or single) pedestals with writing slides at top. Modesty screen between pedestals.

Best period: 1880-1900.

Best size: Medium size about four feet wide.

Colour: Golden brown oak, dark mahogany.

Feet: Plinth.

Features to look for: Count the features — the more the merrier.

Most valuable: American made examples, bearing original makers plaques.

In a word (or two): The original staple of the Brighton antique trade.

Pedestal & Partners' Desks

Quick view: If you have 'arrived' you will have one!

Desirable woods: Period in mahogany or pine; Victorian and later, in pine and walnut.

Restoration: No particular problem areas; care should be taken before leather is replaced — far better a worn original than a less-than-superb replacement. Leather should always be fitted on ultra smooth plaster of paris base.

Fake?: Outright fake unlikely (unless in pine), but could have been 'well-attended to'.

Configuration: A pedestal desk is usually two upright 'units' each containing four drawers, plus a leather-covered work surface containing one long central drawer and a short drawer at either end. A partners' desk is, in effect, two pedestal desks built facing each other — for two partners to sit at!

Decoration/inlays: Stringing and cross-banding, particularly in late examples.

Best period: 1750-1800.

Best size: Almost any size is desirable — with partners' desks, the larger is almost always better.

Features to look for: Quality is everything. If you are in any doubt about the date of a leather-topped desk, check the width of the wood surround. In Georgian examples the wood will be narrow, about 1 inch wide — in later examples the Victorians tended to show more wood, frequently two-and-a-half to three inches wide.

Interiors/drawers: Sliding or rising writing surfaces in central drawer in some examples. Most interesting desks were especially made to the client's individual requirements and incorporate special features, folio racks, special drawer interiors, finely panelled cupboard doors over drawers, etc.

Most valuable: Handsome, original partners' desk in mahogany with finely carved details. The ultimate Partners' Desk is in Nostell Priory in Yorkshire.

In a word (or two): If there was one thing I liked to find on a private call . . !

Some partners' desks are fitted with original brass carrying handles. This example also has a rising reading stand which lays flush with the leather surface when not in use.

Partners' desks are so named as they were originally intended to be used by two people. The drawer and cupboard layout is not usually mirror but diagonally opposite, e.g. drawers on the right whatever side you use.

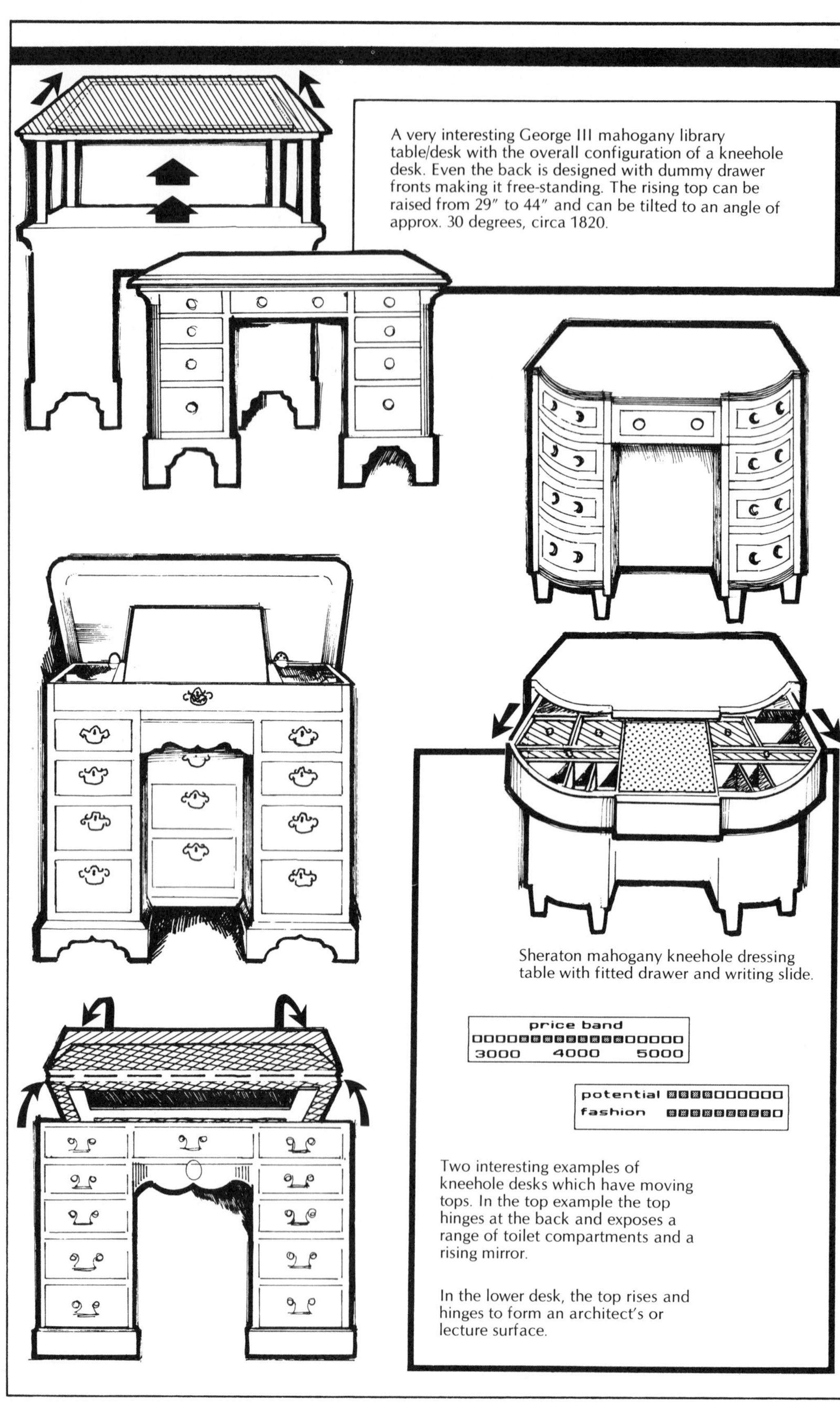

A very interesting George III mahogany library table/desk with the overall configuration of a kneehole desk. Even the back is designed with dummy drawer fronts making it free-standing. The rising top can be raised from 29″ to 44″ and can be tilted to an angle of approx. 30 degrees, circa 1820.

Sheraton mahogany kneehole dressing table with fitted drawer and writing slide.

Two interesting examples of kneehole desks which have moving tops. In the top example the top hinges at the back and exposes a range of toilet compartments and a rising mirror.

In the lower desk, the top rises and hinges to form an architect's or lecture surface.

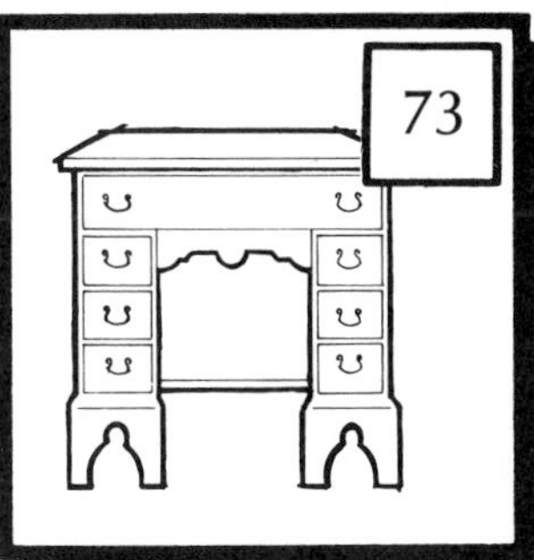

Kneehole Desks

Desirable woods: Mainly walnut.

Handles: One per drawer — plain or simple engraved, shaped plate with a swan drop handle.

Restoration: The feet are much taller than with other pieces of walnut furniture of the same period and are frequently damaged due to their high slender proportions. Drawer fronts will have received fairly constant use over the years and may also require help.

Fake?: Although kneehole desks command regular high prices in the trade and at auction, the very same trade is generally suspicious of this highly desirable small piece of furniture — with very good reason. It is one of those cases where it is a great deal easier not to look too closely and take a profit. In the days when walnut chests-on-chests and chests of drawers were more freely available as breakers, many changed direction somewhat and ended up looking a great deal like kneehole desks. Today, they have matured to a degree where exposure is unlikely.

Configuration: Two pedestals, each with three drawers and a central full-width drawer and a cupboard (or rarely, a further three drawers) below. Oak-lined drawers.

Decoration/inlays: Cross-banded and feathered.

Best top: Quartered and cross-banded top.

Best size: The smaller the better.

Colour: That of the finest heather honey!

Feet: Tall, slim, bracket; sometimes four feet to the front.

Features to look for: The central cupboard pulls forward flush with the pedestals. Tall original feet.

Interiors: Rare lift-up top to reveal fitted interior as dressing table, long false drawer front.

Most valuable: All are expensive! A totally 'right' example even more so.

Oddities: Very rare architect's or artist's top.

In a word (or two): Not a desk in fact, but rather a dressing table from the bedroom or dressing room. Only referred to as such today by the higher echelon of the trade.

In this early English walnut example, the top drawer is pulled forward to show the fitted compartments, all enclosed with a slide which, in turn, provides extra surface area.

Tall bracket feet

price band		
□□□□■■■■■■■■■■□□□□□□		
2000	4000	6000

potential	■■■■■■□□□□
fashion	■■■■■■□□□□

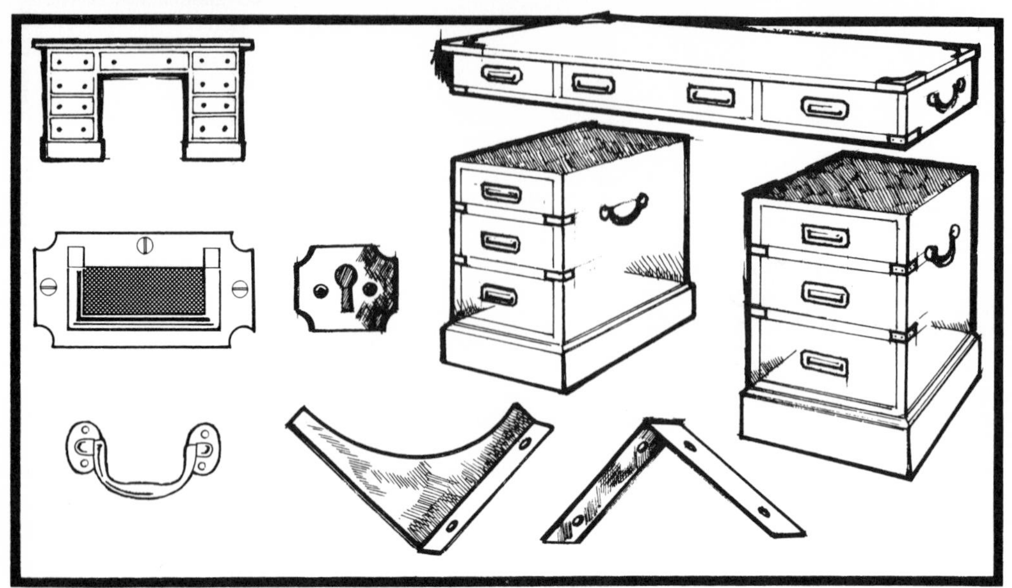

price band
400 500 600

A shopping list of the brass fittings required to change a mundane pedestal desk into a glamorous fighting man's desk. You will need brass straps, recessed handles, carrying handles, corner pieces and brass escutcheons.

A military chest with single carrying handle and recessed handles, on platform feet.

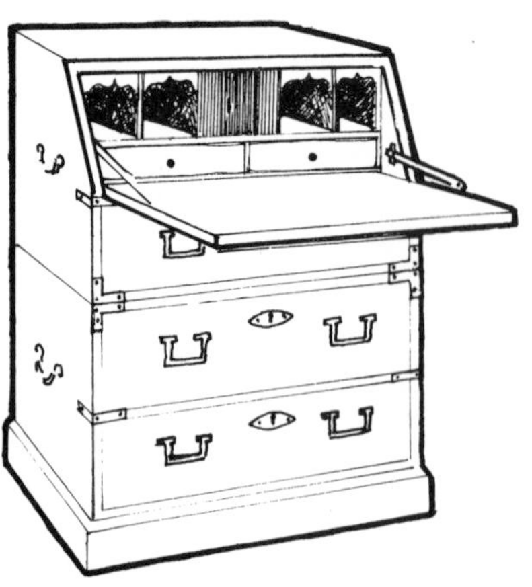

A military bureau, splitting into two parts.

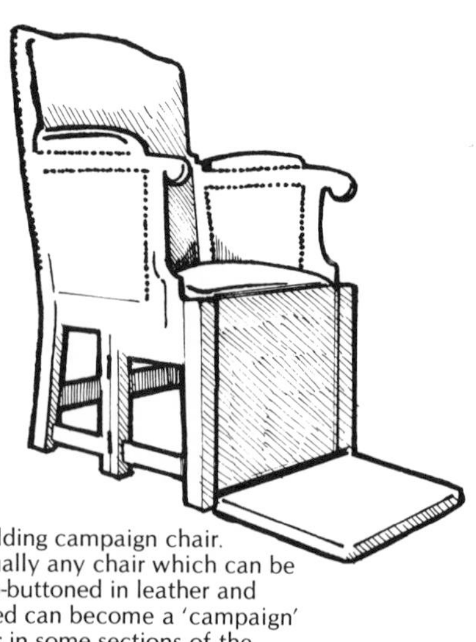

A folding campaign chair. Virtually any chair which can be deep-buttoned in leather and folded can become a 'campaign' chair in some sections of the antique trade.

price band
250 500 750

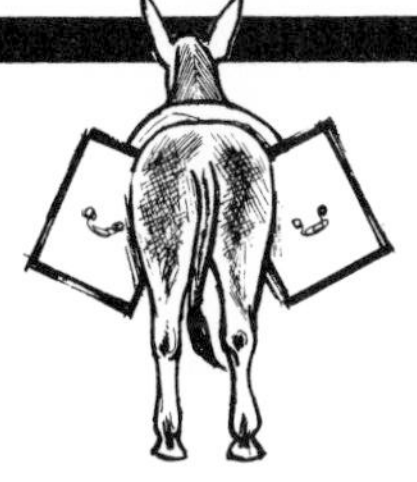

The story goes that military chests split into two equally weighted parts so that they can be carried on either side of an army mule.

Military Furniture

Quick view: A square chest of drawers, usually in red mahogany, furnished with numerous brass fittings and carrying handles, frequently in two parts designed for lifting by 'other ranks.'

Desirable woods: Either mahogany or padouk* (occasionally in pine).

Shape: Very straight — very 'military'

Handles: Recessed brass drawer handles, carrying handles on sides in either brass or iron.

Restoration: Very simple and straight forward; no particular problems — replacement drawer handles, corner pieces, corner straps and carrying handles are readily available. Corners and straps come in both cast and sheet brass.

Fake?: Highly likely. Run your fingers over the surface with your eyes shut — If you feel the brass work standing 'proud' have a closer look and beware!

Best period: 1800-1830 and 1950's onwards!

Best size: usually between 3' to 4' (1-1.2cm) wide — smaller sizes would be preferable.

Feet: Either added bracket feet, Victorian ball feet or carcase sitting in or on a plinth.

Features to look for: Secretaire or other interesting addition — perhaps a name plate or other sign of previous army owner.

Potential: Leave well alone.

Interiors/drawers: Secretaire or other interior fittings very desirable and adding considerably to value.

Most valuable: Totally original with provenance and some history — perhaps proof of ownership by notable soldier.

In a word (or two): The vast majority of military furniture is a total fake — they are so very simple to reproduce using a rather plain chest (or any other 'masculine' furniture) with readily available fittings — (both in cast and sheet brass). However, they can be most attractive and are extremely easy to sell.

*A very dense Indian hardwood. You will know it when you try and pick it up. Almost certainly GENUINE in padouk.

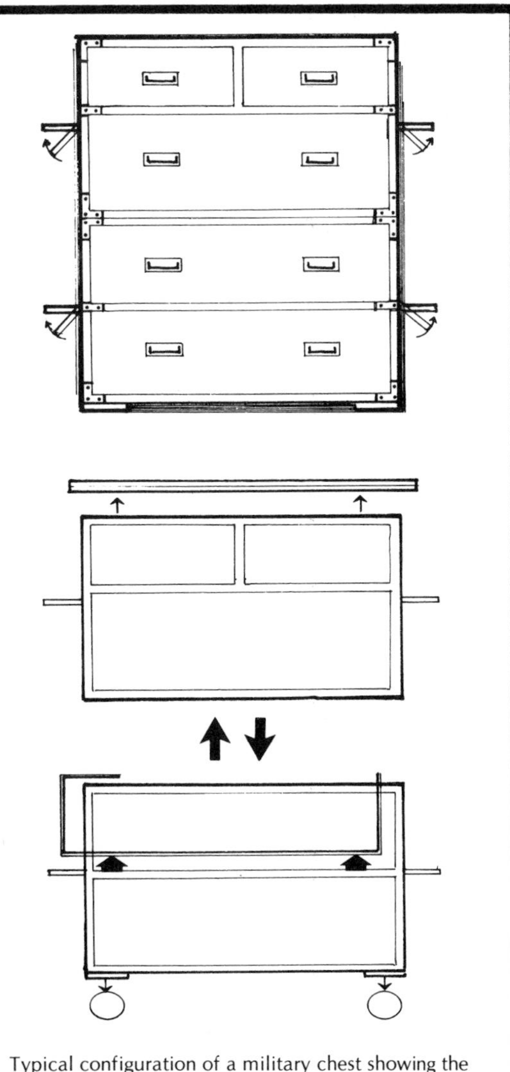

Typical configuration of a military chest showing the division and carrying handles for each section.

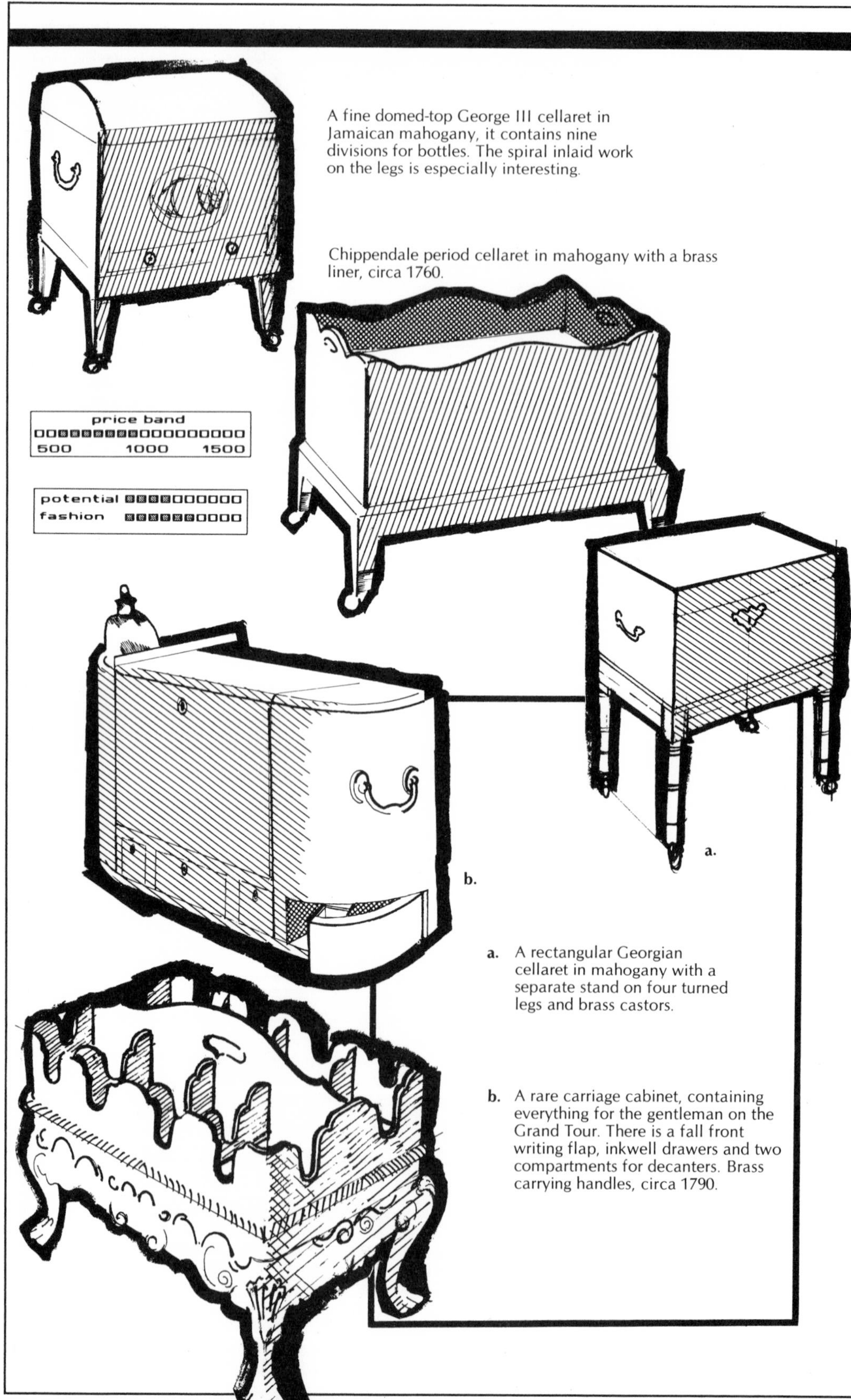

A fine domed-top George III cellaret in Jamaican mahogany, it contains nine divisions for bottles. The spiral inlaid work on the legs is especially interesting.

Chippendale period cellaret in mahogany with a brass liner, circa 1760.

a. A rectangular Georgian cellaret in mahogany with a separate stand on four turned legs and brass castors.

b. A rare carriage cabinet, containing everything for the gentleman on the Grand Tour. There is a fall front writing flap, inkwell drawers and two compartments for decanters. Brass carrying handles, circa 1790.

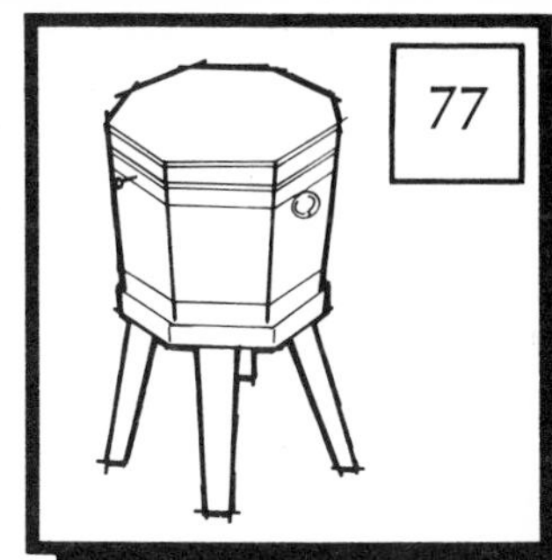

Containers for Wine

Quick view: A wide variety of designs originally intended to keep, store or cool wines.

Desirable woods: Mainly in solid or veneered mahogany.

Shape: Very varied, ranging from bound 'barrels' or 'pails' to elaborate lidded sarcophagus shapes, etc.

Restoration: Specialist services to make good any lead defects may be required.

Fake?: Total fake is unlikely, new stand (as an illustration) possible.

Configuration: A container, usually lead lined, or a 'box' to hold bottles — early examples were frequently designed 'en suite' with side tables (sideboards).

Decoration/inlays: Marquetry or inlaid stringing in Georgian mahogany examples, fine carving, and brass inlay on Regency period examples. Many of the larger and more important examples were produced for major country and town houses by the very best designers and craftsmen of their day. In this respect, some represent the ultimate in design and the highest degree in sheer quality of materials and construction.

Best period: 1780-1830.

Best size: Small generally preferred to large — some sarcophagus cellarets can be very large.

Feet: Cast brass, castors or carved.

Features to look for: Original fittings, lead linings. Many cellarettes held ice or iced water (stored underground from winter or in the estate ice-house) and would have been provided with a tap at the base to drain off water after use.

Oddities: Some were originally used to hold chamber pots in the best dining rooms before it was considered fashionable to place these in a compartment actually in the sideboard.

In a word (or two): As a trade item, all but the very finest are not really considered desirable and they have yet to become popular with the general antique buying public or trade.

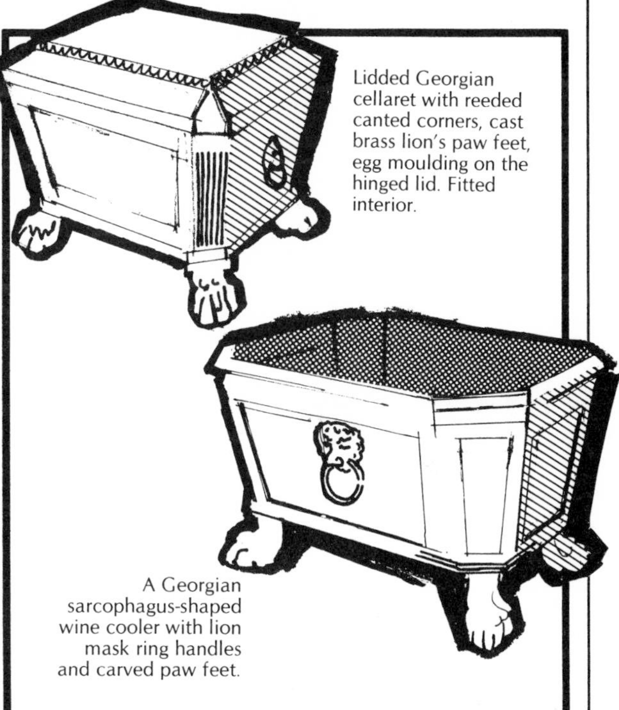

Lidded Georgian cellaret with reeded canted corners, cast brass lion's paw feet, egg moulding on the hinged lid. Fitted interior.

A Georgian sarcophagus-shaped wine cooler with lion mask ring handles and carved paw feet.

price band
1000 1500 2000

potential
fashion

A Georgian wine cooler in mahogany with brass bands.

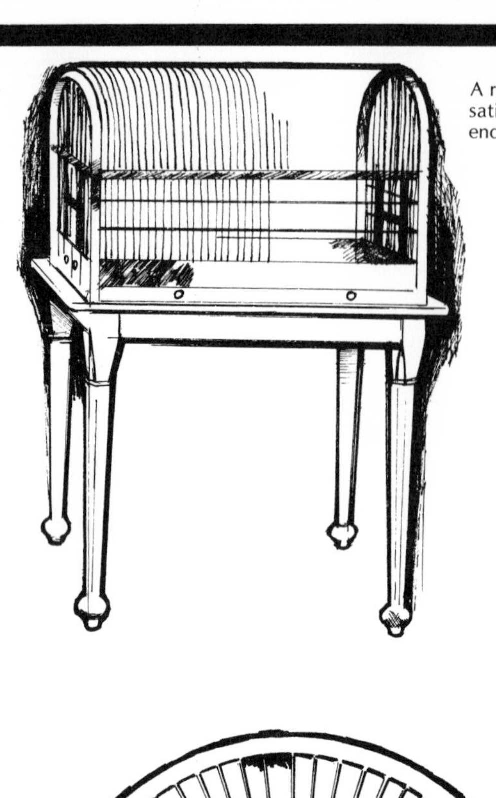

A rare late 18th century cage made in walnut, satinwood and ebony on four turned tapered legs ending in unusual lobed feet.

A fanciful 19th century cage in painted wood and wire some 40″ high.

price band
100 500 1000

potential
fashion

A 19th century example in beech based on the design of the Crystal Palace.

Birdcages

Short description: A mirror image of the home or status of the Victorian bird fancier.

Shape: Almost anything goes — the more outrageous the better.

Restoration: A sympathetic restorer may listen!

Fake?: Highly unlikely, although fairly recent 'show' cages are being offered as antique — probably unwittingly.

Decoration/inlays: All manner of inlays, brass stringings, ivories and fretworks are possible and desirable.

Best period: The most exciting period for birdcage design is the 19th century although earlier examples are rarer and could well be more expensive.

Best size: As big as you can afford or house!

Colour: Most cages are painted or japanned.

Feet: Cast brass or gilded brass where applicable.

Features to look for: Originality and little details like horn drinking bowls, mahogany, teak or pewter seed drawers or dishes.

Potential: They are featured in auction sale advertisements mainly because they are considered eye-catching but they have yet to be collected really seriously. There is no specific Price Guide as yet!

Interiors/drawers: just the functional drawers for seeds or cleaning-out!

In a word (or two): Don't let a live bird near one!

I make no apologies for including antique birdcages with furniture. In many respects they are a reflection of design, style and taste in microcosm. The more vulgar excesses of the Regency and Victorian periods are to be seen in miniature in their owner's birdcages.

Cages were very much a necessity in the Victorian home as a book on the new hobby of bird keeping reports — an owner had left his newly acquired parrot flying free in the house. When he returned after an evening at his club, he found that the bird had completely chewed through one leg of his billiard table!

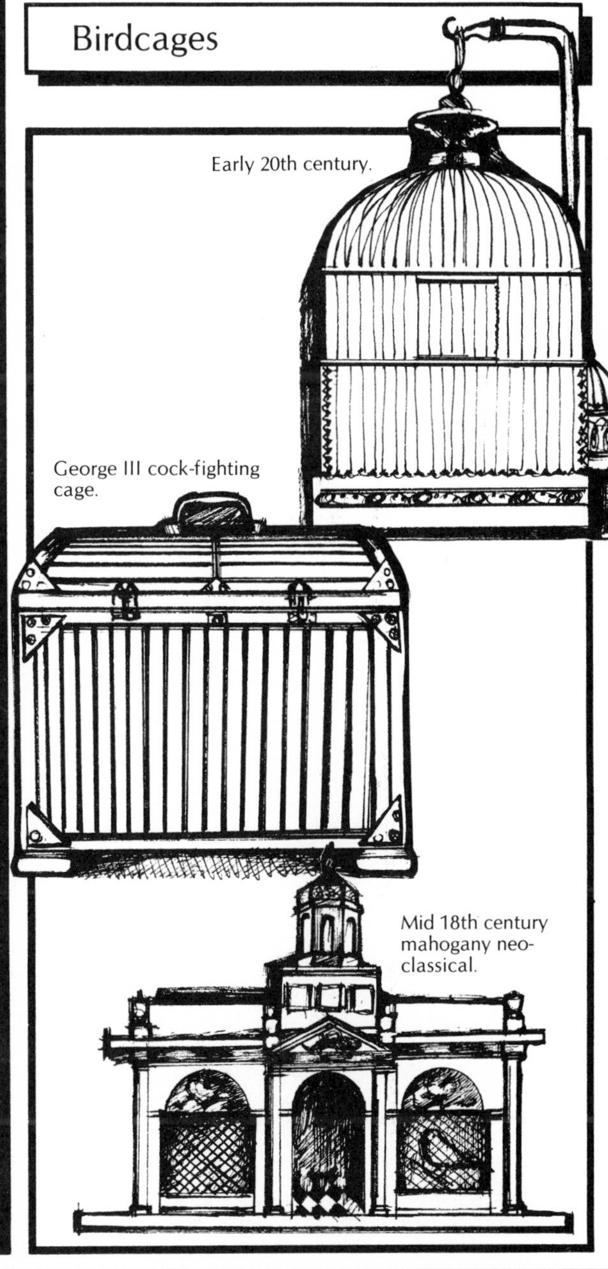

Early 20th century.

George III cock-fighting cage.

Mid 18th century mahogany neo-classical.

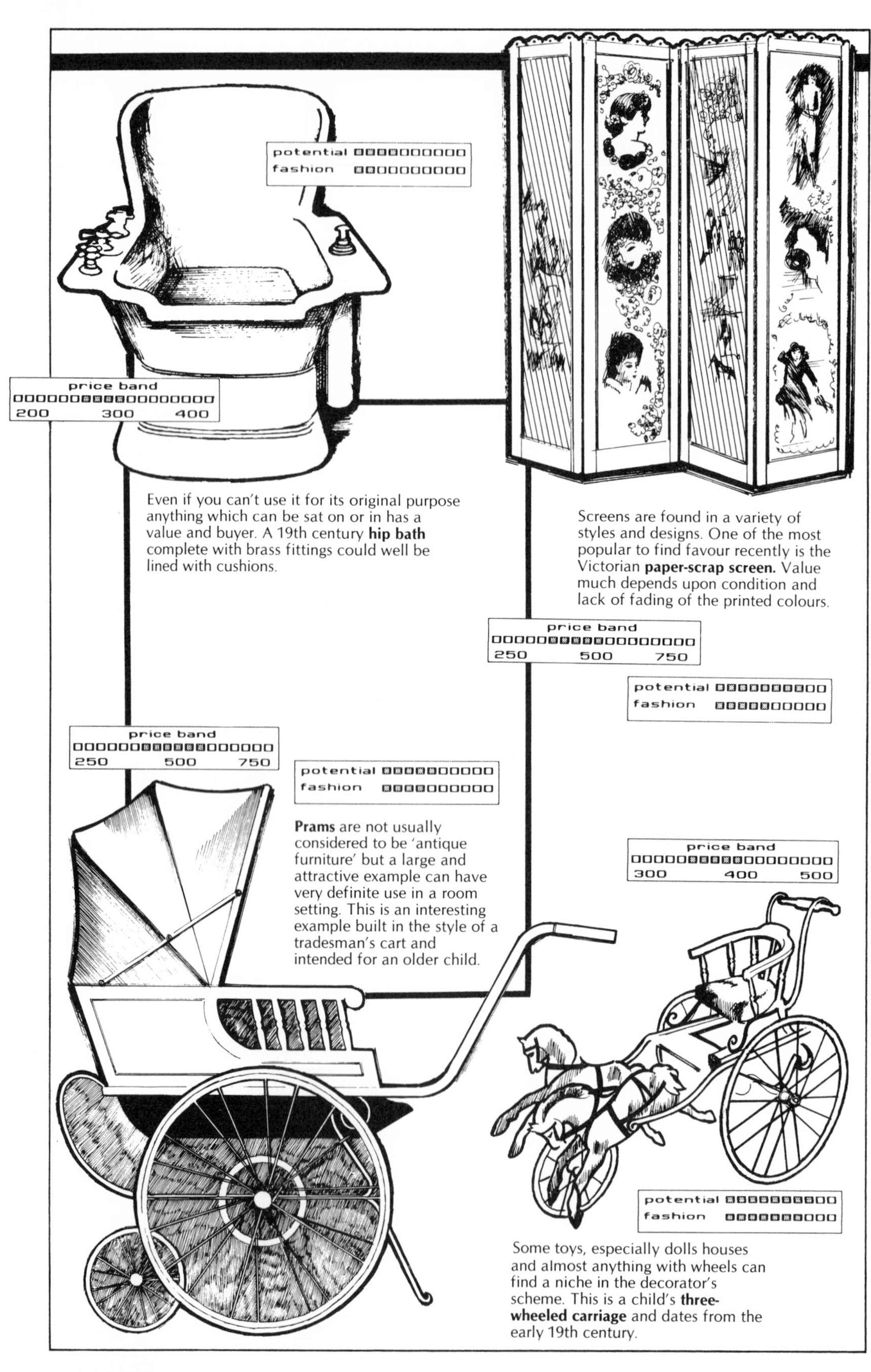

Even if you can't use it for its original purpose anything which can be sat on or in has a value and buyer. A 19th century **hip bath** complete with brass fittings could well be lined with cushions.

Screens are found in a variety of styles and designs. One of the most popular to find favour recently is the Victorian **paper-scrap screen.** Value much depends upon condition and lack of fading of the printed colours.

Prams are not usually considered to be 'antique furniture' but a large and attractive example can have very definite use in a room setting. This is an interesting example built in the style of a tradesman's cart and intended for an older child.

Some toys, especially dolls houses and almost anything with wheels can find a niche in the decorator's scheme. This is a child's **three-wheeled carriage** and dates from the early 19th century.

Miscellany I

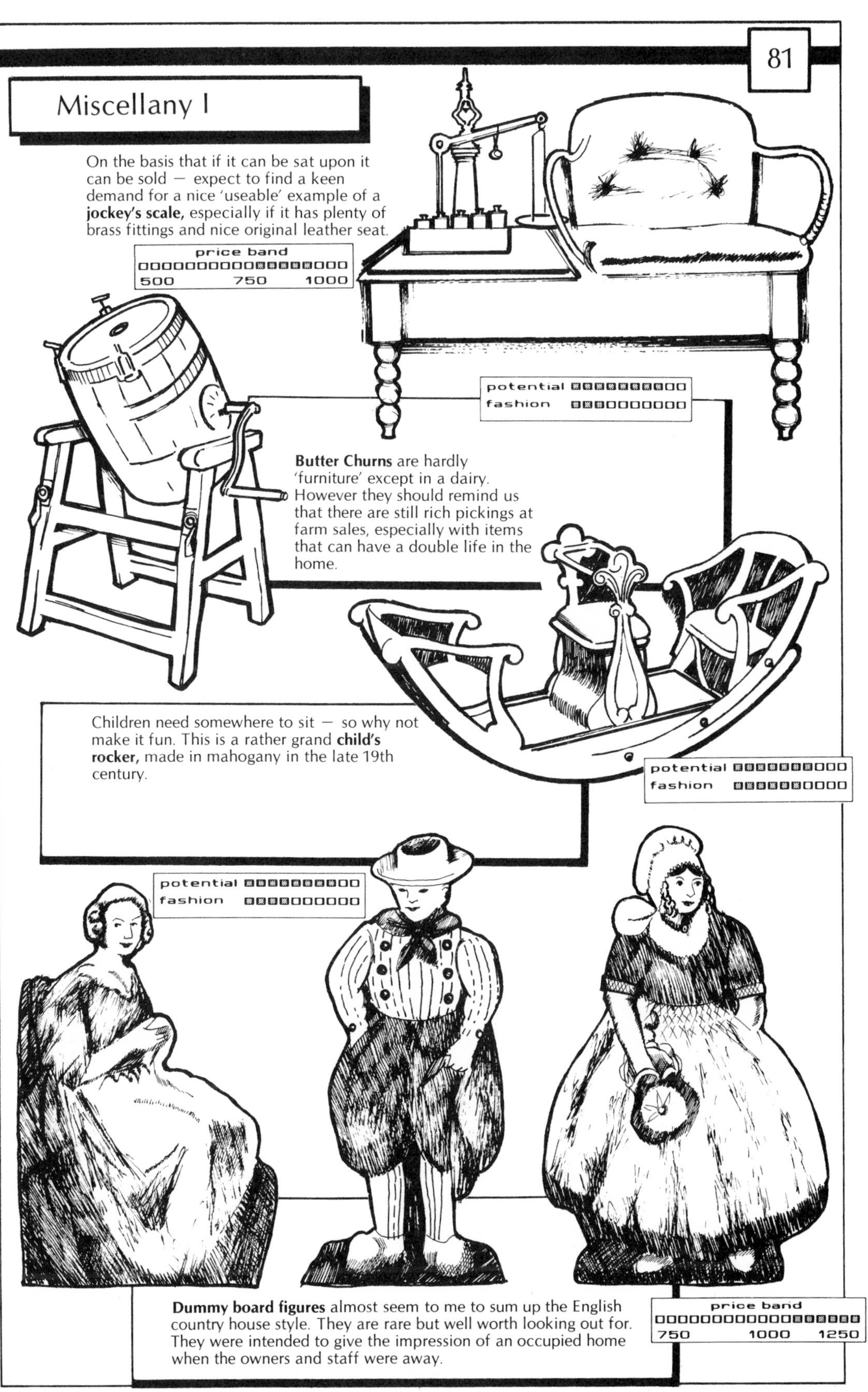

On the basis that if it can be sat upon it can be sold — expect to find a keen demand for a nice 'useable' example of a **jockey's scale,** especially if it has plenty of brass fittings and nice original leather seat.

Butter Churns are hardly 'furniture' except in a dairy. However they should remind us that there are still rich pickings at farm sales, especially with items that can have a double life in the home.

Children need somewhere to sit — so why not make it fun. This is a rather grand **child's rocker,** made in mahogany in the late 19th century.

Dummy board figures almost seem to me to sum up the English country house style. They are rare but well worth looking out for. They were intended to give the impression of an occupied home when the owners and staff were away.

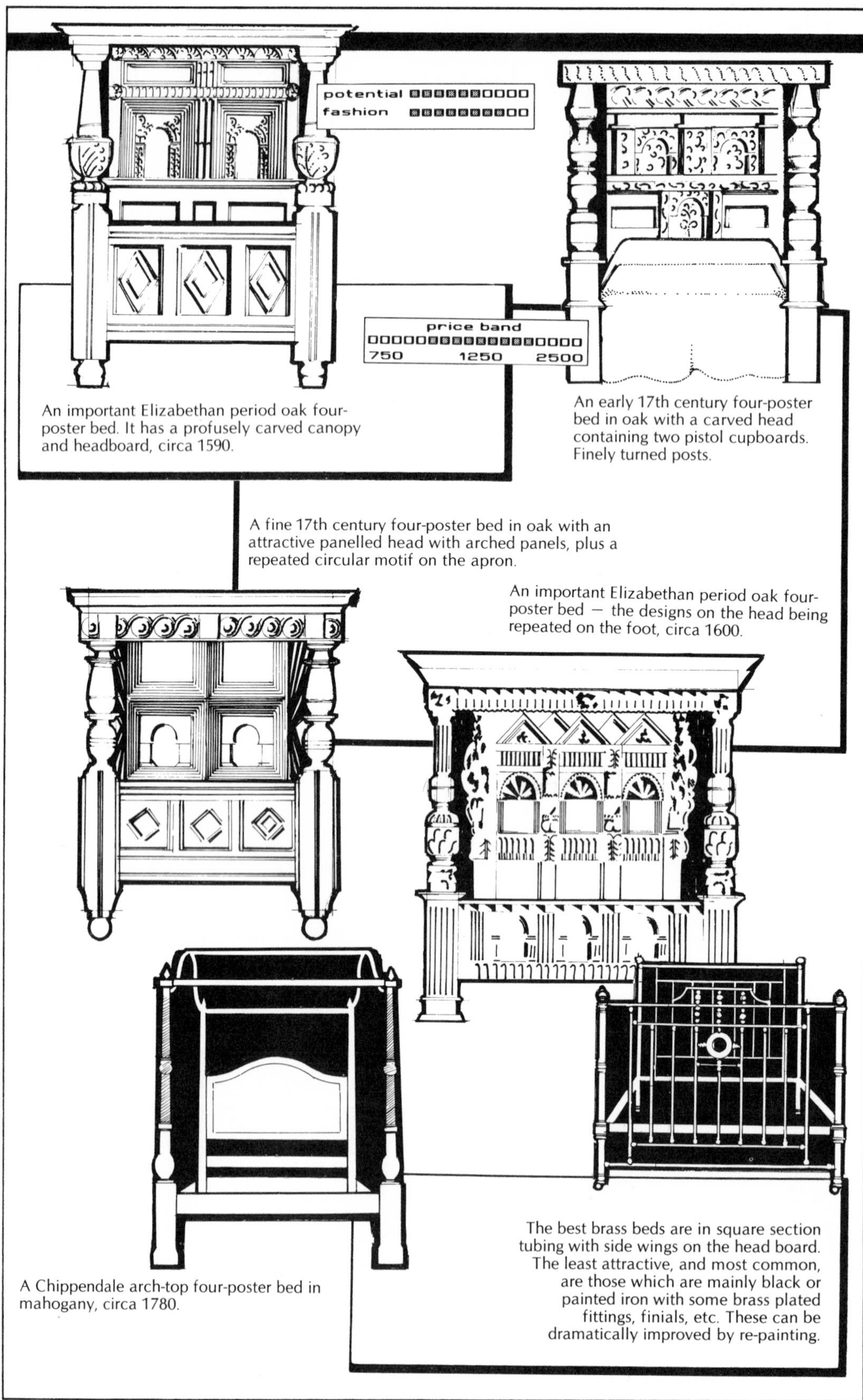

An important Elizabethan period oak four-poster bed. It has a profusely carved canopy and headboard, circa 1590.

An early 17th century four-poster bed in oak with a carved head containing two pistol cupboards. Finely turned posts.

A fine 17th century four-poster bed in oak with an attractive panelled head with arched panels, plus a repeated circular motif on the apron.

An important Elizabethan period oak four-poster bed — the designs on the head being repeated on the foot, circa 1600.

A Chippendale arch-top four-poster bed in mahogany, circa 1780.

The best brass beds are in square section tubing with side wings on the head board. The least attractive, and most common, are those which are mainly black or painted iron with some brass plated fittings, finials, etc. These can be dramatically improved by re-painting.

Beds

Quick view: Antique beds embrace everything from early carved oak four-posters, classic period beds, Victorian half and full testers, brass beds, and now imported pine beds from Eastern Europe.

Desirable woods: Four-posters in oak and mahogany.

Restoration: Many Georgian four posters are, in fact, two genuine posts only — the remainder may be new pine covered with fabric.

Fake?: Many apparently early oak four-poster beds are in fact made-up from old kists, panelling and the like. A close look may reveal keyholes in the most unexpected places. Four-poster beds of all periods went through an unfashionable spell, and many were broken up and made into table stems, torch stems and other, then fashionable, items.

Decoration/inlays: Many early oak beds boast beautiful marquetry decoration as well as evocative carving, panels, etc.

Best size: Size can be very important — a custom-made mattress may be necessary.

Features to look for: Style and quality of design and work — elegance above all with Georgian designs, square section tubing in Victorian brass beds.

Potential: Mainly in the reclaiming of posts which had lost their way — they can be turned back to their original purpose.

Most valuable: Oak four-posters of fine quality and provenance; square section brass beds with high head-boards and side wings, plus decorated porcelain panels.

Oddities: Reproduction early 'oak' beds are available in England made entirely from plastics. They are visually virtually impossible to detect but can be a horrendous fire risk.

In a word (or two): Have fun!

A Victorian mahogany framed bedstead made in the mid-19th century.

price band
150 300 450

potential
fashion

Modern classic fabrics can transform a 'heavy' Victorian bed

Victorian walnut half-tester bedstead.

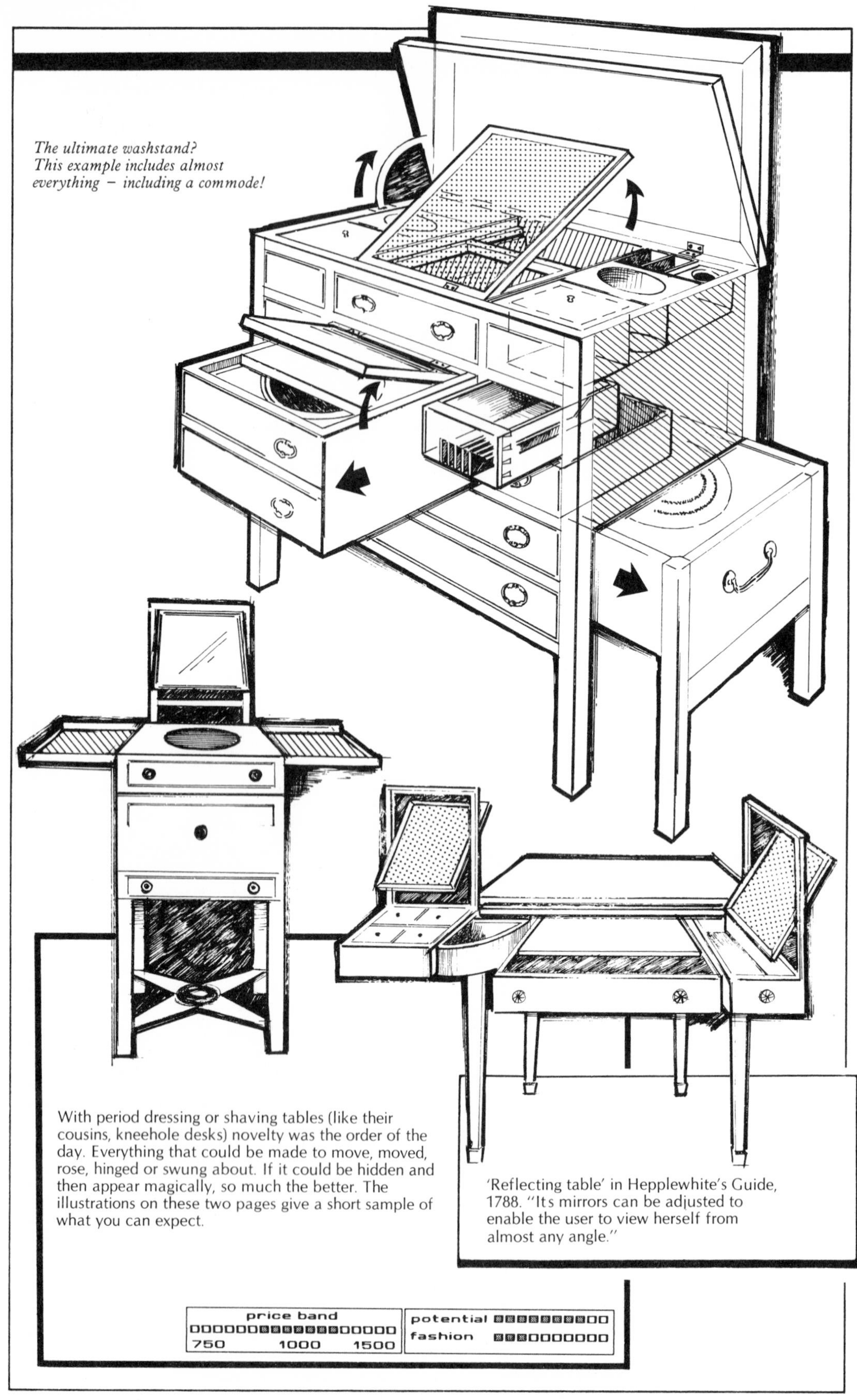

The ultimate washstand? This example includes almost everything – including a commode!

With period dressing or shaving tables (like their cousins, kneehole desks) novelty was the order of the day. Everything that could be made to move, moved, rose, hinged or swung about. If it could be hidden and then appear magically, so much the better. The illustrations on these two pages give a short sample of what you can expect.

'Reflecting table' in Hepplewhite's Guide, 1788. "Its mirrors can be adjusted to enable the user to view herself from almost any angle."

price band	potential / fashion
750 1000 1500	potential fashion

Dressing Tables

Short description: A table or stand incorporating a bowl and other toilet articles used for washing or shaving and incorporating a mirror.

Best woods: Usually mahogany.

Shape: Square, rather masculine appearance, especially when closed.

Fake?: Highly unlikely.

Decoration/inlays: Well figured mahogany would be expected.

Best period: 1780-1830.

Features to look for: Original mirror(s) and toilet accessories; bowl and beakers, dishes and the like. If these were also from a prestigious factory and marked according this should be considered a considerable bonus as it would confirm the quality of the total piece.

Potential: They are not expensive when compared to other similar interesting pieces of Georgian furniture and must have scope for an improvement in value. Their lack of popular appeal may possibly stem from the fact that most look a trifle numb when closed and even less appealing when open. If actually used for their original purpose they could also suffer considerable damage from modern perfumes and cosmetics.

Interiors/drawers: Lots of things happening in the insides! Hinged flaps with rising and swinging mirrors; built-in compartments hiding further hidden drawers and boxes; perhaps a wash bowl with its own water supply including all the plumbing, taps, drains, etc. In the large illustration opposite, even a pull-out commode has been installed in one side.

Most valuable: The example illustrated opposite in the large drawing must be close to the top of the price ladder.

In a word (or two): A piece of Georgian history of great novelty. One can almost see the piece, with all its wonders, being demonstrated for the first time and the comments that would ensue.

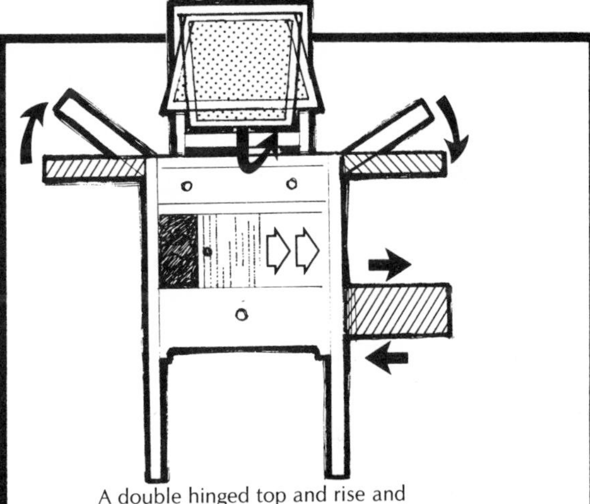

A double hinged top and rise and tilt mirror plus a tambour-fronted compartment for a chamber pot.

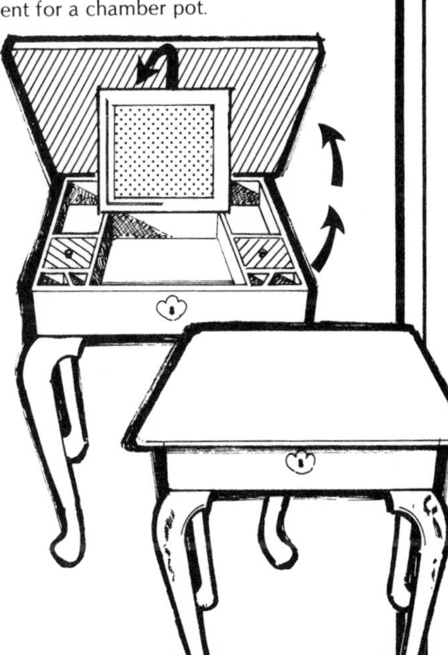

A George II period table combining a dressing and writing table. The cabriole legs are carved on the knee and end in hoof feet, circa 1730.

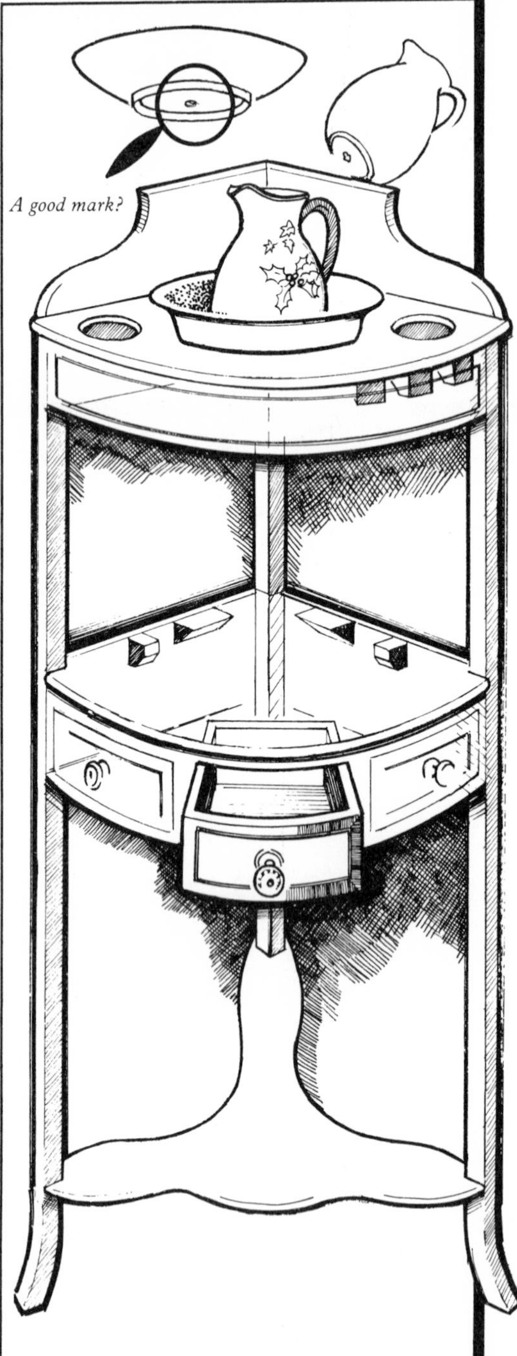

The anatomy of a corner wash stand, showing the single drawer and two dummy drawer fronts. The ewer and basin would stand on the platform base when not in use. The two holes could hold beakers or round soap dishes.

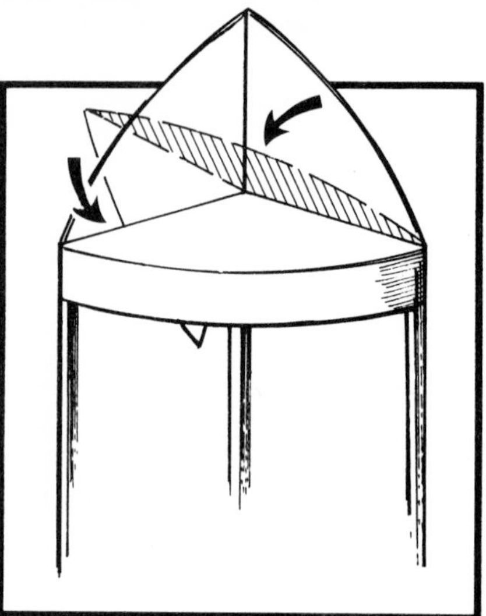

In this clever 18th century design the back 'folds' down on the top surface of the washstand to form a flat polished platform, disguising its true purpose.

Quick view: An attractive piece of furniture designed to stand in a corner of a dressing room or bedroom to hold a hot water jug, basin and two dishes. Many have a stand (to hold the ewer) on the stretcher below.

Best woods: Normally mahogany.

Shape: Top 'work' surface with apertures, drawer(s) below and stretchers; fixed back.

Drawers: Three drawer fronts; one real, two false.

Restoration: No particular problem except, perhaps, repair or matching of missing/broken pottery.

Fake?: Unlikely.

Best Period: 1780-1820.

Features to look for: Original, high quality, pottery fittings.

Most valuable: Fine example with hinged top — see illustration.

In a word (or two): An interesting small piece of bedroom furniture unlikely to be of inferior quality or 'messed about.'

price band
200 300 400

potential
fashion

Washstands

Desirable woods: Mahogany.

Shape: Various — see illustrations for some variations.

Handles: Small wooden knobs or hollow brass on period; pierced cast brass on Edwardian.

Restoration: No problem with period examples — broken marble or tiles much more difficult — you should question finished value!

Fake?: No, not as a washstand — they themselves are much more likely to be transformed into something more desirable.

Configuration: Period examples: Apron top with shallow back and sides, single or two drawers, turned legs. Victorian/Edwardian: higher back, frequently tiled, marble surface, single shallow drawer, brass towel rail at one or both ends. Turned legs with shaped under-shelf as stretcher.

Decoration/inlays: In late Victorian or Edwardian examples the quality of the tiles and marble influence the value.

Best period: Late Georgian.

Best size: All are about 48″ (1.2m) wide.

Features to look for: Look for period examples in fine quality mahogany, stamped **Gillow** on top of drawer front near the lock — equals premium price.

Potential: The period 'washstand' which looks more like a desk is the most desirable.

Interiors/drawers: Usually one or two shallow drawers, or central drawer and two side drawers at either end of the front — see illustration.

Most valuable: Good 'Gillow' example — frequently sold as desks. If stamped **Gillow,** (usually on a drawer top, near the lock), this is the most respected name. However, look also at the sheer quality of the piece — many a 'restorer' has his own Gillow punch!

Oddities: A damaged Edwardian washstand with good tiles may have a value as a 'breaker', Marble is also saleable despite fixing holes in ends.

In a word (or two): Period washstands are useful, many are very well made — all are currently under-rated.

price band
50 125 250

Typical Edwardian washstands with mirror or tile backs and marble tops.

potential
fashion

A much earlier washstand in mahogany.

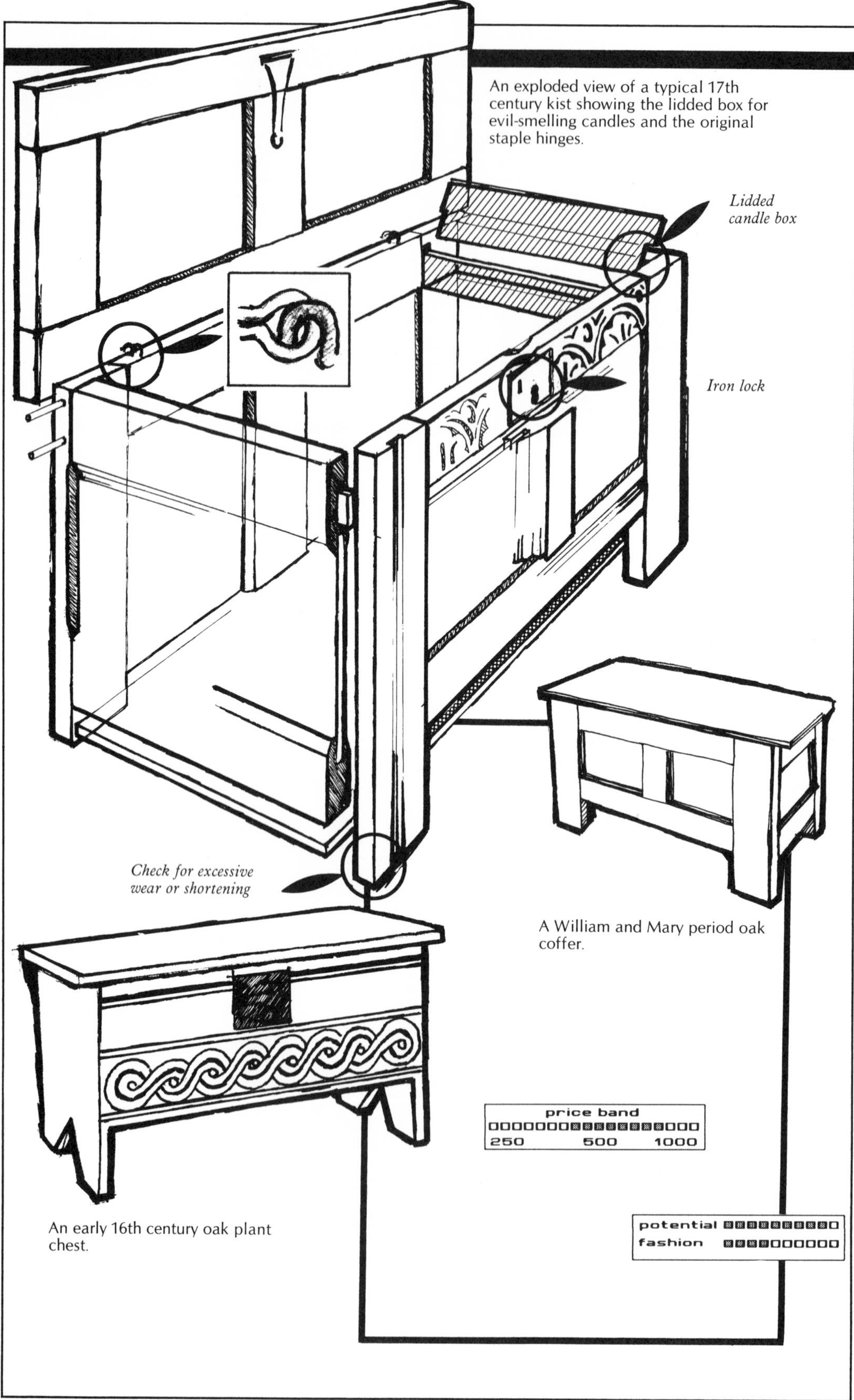

An exploded view of a typical 17th century kist showing the lidded box for evil-smelling candles and the original staple hinges.

A William and Mary period oak coffer.

An early 16th century oak plant chest.

Kists & Boxes

Quick view: Probably the oldest piece of furniture generally available today.

Desirable woods: Kists are usually found in dark oak.

Beware!: Don't be misled by a carved date on a kist — this may not be too accurate.

Restoration: Restoration is best avoided with early oak — split panels and rotted feet are the main restoration areas.

Fake?: Very rare — avoid over-restored old oak; heavily carved examples may have been 'improved' in Victorian times.

Configuration: A box with a small interior candle box at the top, carved front panels. Marriage chests have two drawers in the lower half.

Decoration: Marquetry and carved and linen fold panels.

Best period: 17th century.

Best size: Small, under 36″ (1 m) long.

Feet: We are accustomed to the feet on kists being rather 'low' — however most were probably rather higher when originally made and have rotted away over the years, caused by continual washing of stone floors.

Feature to look for: Original, and frequently beautiful, iron lock plates. Original iron staple hinges — simply a staple in the lip interconnected with a similar staple in the base.

Potential: May have already been exploited! Thousands of boxes, especially those with linen fold panels and nice carving found their way into 'period' four poster beds and library panelling.

Interiors/drawers: Interior candle box. Candles were particularly evil smelling in the 17th century and were stored in the 'candle box' in the kist to keep moths at bay.

Most valuable: Marquetry examples, finely carved panels or, rarely, with very early panels incorporated in front.

Charles II oak coffer with fielded panelling on the top.

Mid-17th century oak chest with applied turned moulding, circa 1655.

A 16th century counter, used for measuring and counting.

A late 16th century cyprus wood coffer.

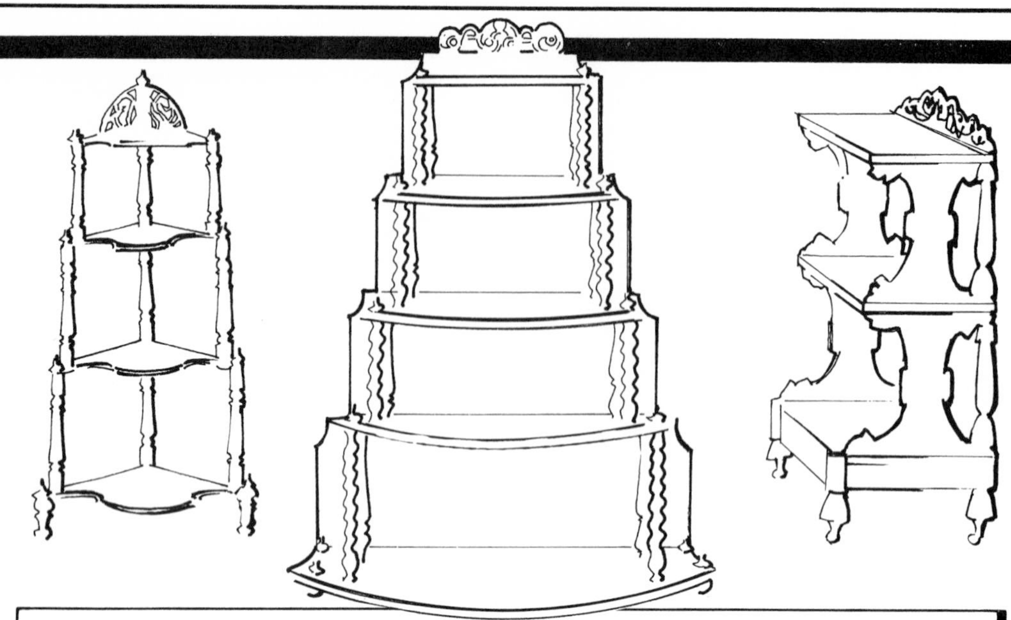

Victorian walnut whatnot.

A fine quality five tier Victorian walnut whatnot.

Fine quality Victorian walnut whatnot.

price band		
■■■■■□□□□□□□□□□□□		
300	800	1500

potential	■■■■□□□□□□
fashion	■■■■■■■■□□

George IV plum pudding mahogany whatnot.

A two-tier mahogany whatnot with a single drawer in the base and a tilting reading top.

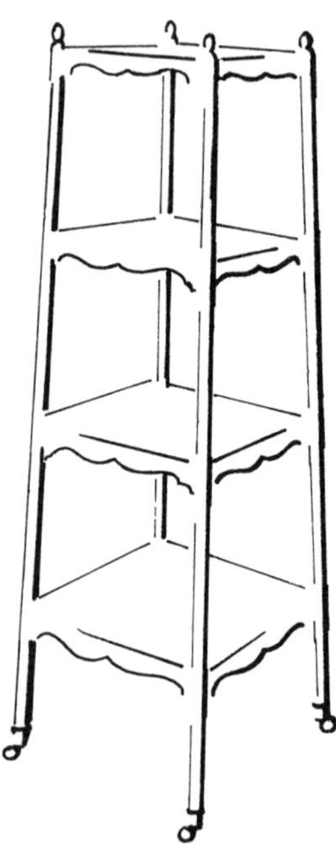

An ususual tapering design of mahogany whatnot with shaped aprons to the shelves.

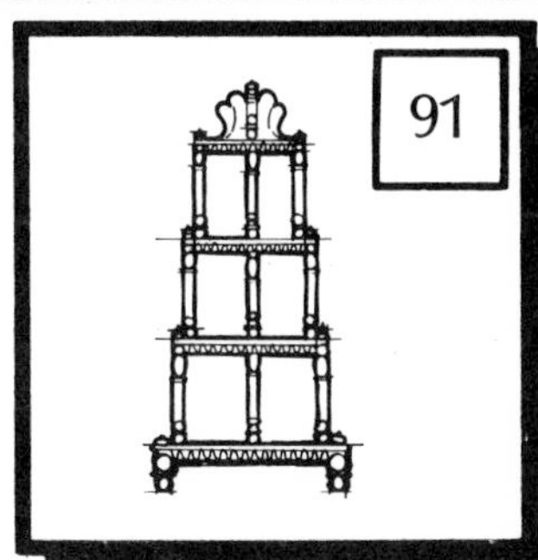

91

Whatnots

Short description: A series of small shelves divided by fretwork or turned supports.

Best woods: Georgian: mahogany, Victorian: walnut.

Shape: Georgian: square, Victorian: triangular or rectangular.

Restoration: No particular problems, which is probably just as well as many Victorian whatnots arrive in the trade as a series of shelves and a 'bag of bits'. Their fragile design and construction make them especially vulnerable during house moving and the like.

Fake?: Copies of Victorian designs were produced in large numbers in England during the mid and late 1970's but they are not considered 'fakes' in the general usage of this Guide.

Configuration: Georgian: three, four or five shelves divided by finely turned supports perhaps with a drawer below and a tilting reading or manuscript top. Victorian: three or four shelves divided by ornate pierced fretwork plus shaped fretted aprons to each shelf and on the rear. It is also quite usual to find serpentine shelves in Victorian designs.

Decoration/inlays: No decoration in Georgian examples — quite the opposite is true with Victorian whatnots. Every type of coloured wood inlay, stringing or 'off the shelf' inlaid panel will be incorporated in every conceivable flat surface.

Best size: Particularly large examples of both periods will command the top prices.

Features to look for: In Georgian whatnots, look for fine turning detail on supports, original castors and moving, tilting top. When considering Victorian examples, a solid 'feel' and good quality inlays and un-broken fretwork should be the rule.

Oddities: A combination of the canterbury with a whatnot configuration on top; known, not surprisingly, as a 'canterbury whatnot'.

In a word (or two): If you want to display lots of little bits and pieces there is no better way!

A tall example with a series of drawers below and a three tier whatnot above. Mahogany, circa 1800.

A single drawer but rather nicely turned baluster supports to the shelves.

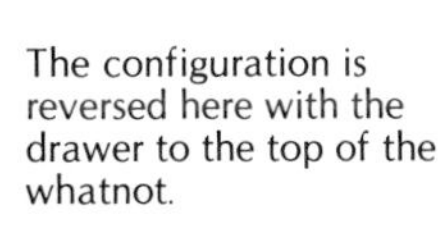

The configuration is reversed here with the drawer to the top of the whatnot.

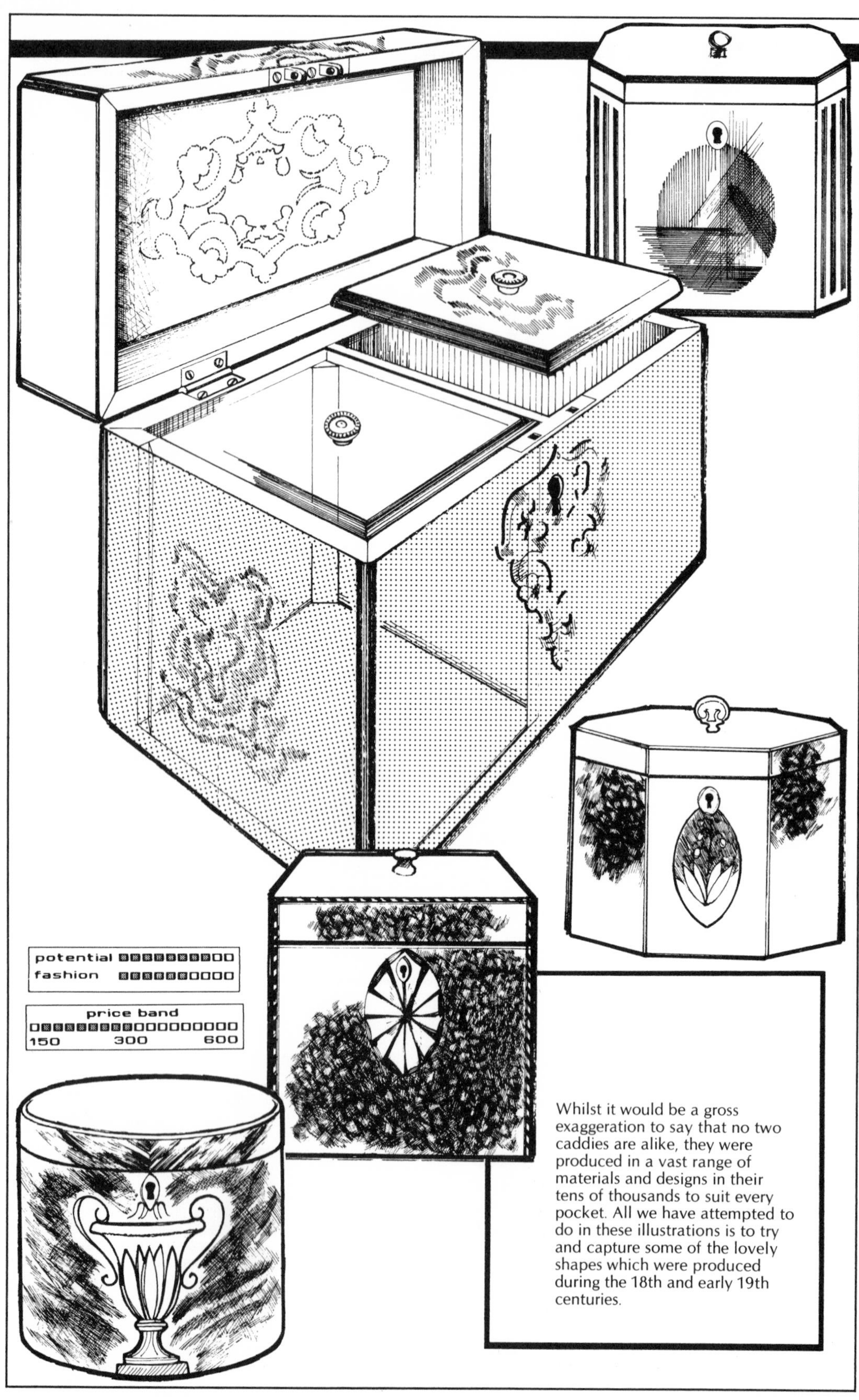

Whilst it would be a gross exaggeration to say that no two caddies are alike, they were produced in a vast range of materials and designs in their tens of thousands to suit every pocket. All we have attempted to do in these illustrations is to try and capture some of the lovely shapes which were produced during the 18th and early 19th centuries.

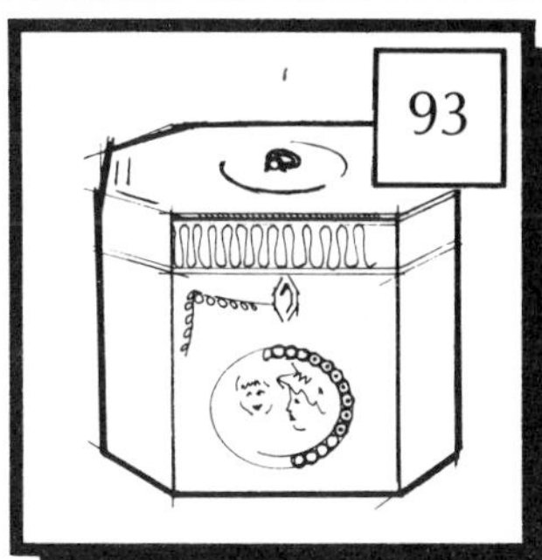

Tea Caddies

Quick view: Lockable little chests for the storage, and frequently mixing, of tea. 'Caddy' is derived from the Malay 'kati' — a unit of (tea) weight.

Desirable woods: Almost every wood will be found in caddy construction, including rare varieties like partridgewood, zebra, amboyna, etc., etc., — the list is endless. Caddies are also made in porcelain, enamels, silver, ivory, tortoiseshell, straw-work, etc.

Shape: The most desirable for the purist collector is probably the 'fruit' caddy — made in the form of an apple, pear, etc. The commonest are square or rectangular shapes with 'cut corners'.

Handles: Comparable quality to caddy — ormolu, gilded brass and cast brass.

Restoration: No particular problem provided suitable exotic materials are available.

Fake?: Not likely, although copies of 'fruit' caddies are possible.

Configuration: Either a box for one, two or more varieties of tea with or without a central mixing bowl. Always lockable due to the original high price of tea — the caddy was kept by the mistress in the drawing room and blended at the tea table when a 'samovar', or spirit kettle was produced by the staff.

Best period: Caddies from the great English designers, plus exotic examples from India.

Best size: Size is not important when compared to design, materials and workmanship.

Feet: Original cast brass.

Features to look for: Original bowl, lead lining intact, lids for compartments present.

Interiors/drawers: Lead paper lining, mixing bowl difficult to replace. Hinges are frequently of poor quality and quite 'right'.

Oddities: The bowl is generally considered to have been used solely for blending — however a late eighteenth century cabinetmakers' catalogue lists "cutting hole for sugar bowl — 6d extra" — scope for research here.

In a word (or two): Highly collectable and desirable. English cabinetmakers' genius in miniature.

Four examples of the ever-popular toilet mirror found in various woods, designs and differing degrees of quality. Look for high quality cross banding and interesting detail; escutcheons, drawer knobs and finials in ivory or bone, etc. Early examples in walnut frequently have charming interiors and are similar in design to the writing bureaux of the period.

Three wall-mounted mirrors or looking glasses. On the left, a pier glass, designed to be positioned over a matching consul table. This is a mid 19th century example with an impressive central urn, flower and garland decoration. In the centre, an imported Venetian mirror, also made in the 19th century, with bevelled mirror panels acting as a decorative frame. On the right, a Victorian overmantel mirror — the straight base to the frame is the clue — the surrounding decoration in carved wood or, more normally, gilded plasterwork (gesso).

Mirrors

Quick view: Look for original glass first, frame second. Early glasses had mercury backs before this practice was stopped in the nineteenth century, due to poisoning in workshops.

Construction: Very thin pine backing on old mirrors. Shaped pine frame with a thick mahogany veneer and cross-banding.

Restoration: Please don't replace old glass — or re-silver — it never looks the same. New silvering looks bright and 'white'. the genuine article is blueish-grey. If you do replace, keep the original glass, backing timber and original pins for the next owner.

Fake?: Very frequently faked. Don't look at the front, look at the back — it's very difficult to fake old pine — look for new pins holding backing. Old glass was always thin. You will sometimes see an expert hold a coin edge or pen point against the glass surface. The distance between the edge or point and the reflection indicates the mirror thickness.

Decoration/inlays: So-called Chippendale mirrors frequently include a Ho-Ho-bird — roughly carved, gessoed and gilded; also shells or feathers.

Features to look for: Bevelled glass — used in very early Victorian mirrors. The difference between early and late is quite easy to distinguish. Early bevelled mirrors were hand made and the corners and edges are 'soft'. Later bevels were machine ground and are 'sharp'.

Oddities: 18th century (or later) decorative picture frames have turned into mirrors by the addition of a (new) glass.

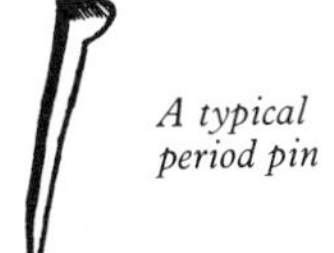

A typical period pin

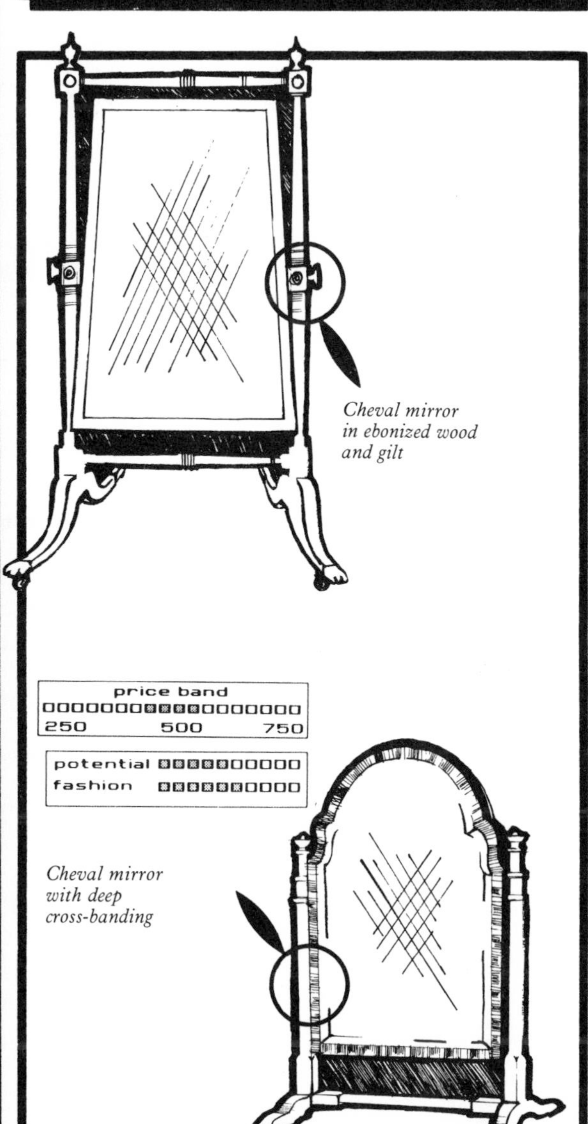

Cheval mirror in ebonized wood and gilt

Cheval mirror with deep cross-banding

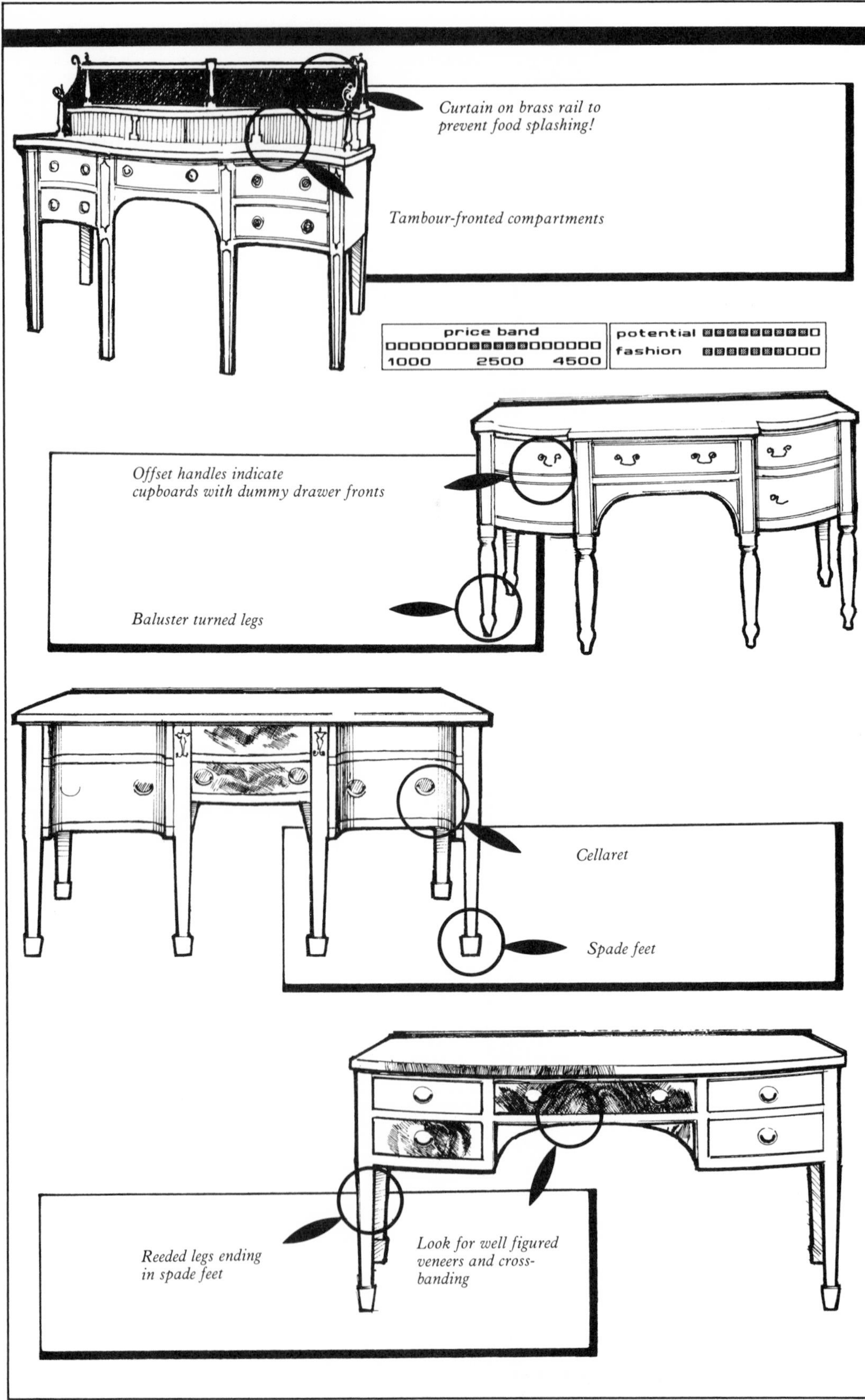
Curtain on brass rail to prevent food splashing!
Tambour-fronted compartments
price band
1000 2500 4500
potential
fashion
Offset handles indicate cupboards with dummy drawer fronts
Baluster turned legs
Cellaret
Spade feet
Reeded legs ending in spade feet
Look for well figured veneers and cross-banding

Sideboards

Quick view: This should be a fine, elegant piece of dining room furniture.

Best woods: Almost always mahogany.

Restoration: The tops and sides are fairly plain solid mahogany. Tops are only half an inch thick onto a pine 1¼″ (3cm). Mahogany veneers on drawer fronts and cupboard fronts are generally of more finely figured wood.

Configuration: Central drawer for flatware, pot cupboard for chamber pot at side, wine cooler (sometimes lead lined); Brass rail with drape; central door, drawers on runners.

Decoration/inlays: Cross-banded in satinwood or tulipwood on drawer and cupboard fronts.

Best legs: Tapered legs ending in spade feet.

Beware: Many were made for big rooms in big houses. Many are (or were) deep and have been reduced in width to make them more acceptable in today's smaller homes.

Best size: Small is best – and if genuine very rare, or of much later manufacture.

Feet: Usually spade.

Features to look for: Original interior, especially intact wine cooler compartment, divided into sections to hold bottles, lined with thin lead, with a small drain plug.

Drawers: Mahogany lined drawers are common.

Special sideboards: Many examples were made-to-order for specific positions in a house. It therefore follows that you should always check to see if the top is totally rectangular or has any special features which might make it difficult to fit into your situation. Some sideboards were made to fit into curved niches in which case the curved back may not sit happily against your flat dining room wall. Such specific sideboards were often made in pairs although are unlikely to have remained together.

In a word (or two): Where else can you possibly put the chafing dishes and the kedgeree?

Two serpentine designs illustrating the traditional – and desirable – 'thick' top

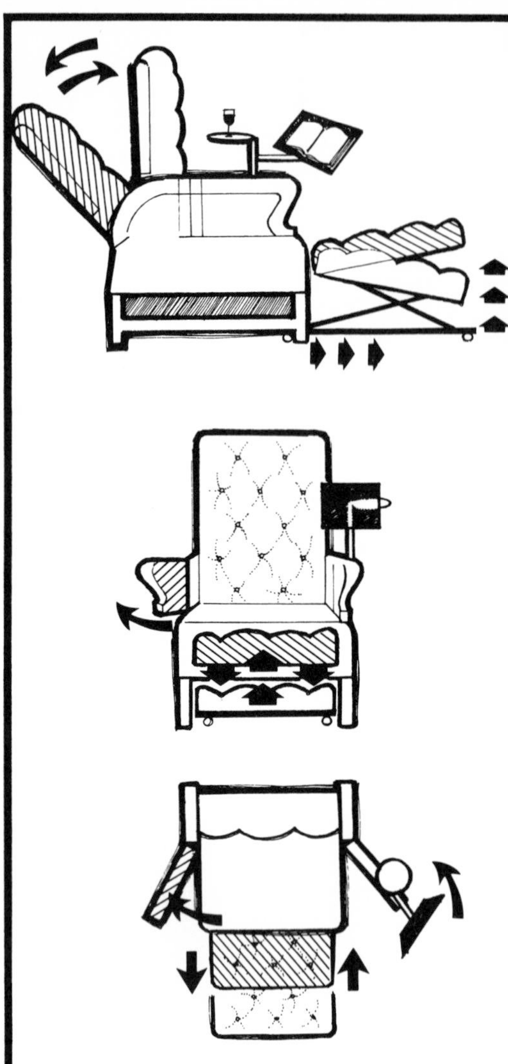

The chair that does everything . . . a rather special Victorian library (or gout) chair — this example upholstered in Dralon — but more usually in deep buttoned leather. Its features include pull-out adjustable rise and tilt foot stool, swing-out arms for ease of access either side. An adjustable swivel bookrest and wine table on one arm. The back of the chair also adjusts down to a horizontal position. Some examples even have brass wheels.

price band
2000 2500 3000

potential
fashion

price band
3500 4500 5000

potential
fashion

A Georgian mahogany architect's cabinet with a rising top which pulls forward, tilts and folds.

price band
2000 2500 3000

An 18th century library table in mahogany which opens to form six library steps. Chairs which performed the same function were also popular.

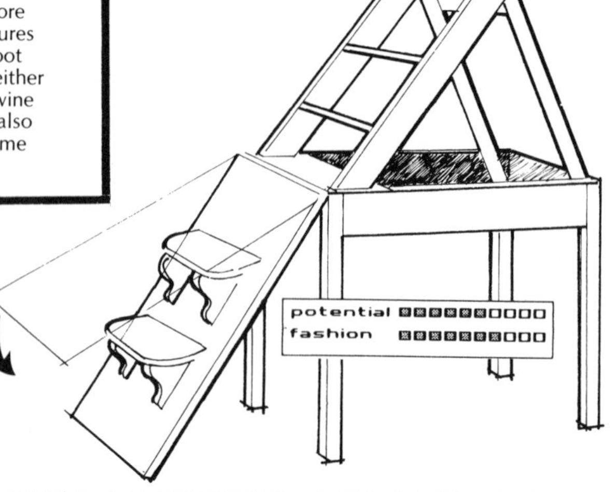

potential
fashion

Mechanical Furniture

A mid-Victorian, figured walnut cabinet/writing desk designed specifically for an artist, with a rising easel.

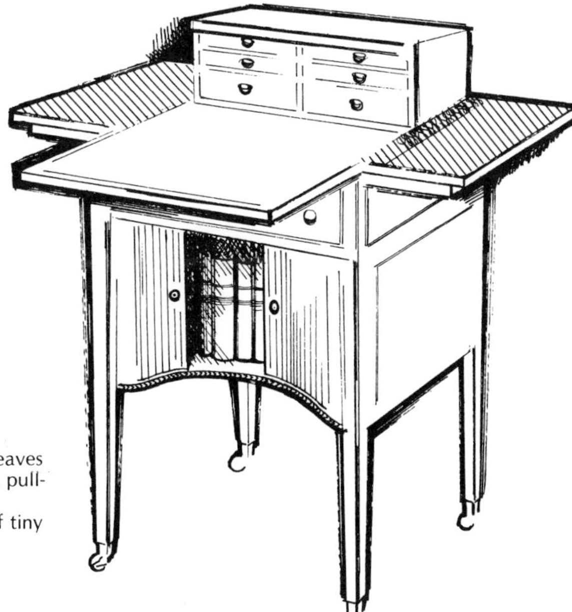

A ladies' writing cabinet featuring a double tambour front, two folding leaves on either side of the top, revealing a pull-forward writing surface and an automatically rising compartment of tiny drawers.

An unusual two-part military secretaire/chest of drawers, the 'middle' drawer pulling out to become a complete campaign office.

price band
250 500 750

potential

fashion

price band
2000 3000 4000

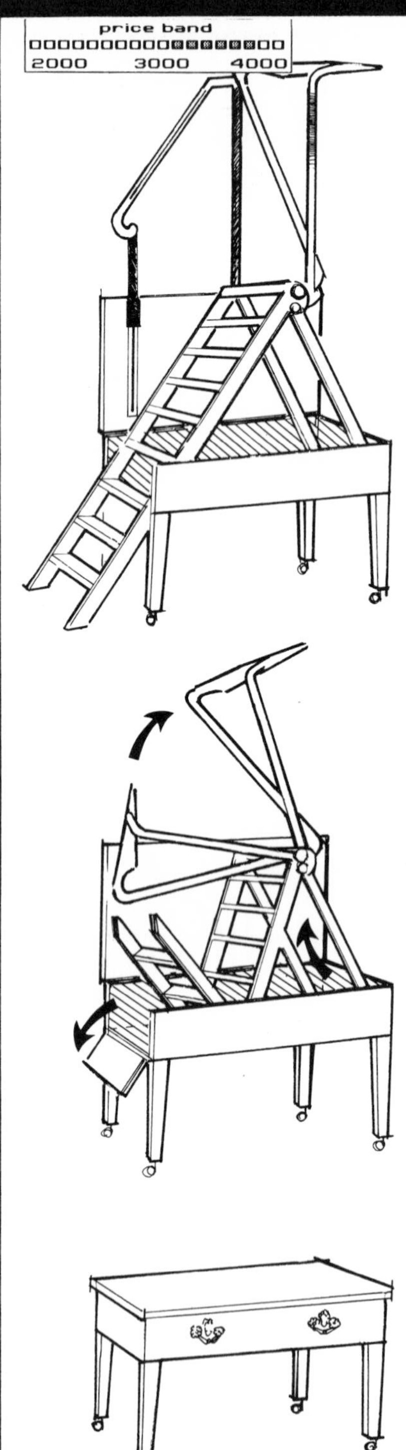

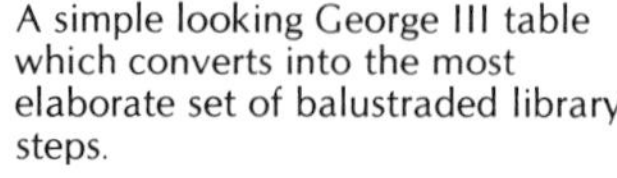

A simple looking George III table which converts into the most elaborate set of balustraded library steps.

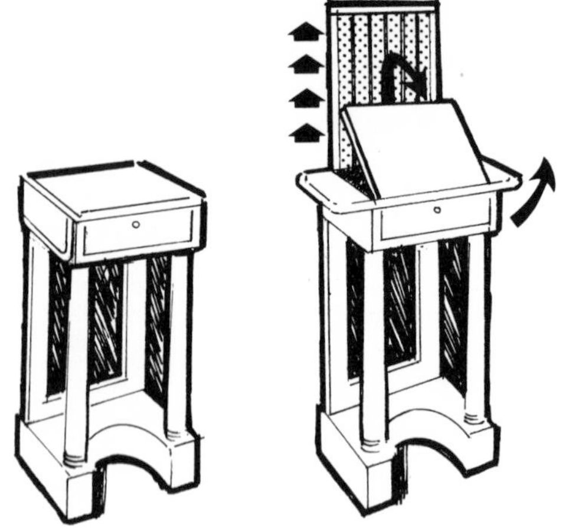

A Regency period writing stand which contains two tiny leaves either side of the writing surface, plus a tilt writing desk and a pleated silk fire screen.

price band			
750	1000	1250	potential fashion

A very rare and important early 18th century George I figured walnut reading-cum-writing chest of drawers, the top drawer and side rails pulling forward and the top tilting. Candle slides swing out from either side.

price band			
3500	4000	4500	potential fashion

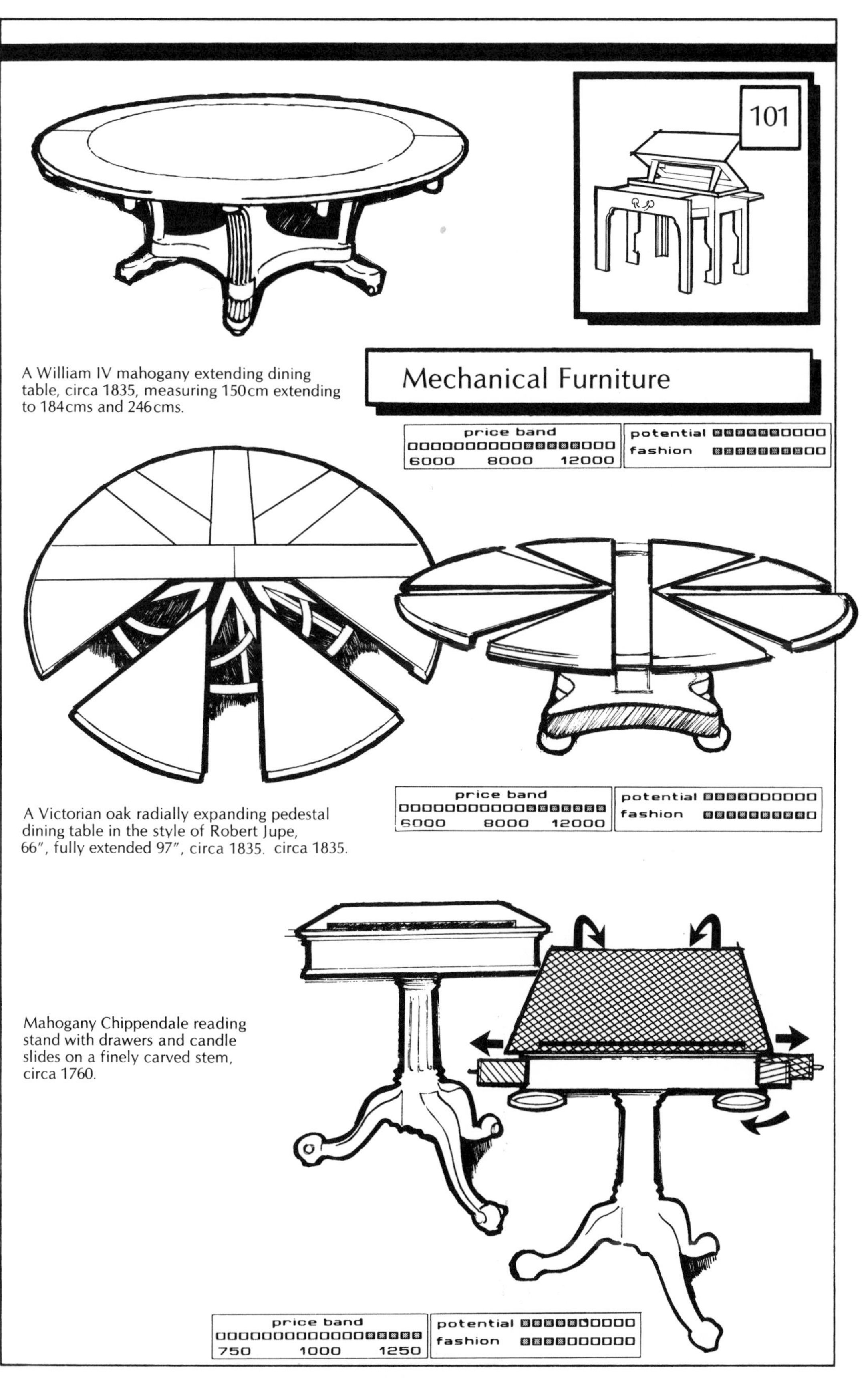

Mechanical Furniture

A William IV mahogany extending dining table, circa 1835, measuring 150cm extending to 184cms and 246cms.

price band
6000 8000 12000
potential
fashion

A Victorian oak radially expanding pedestal dining table in the style of Robert Jupe, 66″, fully extended 97″, circa 1835. circa 1835.

price band
6000 8000 12000
potential
fashion

Mahogany Chippendale reading stand with drawers and candle slides on a finely carved stem, circa 1760.

price band
750 1000 1250
potential
fashion

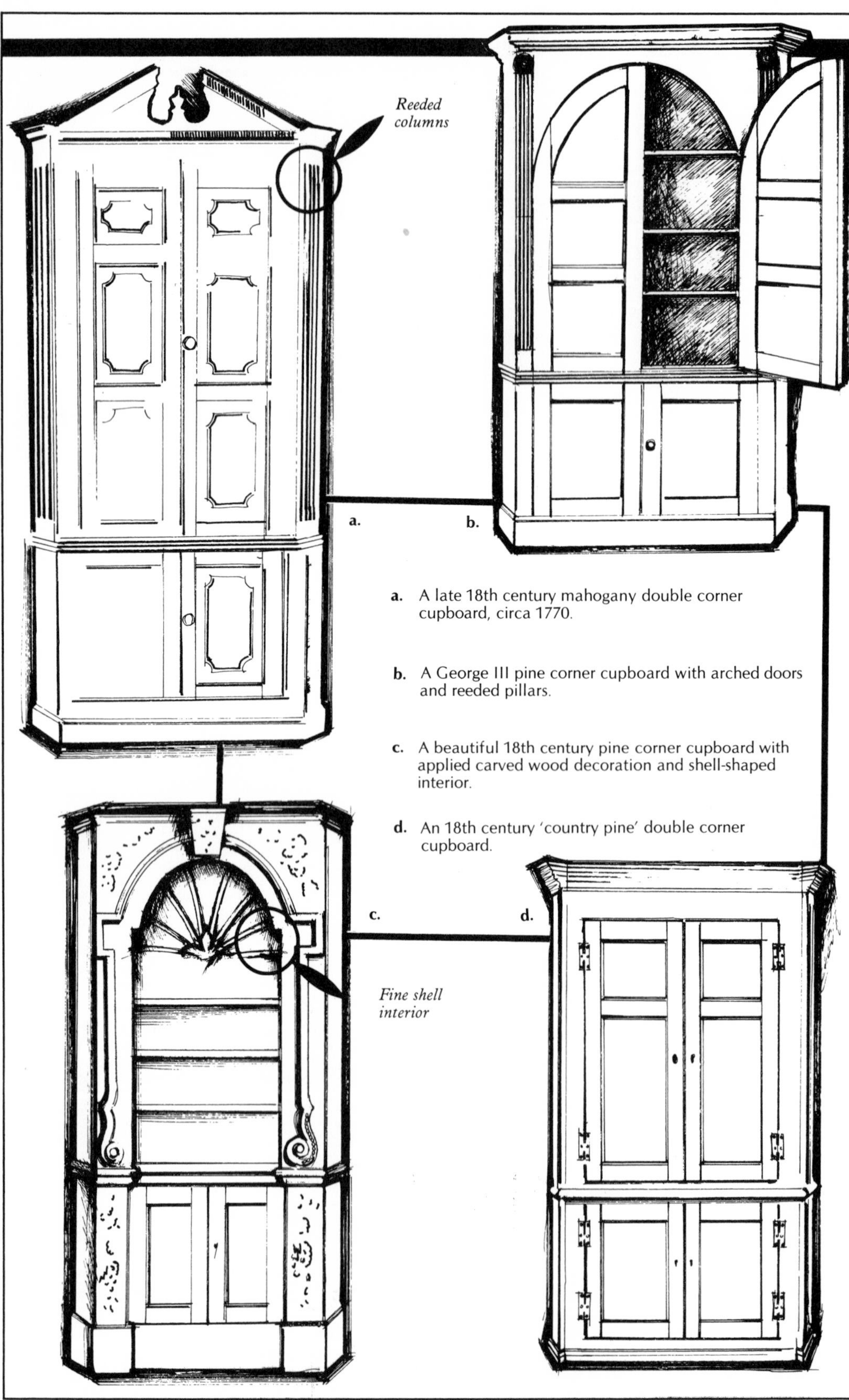

a. A late 18th century mahogany double corner cupboard, circa 1770.

b. A George III pine corner cupboard with arched doors and reeded pillars.

c. A beautiful 18th century pine corner cupboard with applied carved wood decoration and shell-shaped interior.

d. An 18th century 'country pine' double corner cupboard.

Corner Cupboards

Quick view: Panelled or glazed doors.

Desirable woods: Oak, mahogany, pine or satinwood.

Shape: Straight-fronted or bowed.

Fake?: Very small is frequently faked — usually from commodes or end portions of Victorian chiffoniers. Many double corner cupboards have genuine tops and suspect bases.

Configuration: Base, usually blind cupboards with glazed cupboard above, either with single or double doors.

Decoration/inlays: Cross-banding, sometimes star inlay in centre oak door.

Best top: Look for the best design in glazing bars.

Best size: Many genuine examples are fairly substantial, about 3′6″ (1 m) across.

Features to look for: Some of the most attractive glazed or open corner cupboards are in pine, which were frequently built into their original homes. Many have superb interior domed or shaped tops. In these examples a new back (hopefully in old pine) may have been added — this is probably permissible. Shaped shelves are also a bonus in any corner cupboard.

Interiors/drawers: Interior in pine corner cupboards may be painted — the most attractive Georgian colours are pale green or light blue.

In a word (or two): A superb setting for any collection.

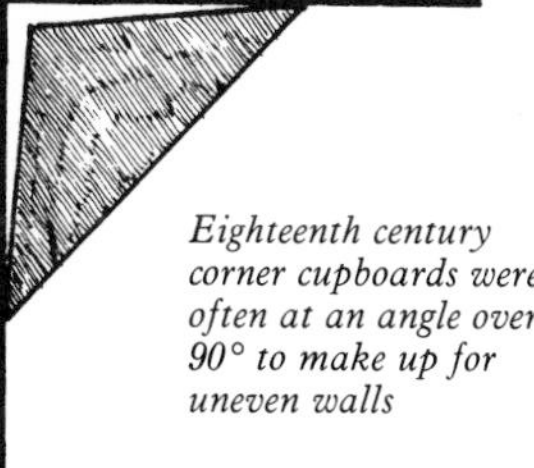

Eighteenth century corner cupboards were often at an angle over 90° to make up for uneven walls

price band		
600	1500	2500

potential ■■■■■□□□□□

fashion ■■■■■■□□□□

A mid-18th century pine domed-top corner cupboard with four glazed doors.

Hanging corner cupboard. 50% of which are fake!

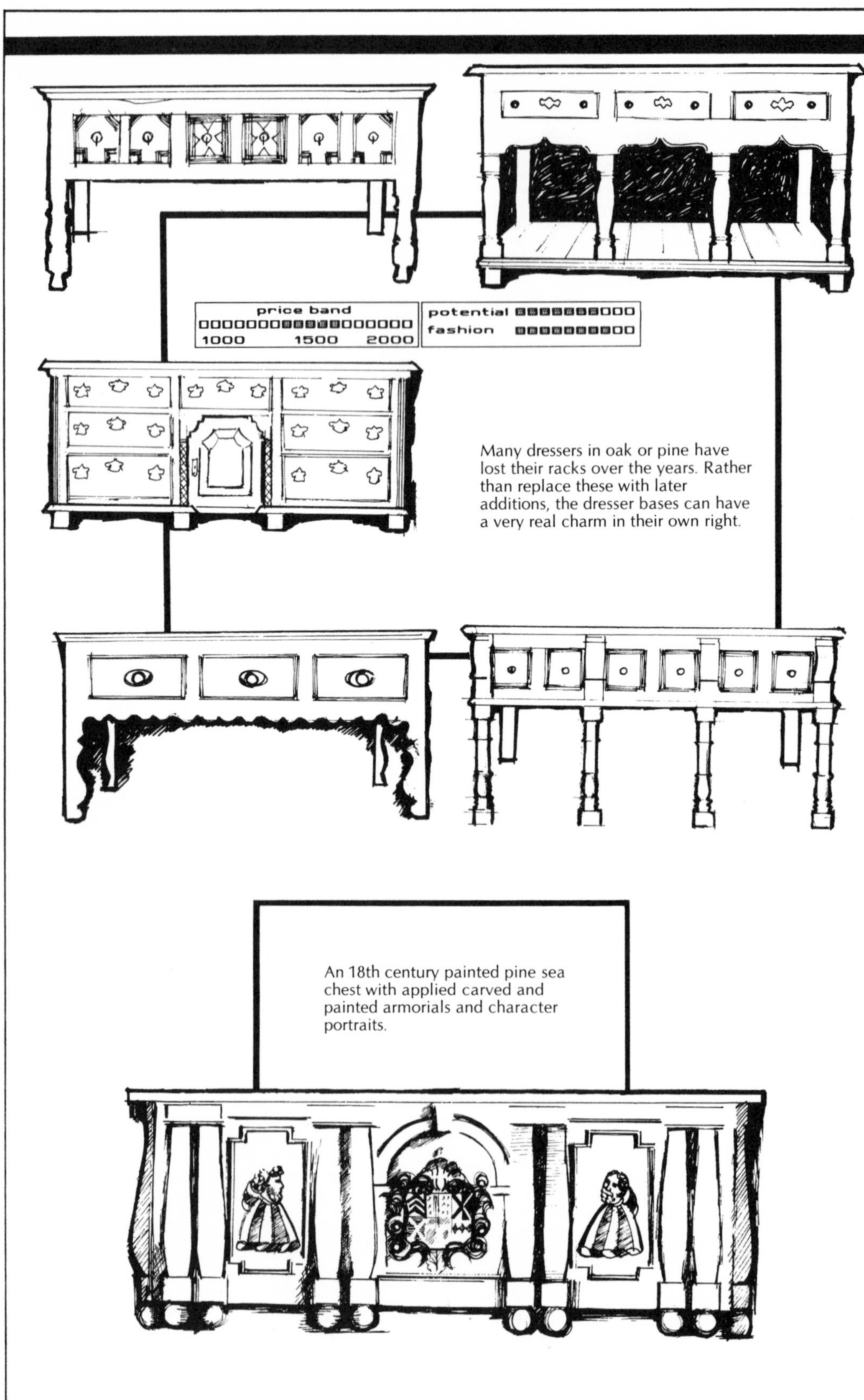

Many dressers in oak or pine have lost their racks over the years. Rather than replace these with later additions, the dresser bases can have a very real charm in their own right.

An 18th century painted pine sea chest with applied carved and painted armorials and character portraits.

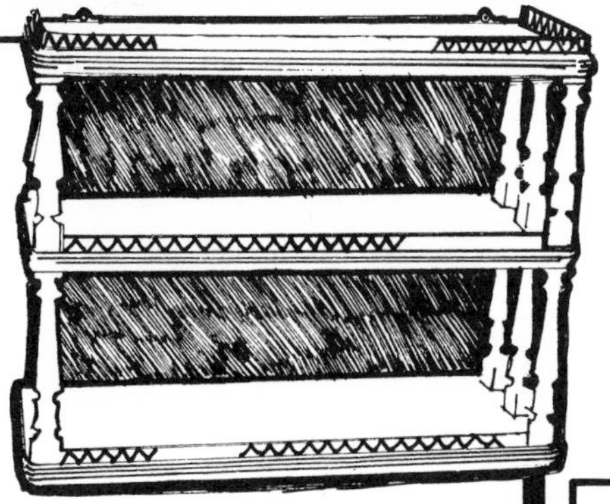

Regency rosewood hanging wall shelves with turned supports and cast brass pierced galleries.

Miscellany II

18th century Chinese Chippendale fretted hanging wall shelves in mahogany.

Hanging wall shelves in painted pine with gilded mouldings.

18th century wall hanging spoon rack. A relic of the days when spoons were made in soft metals and would have become damaged if kept loose in a box.

18th century wall hanging candle box.

price band

□□□□□■■■■■□□□□□□□□

150 200 250

potential ■■■■■■■□□□

fashion ■■■■■■■■■□

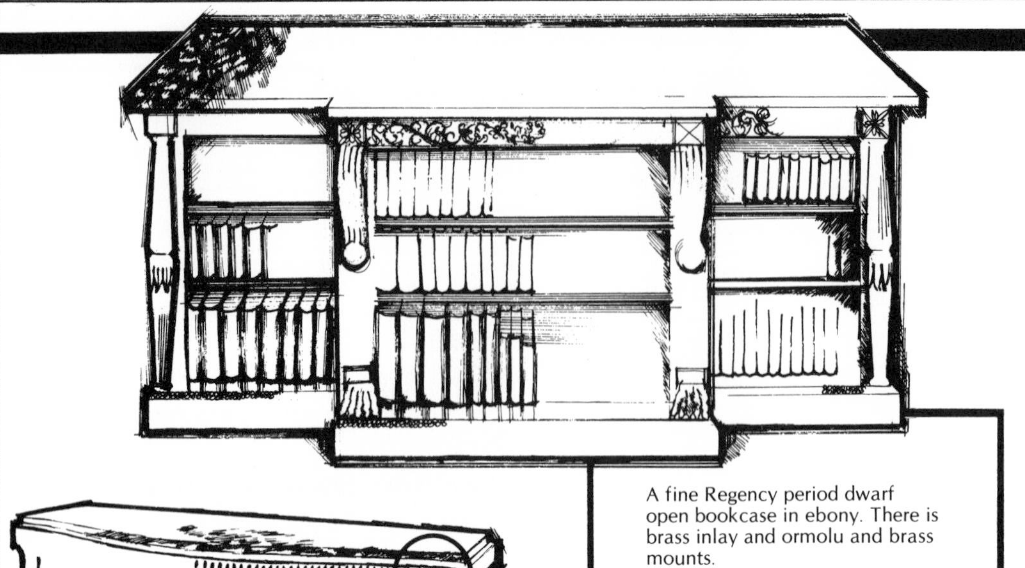

A fine Regency period dwarf open bookcase in ebony. There is brass inlay and ormolu and brass mounts.

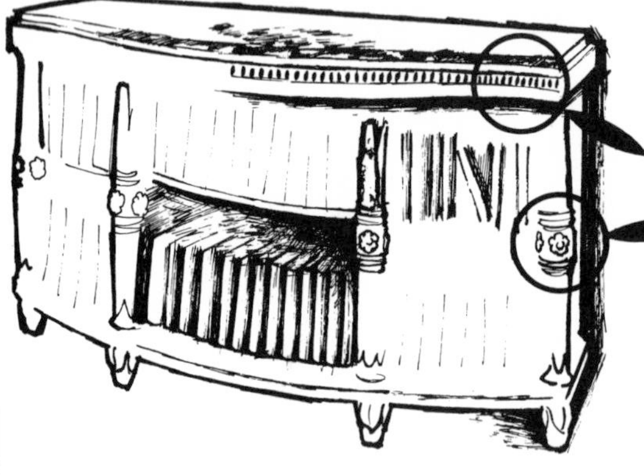

Brass galleries and ormolu mounts

price band
500 1000 1500

A small open bookcase in walnut and figured oak with adjustable shelves and a marble top.

potential
fashion

An interesting small open bookcase in satinwood with a marble top. The single door is fretted and has an oval needlework panel in its centre.

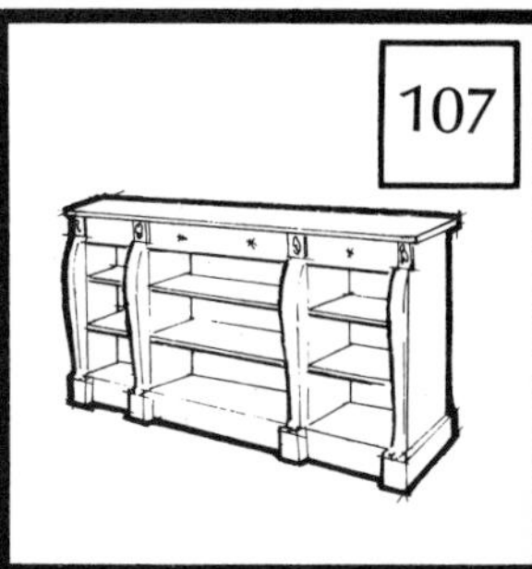

Open Bookcases

Best woods: Georgian - mahogany; Regency - rosewood; Victorian - walnut.

Shape: Straight or break-fronted cabinets containing a series of shelves; free standing examples are usually tall and stepped with shelves on one or both sides, frequently with a single or pair of drawers below.

Restoration: No particular problem areas other than replacement of missing ormolu or cast brass mounts. If the 'marble' top turns out to be painted simulated marble a specialist artist or decorator will be required.

Fake?: Unlikely, although there may originally have been doors rather than an open front. Look for traces of hinges or replaced fillets on 'door' sides.

Decoration/inlays: When marble-topped the colour or rarity of the marble can dramatically affect the value — white is the least attractive; green the most valuable. Expect to find ormolu mounts and masks, cast brass galleries, etc., especially on Regency rosewood examples.

Best period: 1770-1830.

Best size: Unimportant! Quality is more important than size.

Look for: Open bookcases are frequently found in pairs and, as such, are worth considerably more than twice the single example.

Potential: A dull example might be improved by the addition of mounts or ormolu trimmings.

Interiors: If the shelves are adjustable, the method employed can be used to establish date of manufacture.

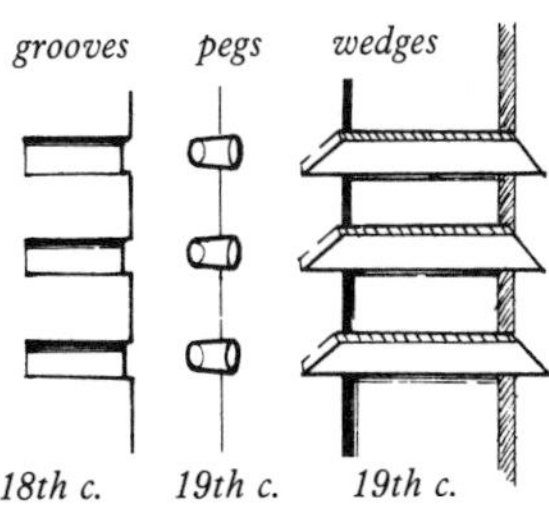

Most valuable: A pair of 18th century decorated satinwood breakfront bookcases.

In a word (or two): Less may be more! Compared to the identical cabinet with doors, the open version may well be more expensive!

A Sheraton period bow-fronted open standing bookcase with a single drawer below.

Superb Regency rosewood open bookshelves with lattice ends and tapered and reeded uprights, circa 1815.

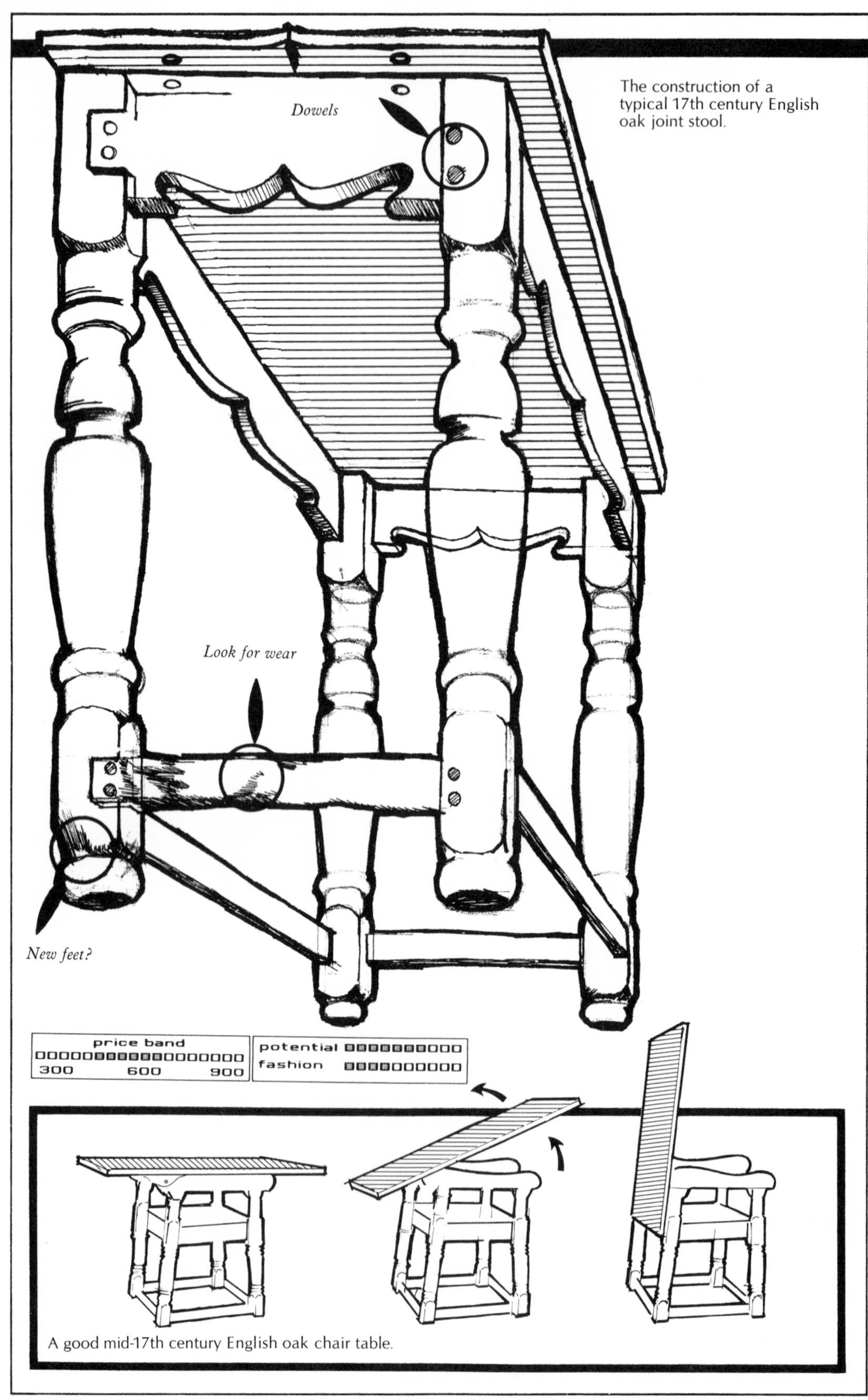

The construction of a typical 17th century English oak joint stool.

A good mid-17th century English oak chair table.

Stools

Quick-view: Joint, joined (or if you are very posh, joynt) or coffin stools are not common today and walnut stools are comparatively rare items. Many walnut or cabriole leg stools have been made-up from a pair of chair bottoms. Only the legs and front rails are used — new side rails being added. If you are offered a stool (or, in fact, any 'stuffed over' furniture) with a base cover, always insist on seeing under it; all good dealers will always want to see under the base cover — by the same token 'good' dealers will never offer stuffed over furniture with base covers.

Fake?: A great many Victorian walnut or mahogany stools have also started life as a couple of broken balloon back cab. leg chairs — with these, however, it probably doesn't really matter.

Cover: Damask or tapestry with some age.

Features to look for: If you see under the cover or if you are considering buying a frame, look to see the number of nail holes in top rails. This will indicate the number of times re-covered (the rails, not the stool!) Rails with only a few holes do not necessarily indicate original upholstery, as rails of beech or birch are frequently enjoyed by woodworm and could have been replaced. You should also find the original glue bandage — a piece of hessian soaked in animal glue, used to reinforce the two leading edge joints.

In a word (or two): A walnut stool — a rare and desirable piece, it should be approached with a degree of caution.

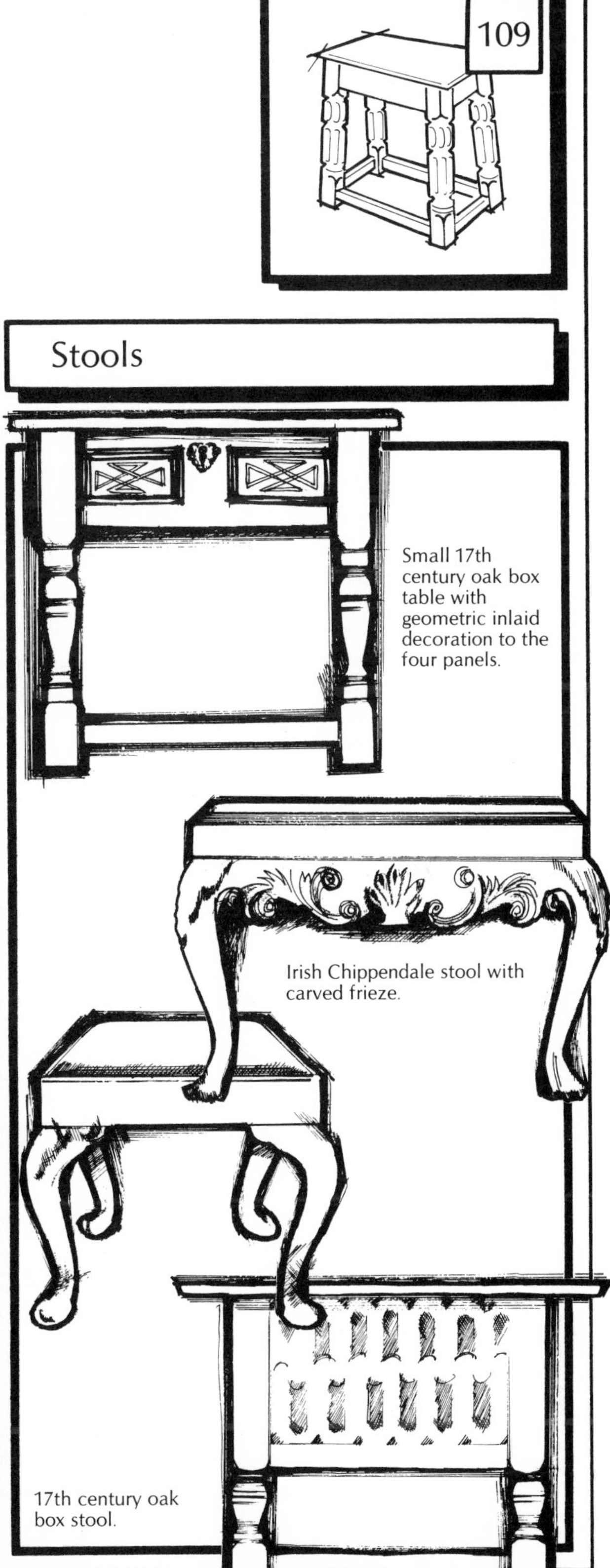

Small 17th century oak box table with geometric inlaid decoration to the four panels.

Irish Chippendale stool with carved frieze.

17th century oak box stool.

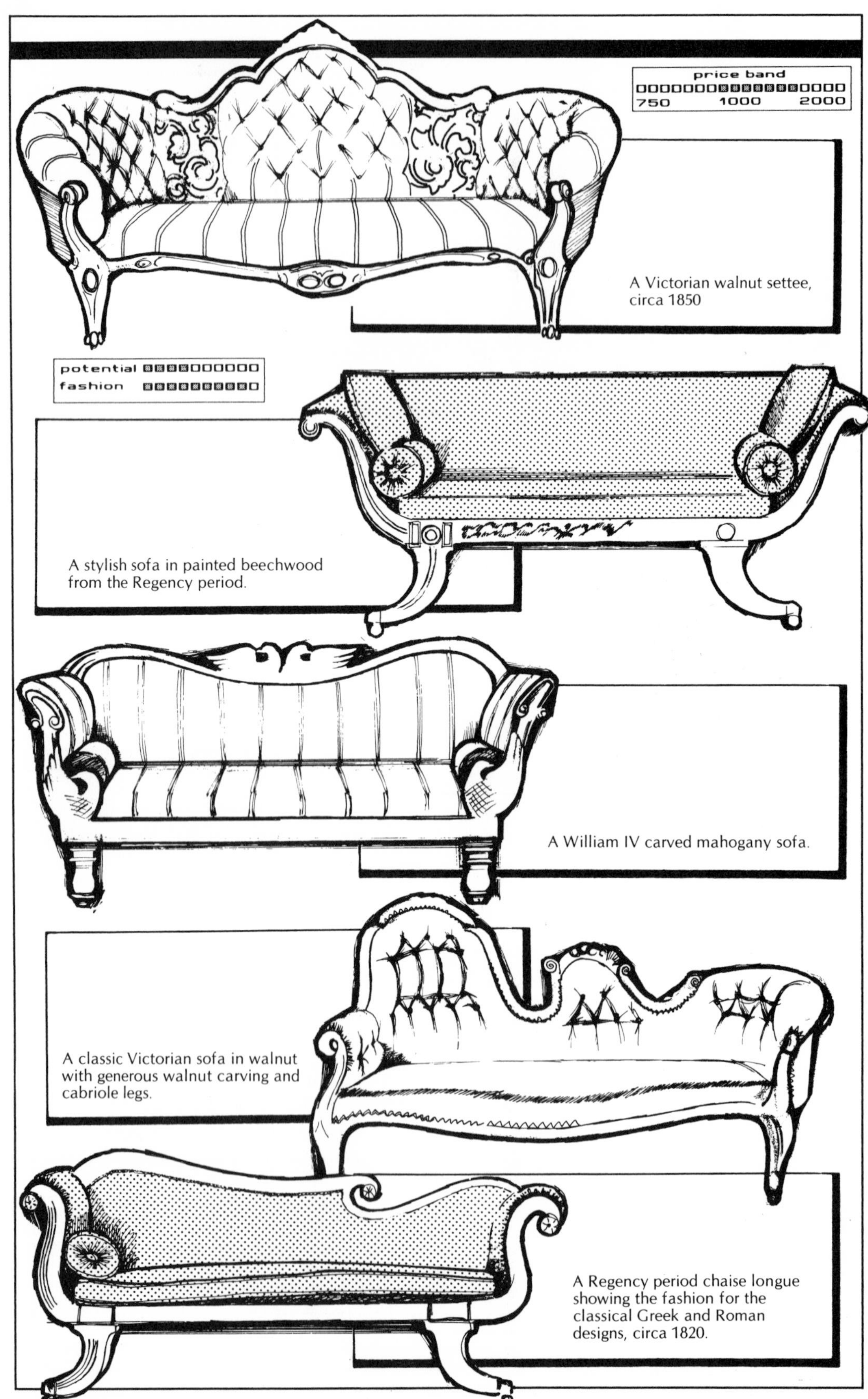

A Victorian walnut settee, circa 1850

A stylish sofa in painted beechwood from the Regency period.

A William IV carved mahogany sofa.

A classic Victorian sofa in walnut with generous walnut carving and cabriole legs.

A Regency period chaise longue showing the fashion for the classical Greek and Roman designs, circa 1820.

Sofas & Settees

Name(s): Sofas, settees and 'stuffed over' furniture. In many cases the Victorian sofa would be sold as part of a larger drawing room suite. This suite could consist of a sofa, a ladies armchair, a slightly larger gentleman's armchair, four (or six) single chairs and a footstool. A smaller matching two-seater sofa might be included in later examples.

Best woods or materials: Rosewood, walnut or mahogany, on a beech frame.

Shape: The illustrations tell some of the story — many show the influence of the fashionable French designers and furniture makers of the day.

Restoration: Apart from re-upholstery, restoration in the antique furniture sense would be confined to the visible wooden parts. The main problem would then be the replacement of any major carved areas — the sheer bulk of seasoned walnut or mahogany being difficult and expensive to find today. The days of the restorer's storerooms full of billiard table legs is long gone.

Decoration/inlays: Brass inlay on Regency examples, quality of carving and design of exposed timber parts frequently dictate the desirability and price of the particular example.

Best period: 1800-1860.

Best size: Size is less important than comfort.

Features to look for: Pierced and well-carved panels on the back — rather like the illustration at the top of the page opposite. Curved ends to accept bolster cushions.

Potential: A good frame with good quality carved walnut cabriole legs will command a very good price — the choice of upholstery is then up to you.

Most valuable: From the purist's point of view, an example with totally original fabric in good condition.

In a word (or two): Definitely a piece to look at rather than actually sit on. I have never owned a Regency or Victorian sofa which could remotely be described as comfortable by modern standards. Quite the opposite of Noel Coward's definition of television: "Something to be on, not to watch."

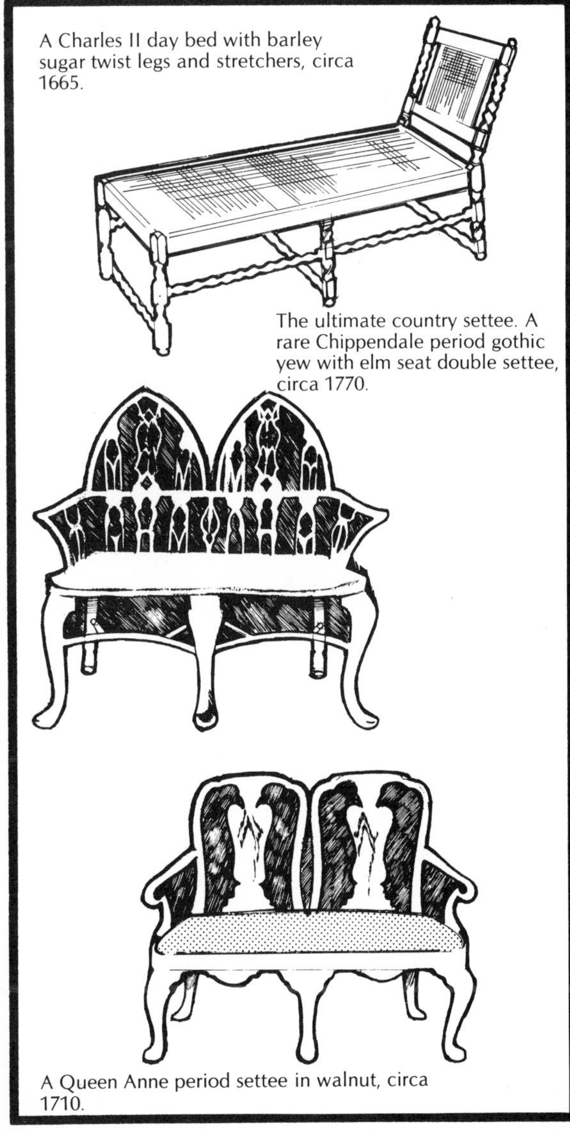

A Charles II day bed with barley sugar twist legs and stretchers, circa 1665.

The ultimate country settee. A rare Chippendale period gothic yew with elm seat double settee, circa 1770.

A Queen Anne period settee in walnut, circa 1710.

Anatomy of the Chair

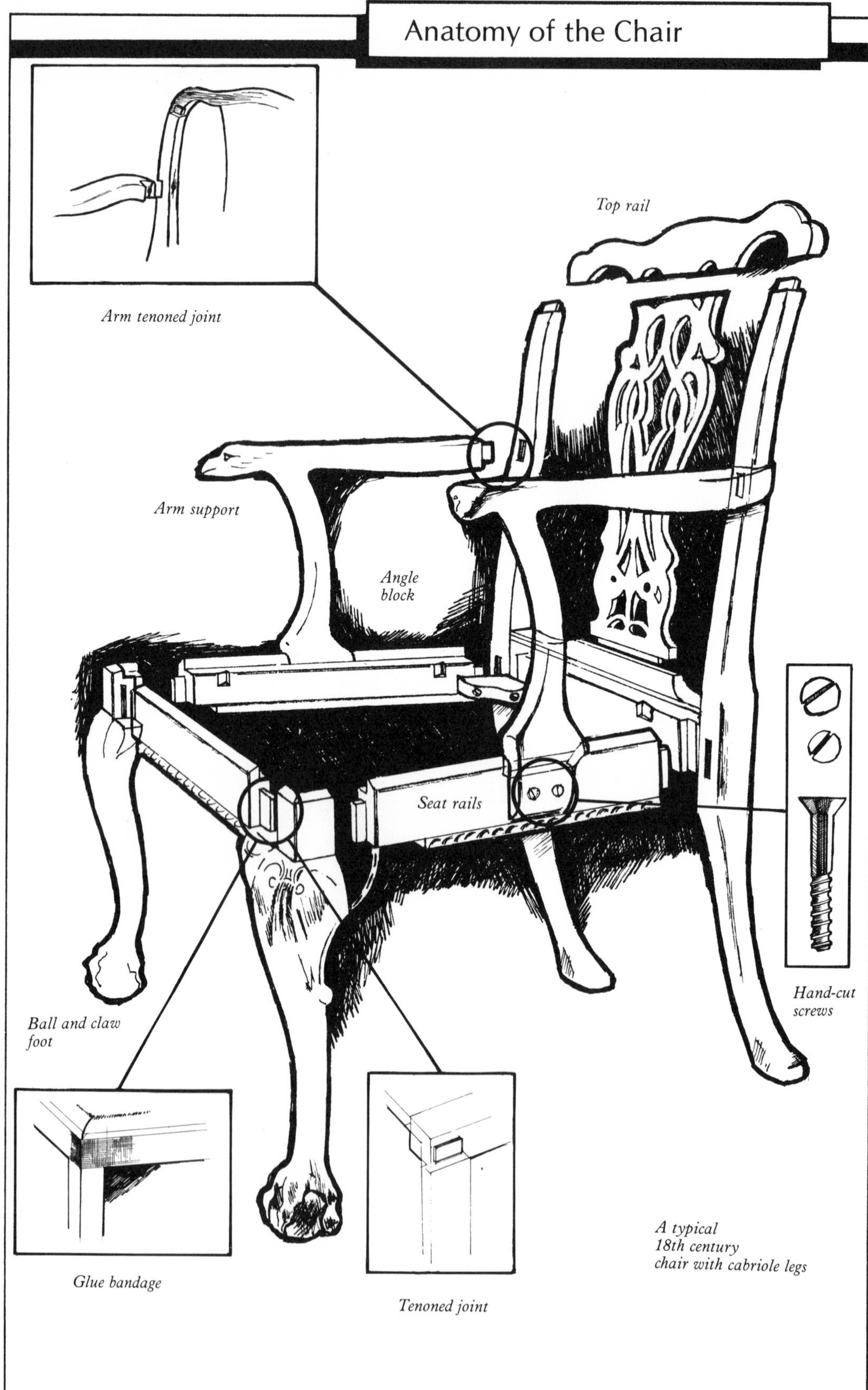

A typical 18th century chair with cabriole legs

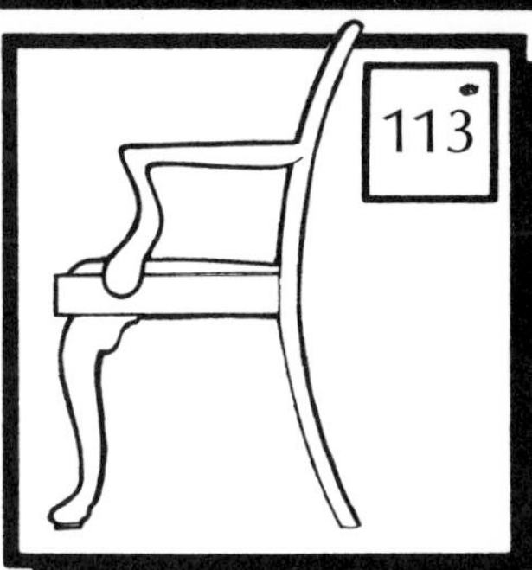

Chair Basics

Chair points: Check the seat rails of stuffed over chairs. Look for the number of upholstery tack holes — this **can** be a clue to the number of times the chair has been re-covered. Beech or birch rails are, however, very likely to have suffered from woodworm attack and been replaced in the past.

If the owner of an 18th century chair contends that the rails and cover are both original expect to find discolouration in the wood around the angular section blacksmith nails. If the nails you find are round, they were made in the late 19th century or even later. The screws fixing the arms (see illustrations opposite) would be hand made if original mid-18th century.

Most 18th century sets are numbered (usually in chiseled Roman numerals) on the back of each chair. They can be rather annoying if you find that you own III, IV, VII, XII and, maybe, XVI out of a fantastically long set.

Chair beware: Your choice will probably hinge on price and design but should also include comfort and strength. A dining chair should be comfortable and also strong enough to absorb the treatment following a well lubricated dinner party.

Sets of slender, fashionable, Victorian balloon-back 'salon' chairs are frequently used as dining chairs today — a role for which they are totally unsuitable. They were originally intended to be more decorative than actually heavily used and their legs and backs can be easily broken.

Chair fake areas: Single dining chairs are unlikely to be total fakes. The danger areas are in sets of six or over where extra chairs will have been made to build a set. A simple test is to hand weight them against each other — suspect the light ones! Examine the arms on carver chairs — these could be later additions; check the seat width on these against the single chairs — the carver seats should be 3" to 4" wider, (4cm).

Chippendale design chairs are not always 18th century. Many more were made in the 19th century than ever were during Chippendale's lifetime.

Faced with the restoration of a set of chairs, restorer Rod Dunning will first make a complete examination of every chair. He will be looking for previous repairs or work and, at the same time, identifying possible problem areas.

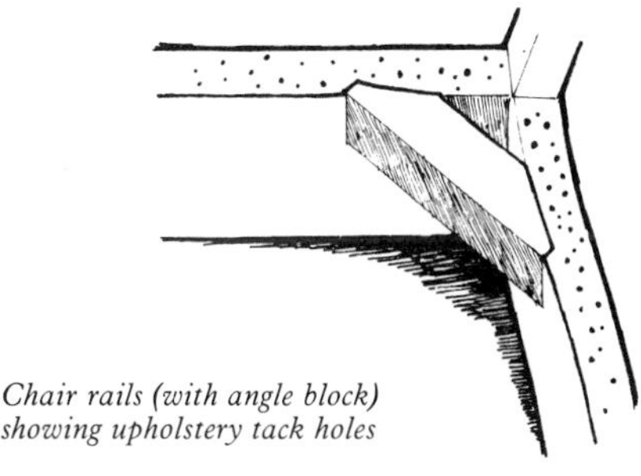

Chair rails (with angle block) showing upholstery tack holes

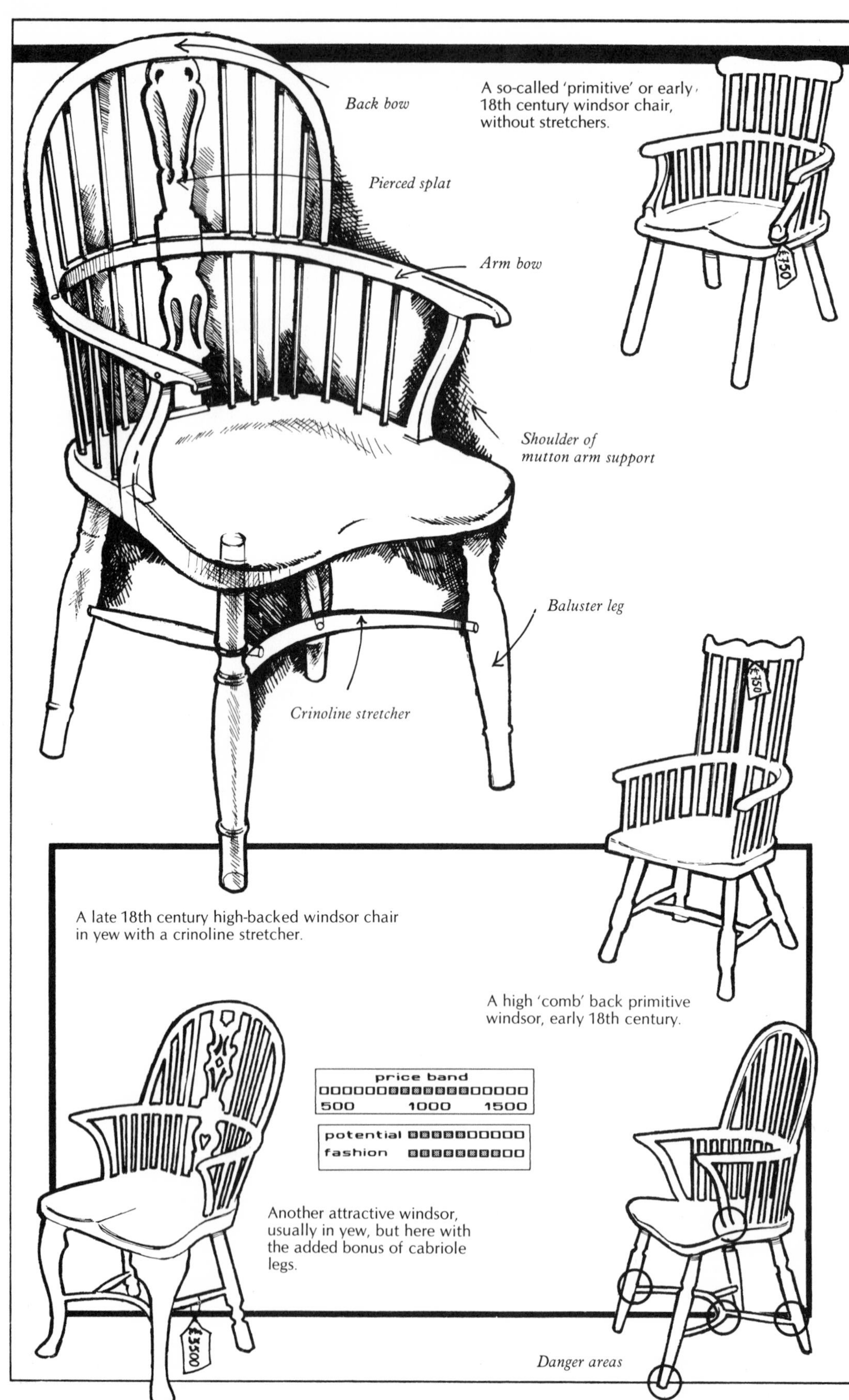

A so-called 'primitive' or early 18th century windsor chair, without stretchers.

A late 18th century high-backed windsor chair in yew with a crinoline stretcher.

A high 'comb' back primitive windsor, early 18th century.

Another attractive windsor, usually in yew, but here with the added bonus of cabriole legs.

Windsor Chairs

Quick view: The most comfortable of all period wooden chairs.

Desirable woods: Yew wood with fruitwood as a second choice; most however, are made in elm or ash; seats in elm, turned parts in beech and 'bent' parts in ash.

Shape: Most desirable design is 'Gothic', with cabriole legs, crinoline stretcher and gothic high back. Best trade windsor is heavy, late, Lancashire high back, in yew with good figuring on broad, well curved, arms.

Restoration: No particular problem — new yew, however, is considered quite difficult to age and colour.

Fake?: Very high quality windsors are made today — not specifically as fakes but they could well be passed off as old. Many windsors are, however, totally made up of bits and pieces collected over the years. They were very common some years ago and subjected to hard wear; many restorers keep collections of seats, stretchers, old legs, etc.

Decoration/inlays: No inlays, however armorials are (very rarely) possible on back, splat shields on knees, little 'knops' under arms, and especially attractive legs are all 'plus' features.

Best size: A wide-seated chair — 18" (45cm) across seat — is to be preferred to a cramped narrow example.

Colour: One of the prettiest colours in the antique business is the apricot 'flash' of yew wood.

Features to look for: Total yew construction, including back legs. Seat, however, in elm. Crinoline (or curved) stretcher.

Potential: Sets of matching chairs make premium prices — BUT THEY REALLY SHOULD MATCH. Less than perfect matching collections are known as 'composite' or 'harlequin' sets; remember to check both overall height and height to seat.

Worth mentioning: Mrs. Beeton suggests using elm windsor chairs in maids' bedrooms (cost 1/- each,) and yew wood examples for housekeepers' and butlers' rooms (cost 5/- each).

Read: *"English Windsor Chairs"* by Ivan G. Sparkes. (Shire Publications.)

A smoker's bow chair but lacking nice thick club arms and consequently less valuable.

The classic 'smoker's bow' or 'captain's chair' which has now replaced the windsor with buyers who can no longer afford the former. Some captain's chairs were made in yew which can take them almost into the windsor price catergory.

An office chair rather similar in design to the smoker's bow but much 'thinner' in construction.

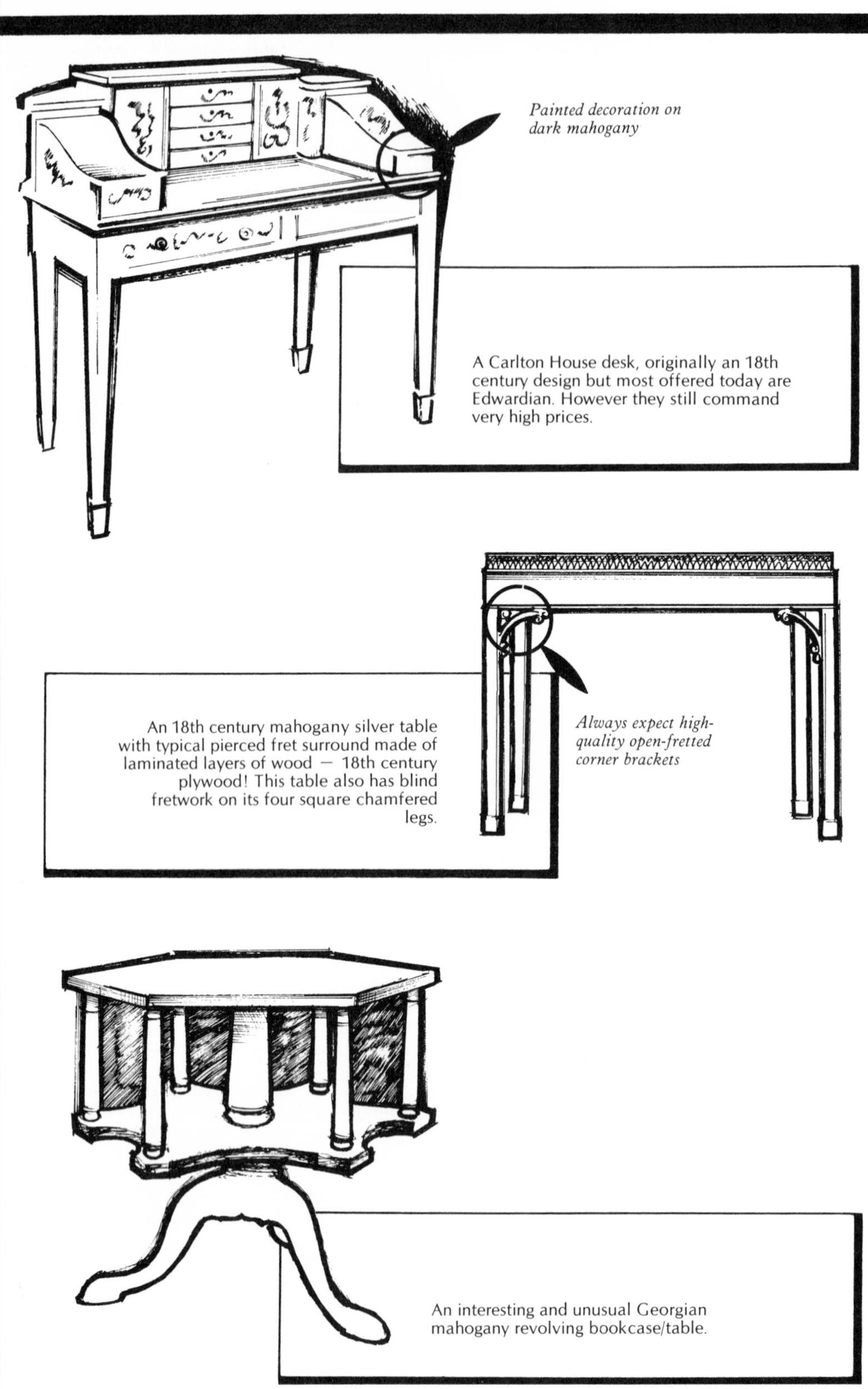

A Carlton House desk, originally an 18th century design but most offered today are Edwardian. However they still command very high prices.

An 18th century mahogany silver table with typical pierced fret surround made of laminated layers of wood — 18th century plywood! This table also has blind fretwork on its four square chamfered legs.

An interesting and unusual Georgian mahogany revolving bookcase/table.

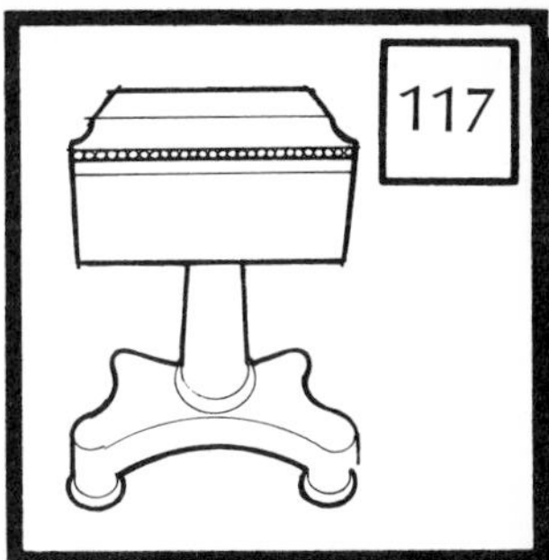

Miscellany III

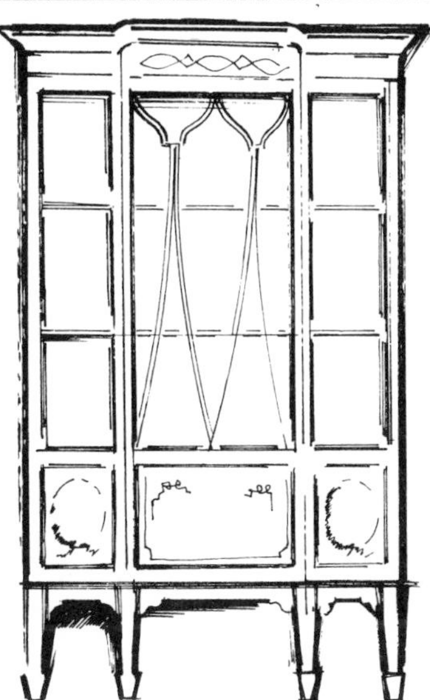

A fine Edwardian display cabinet in mahogany decorated with painted swags of flowers.

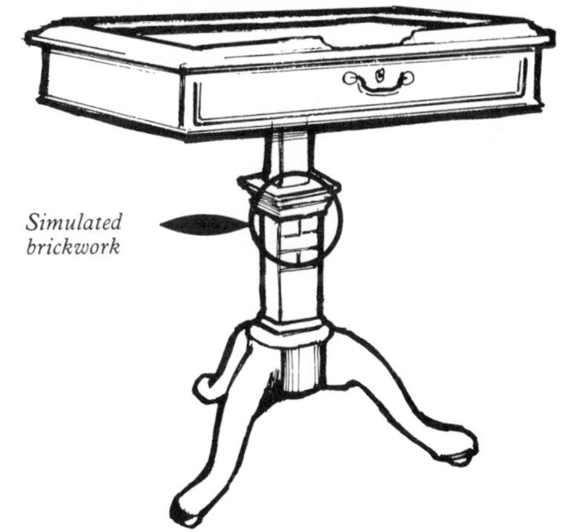

A fascinating 19th century lecturer's table. The especially interesting feature is the simulated brickwork adjustable column.

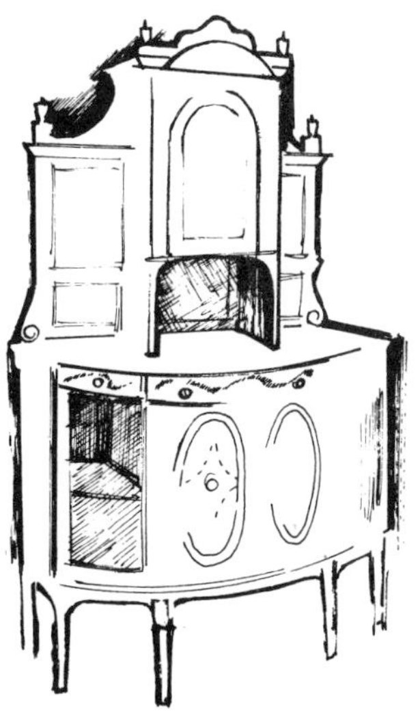

Edwardian period side cabinet in dark mahogany with painted swags and inlaid panels; glazed and mirrored top.

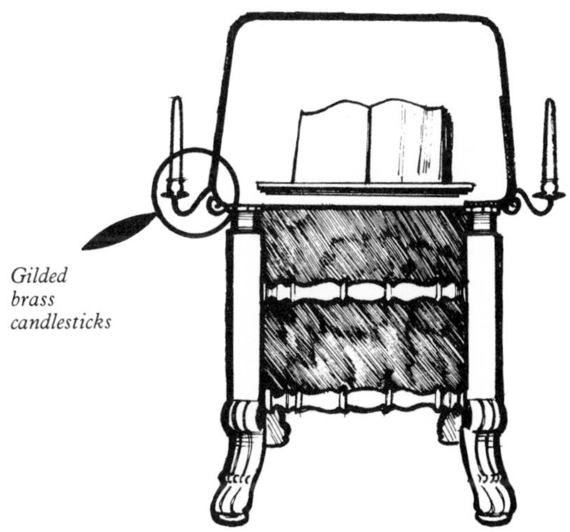

A late 18th century writing table/reading stand with ormolu candle holders.

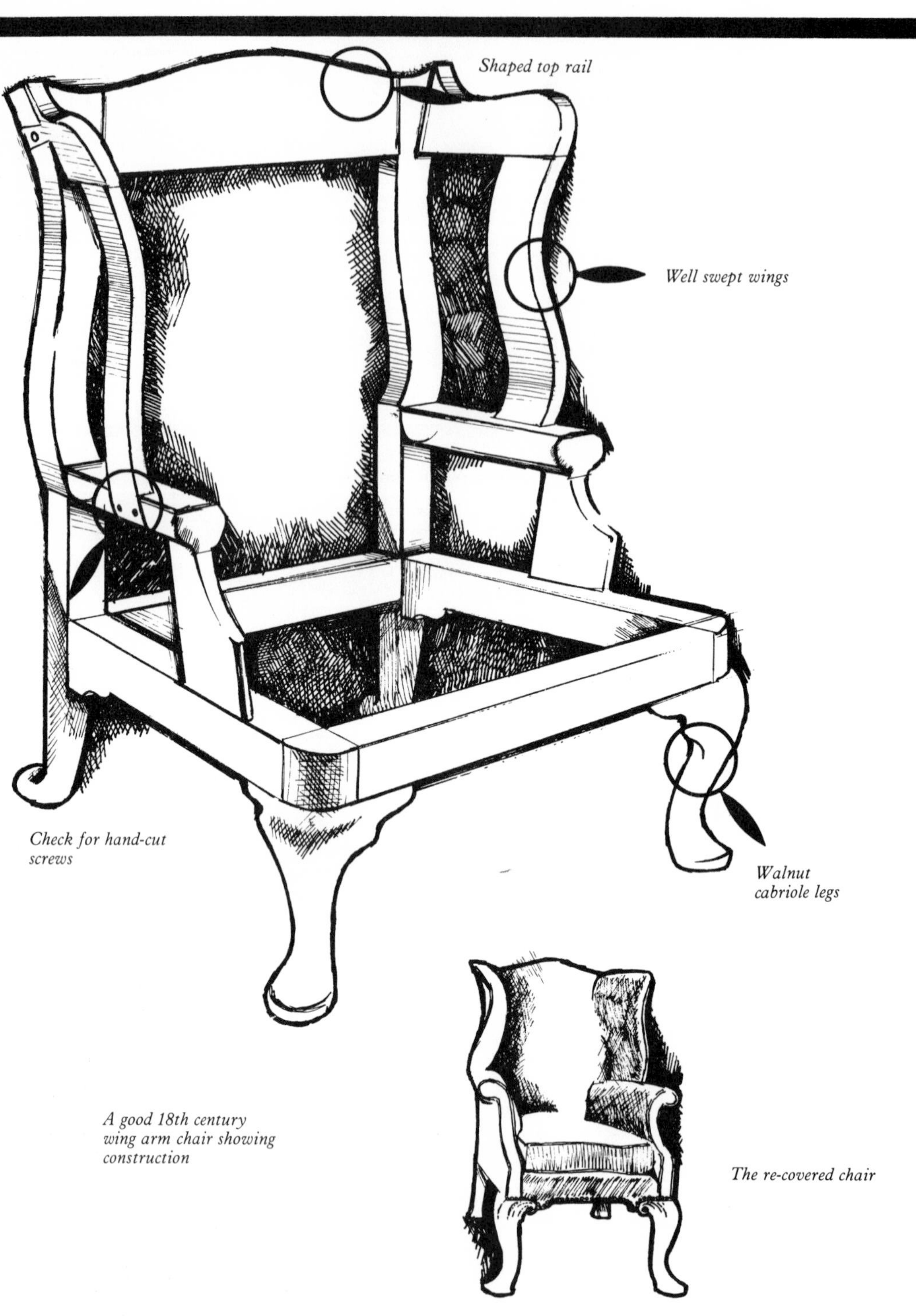

A good 18th century wing arm chair showing construction

The re-covered chair

price band
1000 1500 2000

potential
fashion

Arm & Wing Chairs

Best woods or materials: Mahogany or walnut.

Restoration: The restoration of timber parts present no particular problems. Great sympathy and knowledge must be displayed, however, when recovering. Period upholstery is totally different to modern methods and materials. It is simply no use taking your nice genuine period frame to the local friendly upholsterer. The work must be undertaken by an expert and research is necessary to find the man capable of the job. Much the same sentiments apply to the fabrics employed. Whilst you will, no doubt, have a specific colour or shade in mind, some research into contemporary fabrics which match, in style and treatment, the originals, can be rewarding. In England and the United States there are a great many fabrics available which echo perfectly the colours and designs of the 18th century.

Having said all this, re-covering in something less than acceptable to a new owner is no great lasting disaster. Everything can be undone again.

Fake? Assuming that the visible wood is genuine, the amount of reconstruction and re-placement 'under the covers' may never be known to you.

Configuration: The main important components are the frame, the visible wood — usually mahogany or walnut — and the covering.

Best period: Late 18th century.

Best size: Most period wing or arm chairs are fairly substantial by modern standards.

Feet: Typically ball and claw or square tapered feet.

Features to look for: Original covering. Dramatically shaped 'thin' wings.

Potential: Lots of potential if you can spot a period frame hiding under a modern Victorian covering.

Most valuable: A totally original fine early 18th century example with an arched back and well shaped wings all in contemporary tapestry covering.

In a word (or two): Great satisfaction if you can get a genuine frame and then transform it to something resembling its original glory.

Eighteenth century open arm chair in mahogany

Eighteenth century stuffed-over arm chair

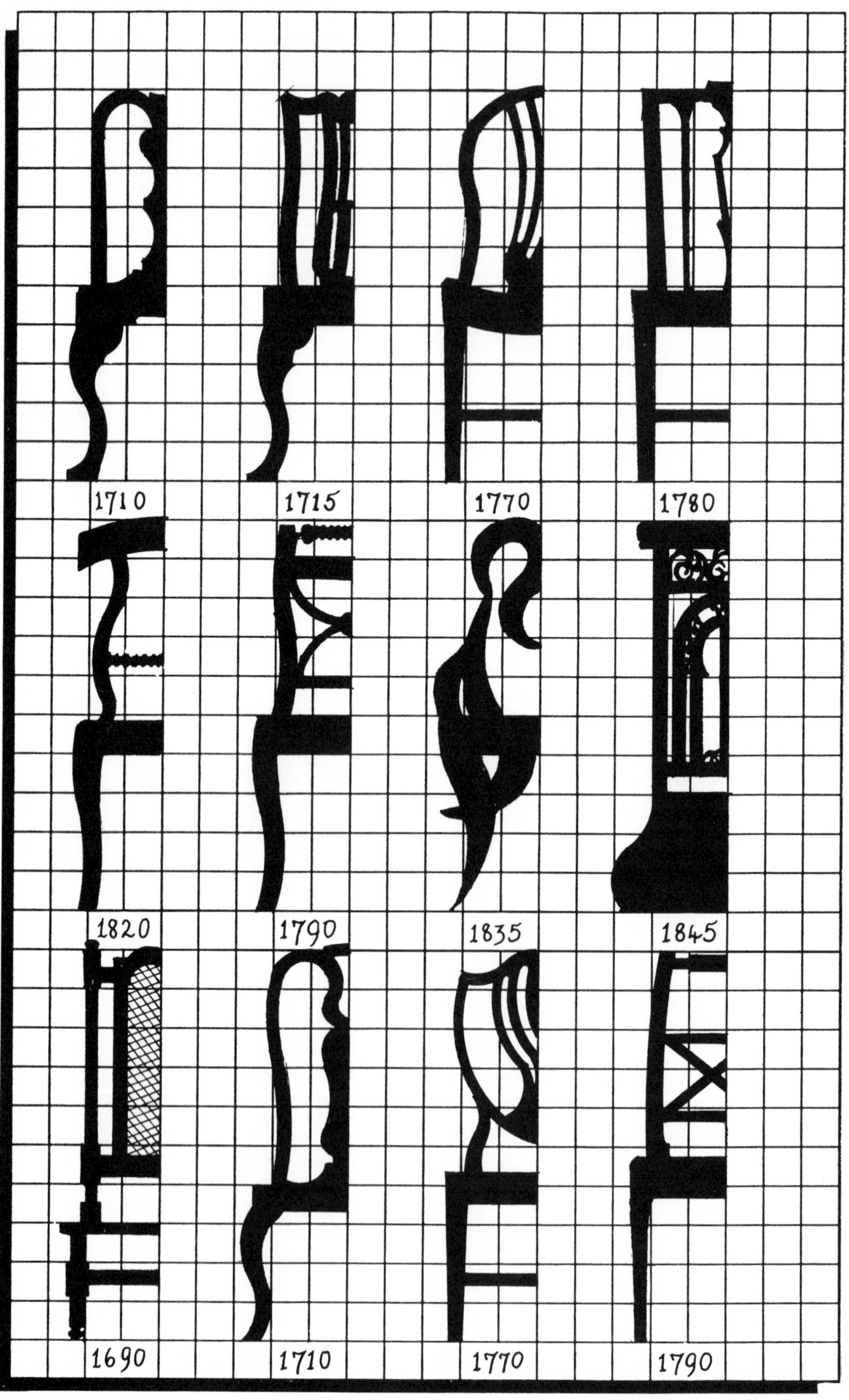
1710
1715
1770
1780
1820
1790
1835
1845
1690
1710
1770
1790

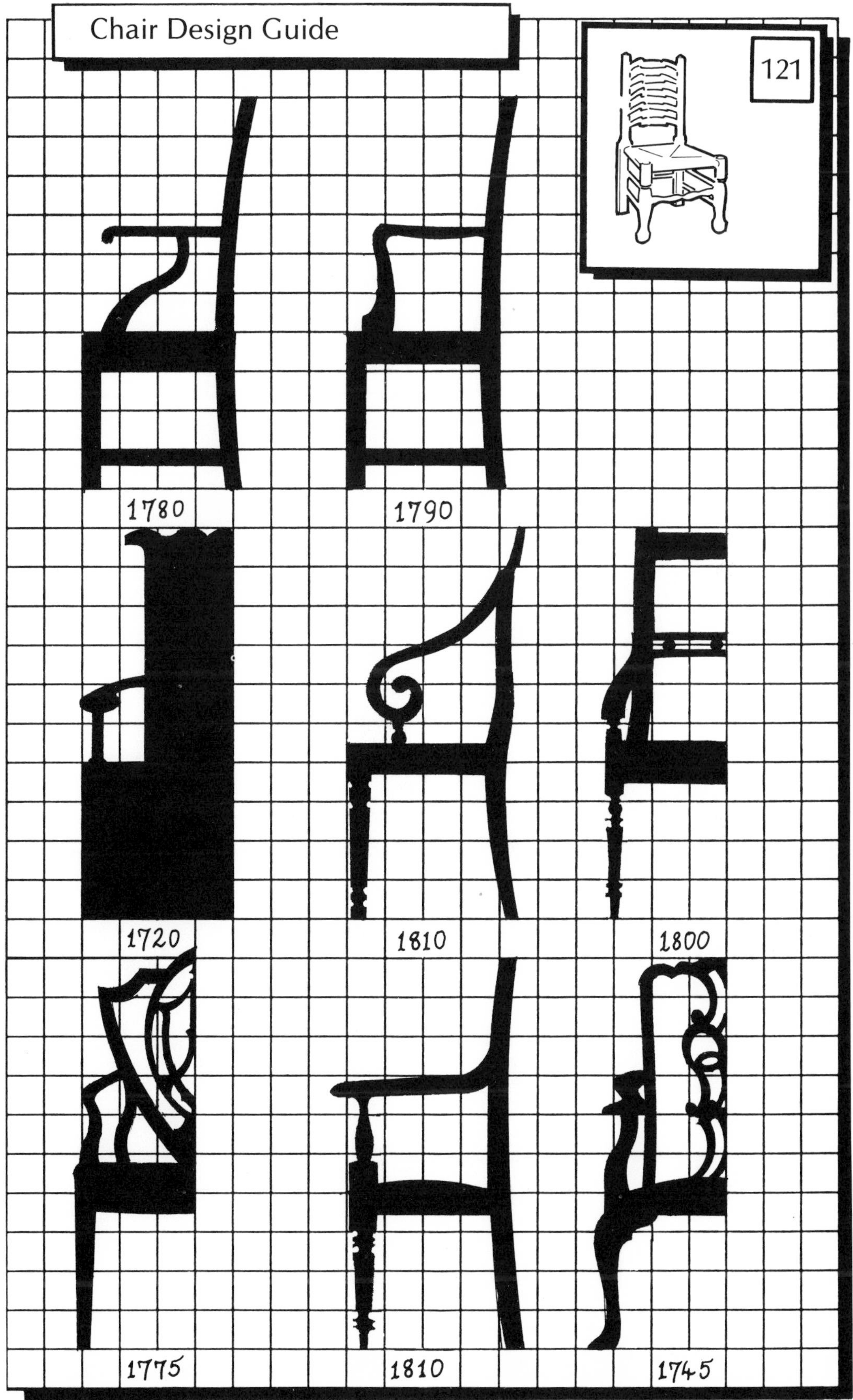
Chair Design Guide
121
1780
1790
1720
1810
1800
1775
1810
1745

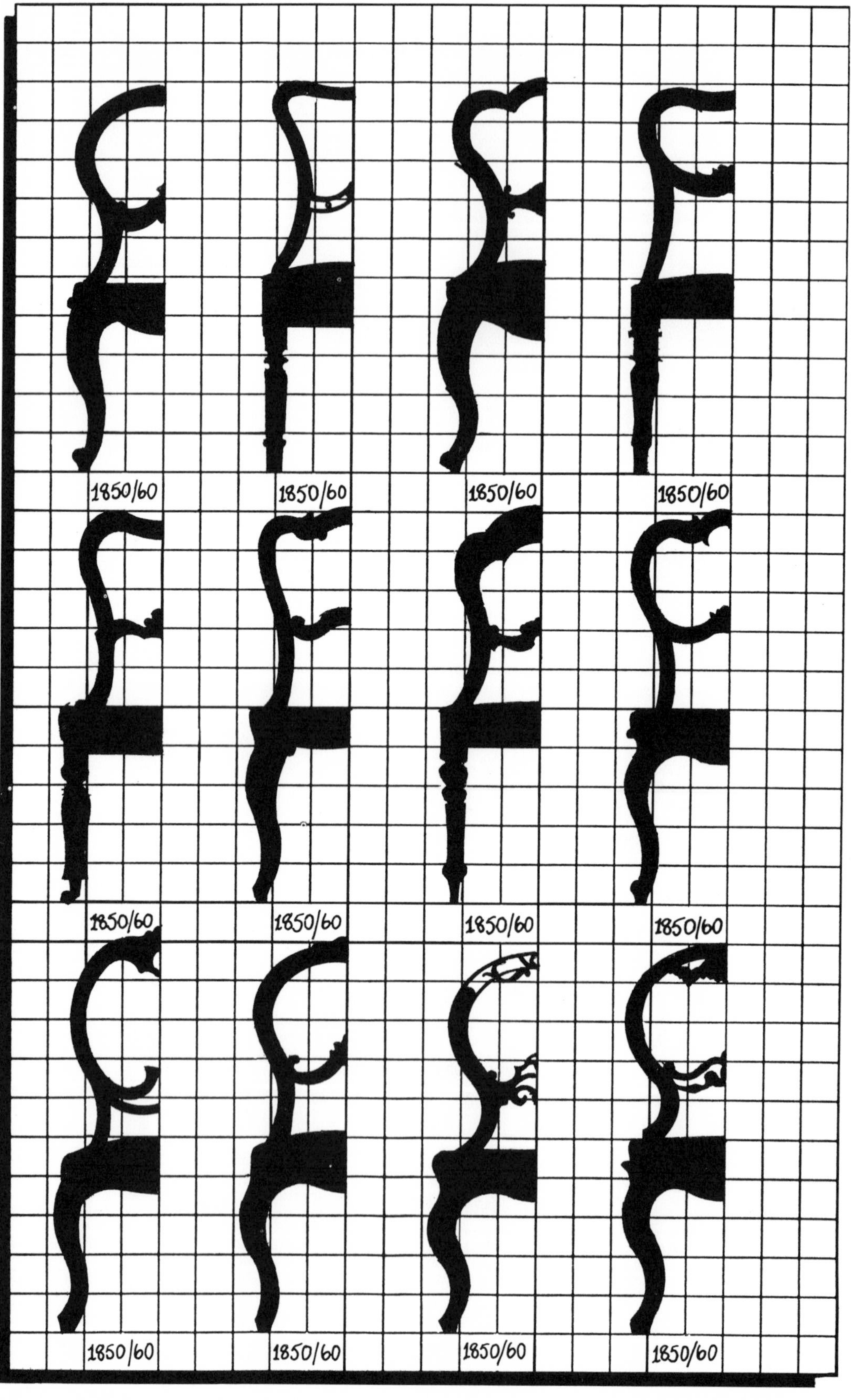

1850/60
1850/60
1850/60
1850/60
1850/60
1850/60
1850/60
1850/60
1850/60
1850/60
1850/60
1850/60

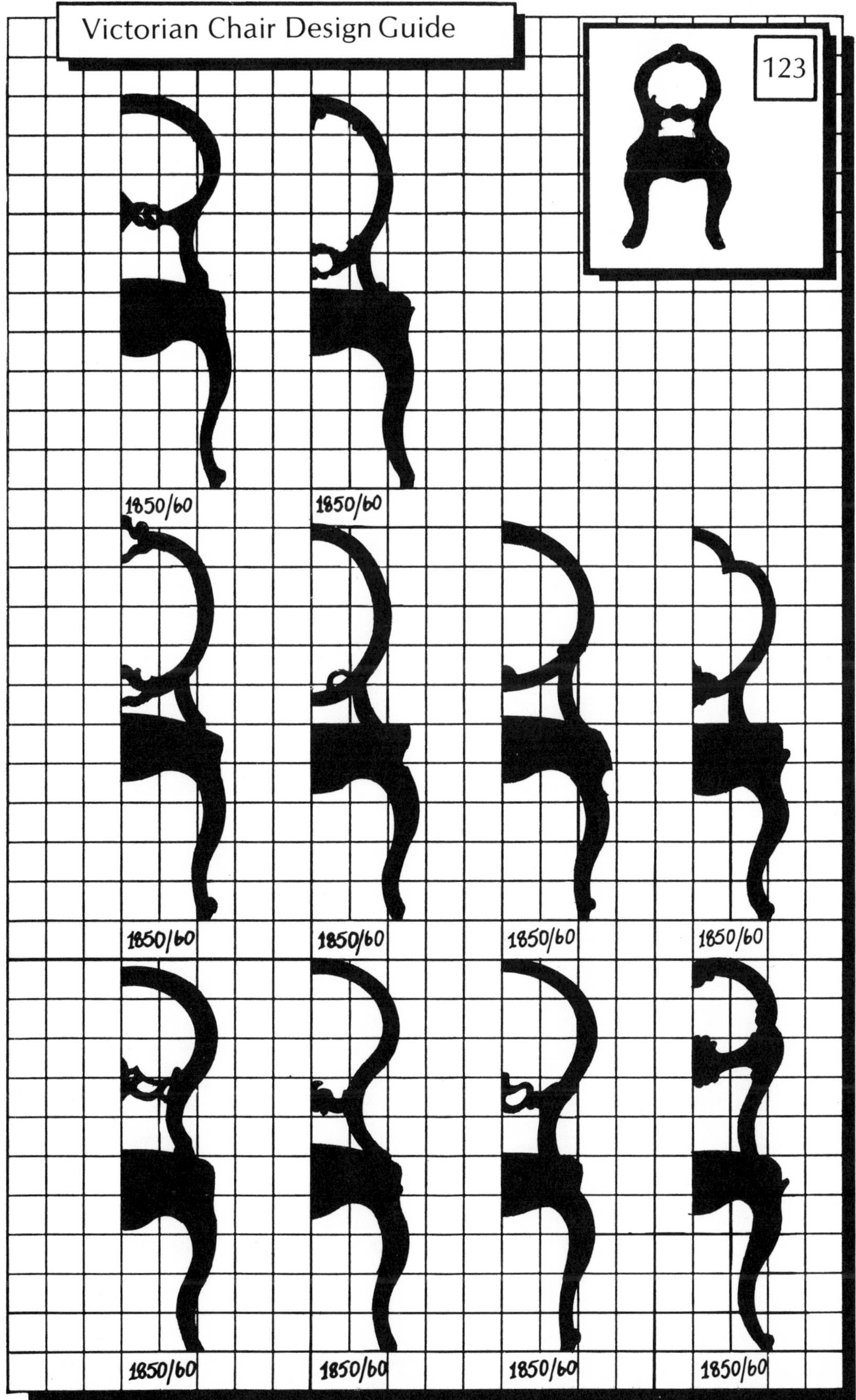
Victorian Chair Design Guide
123
1850/60
1850/60
1850/60
1850/60
1850/60
1850/60
1850/60
1850/60
1850/60
1850/60

GRANDFATHER CLOCKTAIL CABINETS

In the good old days when big, wide Yorkshire clocks could not be sold, some were lined with green baize, shelves and strip lights fitted and sold as **grandfather clocktail cabinets.** A refinement would be automatic lights when the door was opened or when the clock chimed! Happily, this practice is not required today when any longcase clock is saleable.

CHESTS THAT SHRINK

Tall chests with 'too many drawers' can be cut down to a more saleable size by the simple expedient of removing the bottom drawer. Victorian examples with turned feet can find these replaced with bracket feet.

A fitted secretaire can find its way into an especially deep single top drawer. These secretaire interiors are frequently genuine in themselves, but have become divorced from their original carcase.

HELLO SAILOR

Any pine box can be transformed into a so-called **sea chest** or **seaman's chest** with the addition of a primitive ship portrait and a spurious vessel's name and owner. More sophisticated versions are lined with genuine stained sea charts, fake, torn labels on the front and sides, and rope carrying handles. For the record, genuine sea chests always had any picture on the inside of the lid.

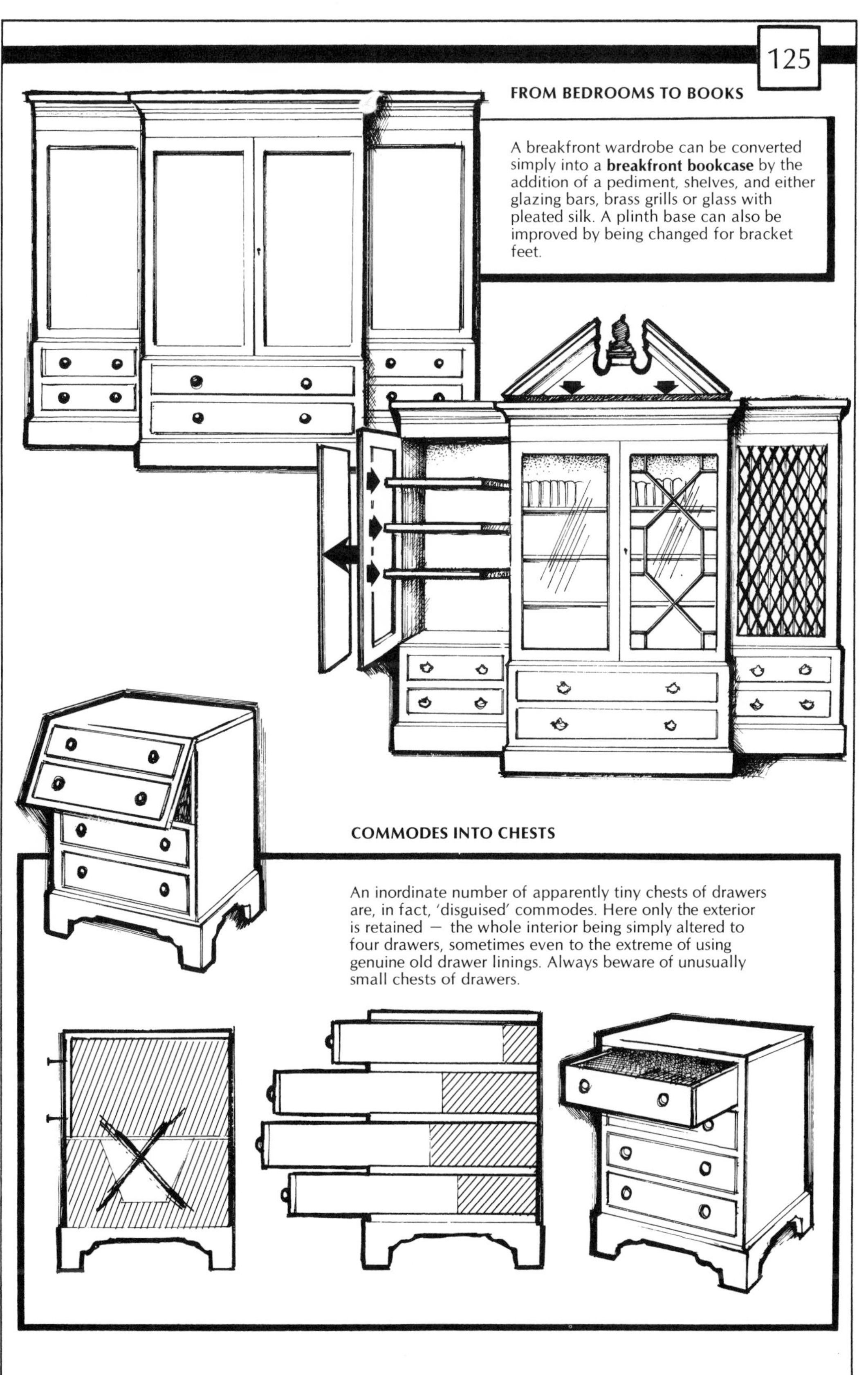

FROM BEDROOMS TO BOOKS

A breakfront wardrobe can be converted simply into a **breakfront bookcase** by the addition of a pediment, shelves, and either glazing bars, brass grills or glass with pleated silk. A plinth base can also be improved by being changed for bracket feet.

COMMODES INTO CHESTS

An inordinate number of apparently tiny chests of drawers are, in fact, 'disguised' commodes. Here only the exterior is retained — the whole interior being simply altered to four drawers, sometimes even to the extreme of using genuine old drawer linings. Always beware of unusually small chests of drawers.

Improving Furniture

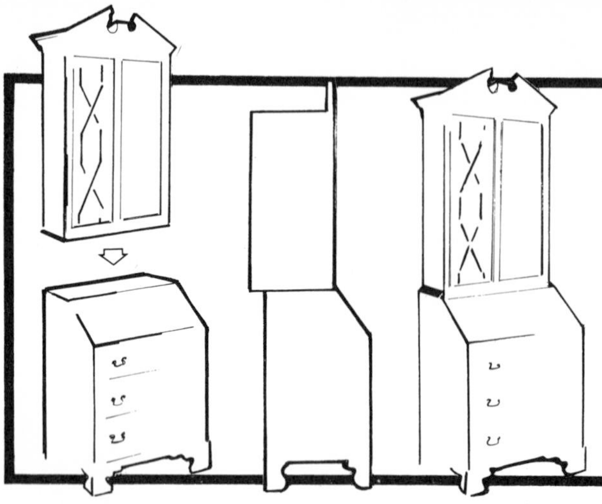

UN-HOLY MARRIAGES

The most common of all antiques improvements is the **marriage** of two pieces — usually a bureau bookcase, but can also be a chest on stand or a secretaire bookcase, etc. Some bureau marriages are very hard to detect. Look, for example, for moulding around the base of the top to compensate for extra width or an overhanging back — this should always be the same width on all three sides. If the top of a bureau is more than about 11″ deep (back to front) it probably originally had a bookcase on top.

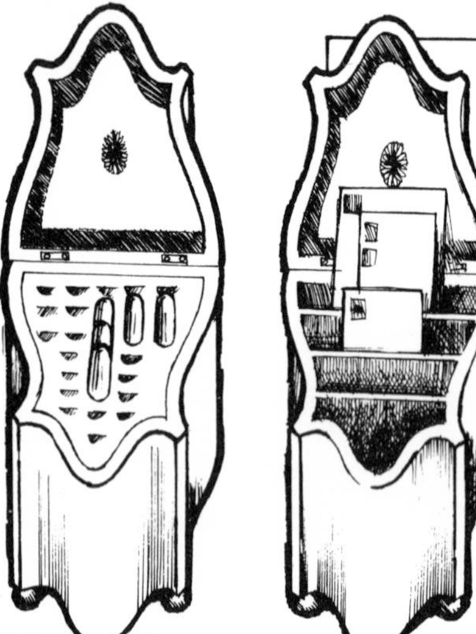

ALL KNIFE BOXES THAT ARE NOT WRITE

There is little demand for genuine knife boxes — a relic of the days when knives were steel and kept separately from the rest of the flatware. Today they are converted into stationery boxes or letter racks. Almost a permissable improvement as they can be re-converted simply by the purist.

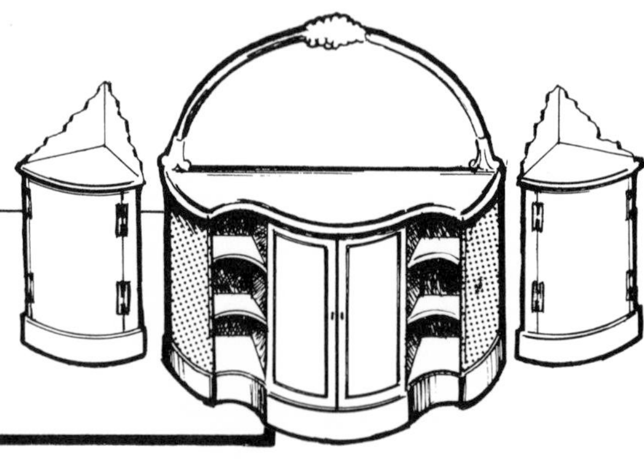

CORNER CUPBOARDS

A popular example is the pair of hanging corner cupboards from Victorian chiffonier. This did happen at one time but today the chiffonier is easier to sell, (usually into the export trade), than it is to sell two suspect cupboards.

CHAIRS THAT GROW

Few buys are more frustrating for the dealer than the split set of chairs. It is one of the most common 'finds' in the business. "The other three were given to my sister years ago," "Two got broken and were thrown out." The buyer has almost a duty to restore the set to its former glory.

CIRCULAR COMMODES OR POT CUPBOARDS

When they are not being converted into corner cupboards. Victorian circular commodes can be sold as drinks cupboards, as can three-step commodes which are especially popular in France.

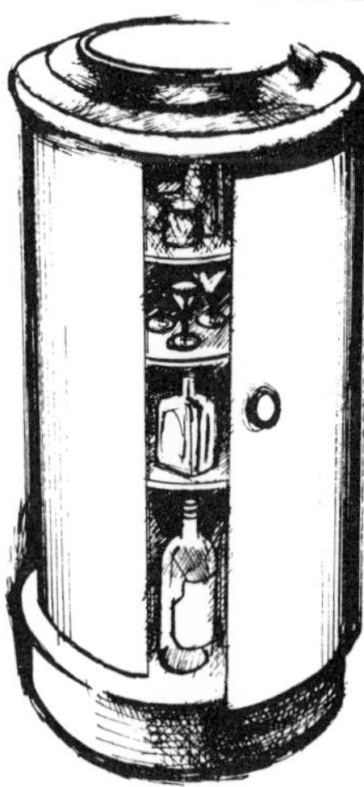

MORE COMMODES THAT TAKE TO DRINK

When the small straight-fronted pseudo-chest-commode has two false cupboards it does not lend itself to improvement as a chest of drawers. Another **drinks cabinet** is the result — seems almost appropriate somehow!

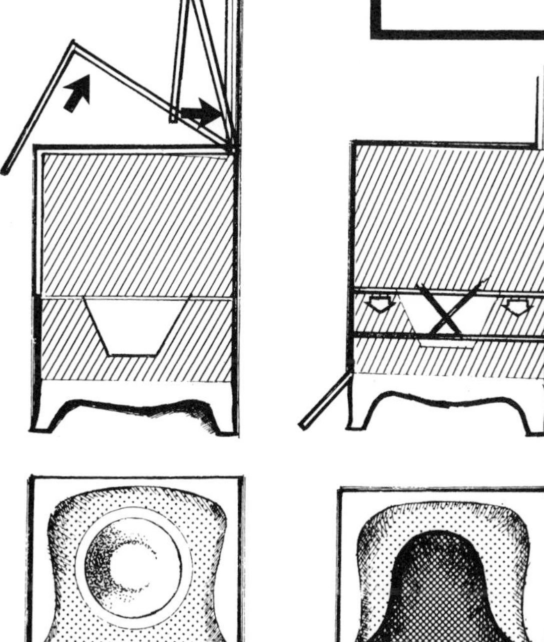

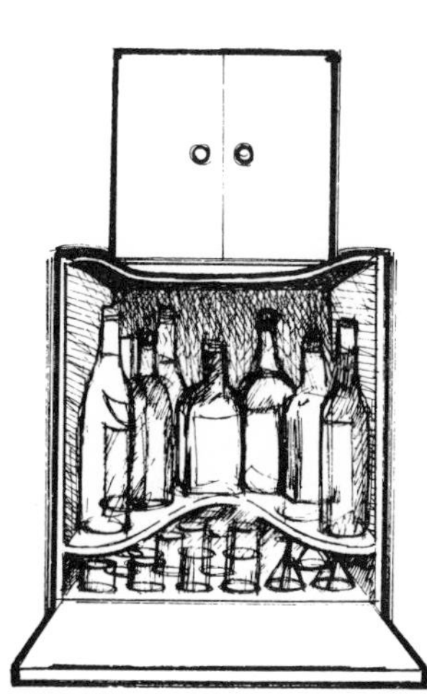

secrets of the antique trade

introduction

Every guide has to be written from a particular point of view and this section of *The Insiders' Guide To Antique Furniture* has been compiled from the position that the reader might be interested in becoming a full or part-time antique dealer or would simply like to know more about a trade that is so shrouded in mystique.

In doing so, it tends to focus on what might be considered to be the less savoury aspects of the trade. Even if the reader has no interest, or intention, of becoming a dealer, some of the points and comments can be taken as an insight into the 'dealer mind' and as a warning of the forces ranged against him as a buyer or a seller.

Like very many traders, antique dealers relish a 'them and us' attitude. With the heavy emphasis on ongoing business with other dealers and the camaraderie at regular auction sales, it is easy to understand how these attitudes have grown. To say that the trade has total contempt for the public might be too strong a generalization, but it is unfortunately near the mark with many individuals.

It should not be thought that every antique dealer is a rogue. That all depends on one's definition of the word. Many people totally resent the whole idea of 'profit', especially when it is apparently made at their personal expense. The dealer makes his living buying from one individual and selling to another — the arch middle man. As a consequence, perhaps, the dealer has been seen, traditionally, as someone who profits from, and takes advantage of, the ignorance and greed of the buyer and the seller. This is no less true of the back street buyer off a barrow or the curator in the marbled halls of the national museum collections. It all depends on your point of view. Added to this is the fact that antiques are often sold at a time of personal stress, death, moving house, etc, and profits are even more resented after emotions have cooled.

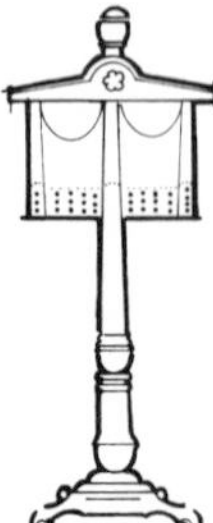

The profit motive is behind every commercial activity in a free society. When one buys a washing machine, a new dress, or even a bar of chocolate, there has been a profit at every stage of its production. This profit is not seen and is seldom grudged. However, the antique dealer (and to a similar extent, the used car dealer) is in a slightly different situation, as the ordinary householder is his source of stock. In theory, at least, it is possible for Mrs. Average to sell her sideboard, loved and polished and handed down through the family from her maternal grandmother, to a dealer, and then see it in his showroom the following day, virtually untouched and marked at twice the price she received for it.

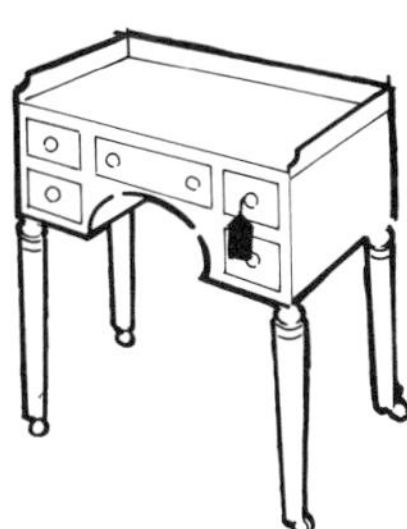

I am not suggesting that there is anything morally wrong with this — I earned my own living doing just this for some considerable time — it is just an unfortunate fact of life of the antique trade. The disenchanted sideboard seller will never consider for a second the frequently enormous overheads levied on every business through salaries, city rates, rent, bank interest, lighting, heating, insurance, and all the other hundred-and-one inroads into profit margins.

statements in 'the guide'

In attempting to compile a visual reference guide, specific statements have to be made without qualification. But almost without exception every one of these statements can just as easily be totally, and quite correctly, contradicted. If there is one rule which applies to every aspect of dealing with the multitude of objects, furniture, and works of art in this trade, it is that there is no rule at all.

pricing in 'the guide'

I was asked by my Editor to include some prices or, at the very least, some indication of 'price bands' for the furniture featured. We both agreed that this would be helpful to the reader if it could be done in a meaningful way.

But which price?

The original price paid by the first knocker? The country auction price? Perhaps the London auction price or the price asked by any one of a hundred different strata of dealer?

If this seemingly simple request has so many answers — which is the 'right price'? The boxes in the Price Bands attempt to illustrate the typical range of prices for each piece or group. Any absolutely specific price can only tend to be too dogmatic and lead the unwary into dangerous areas both buying and selling.

What about all the antique price guides which fill every shelf in the bookshop? Are all these prices correct? These guides have been the antique publishing success of the last ten years or so. In this period I have bought my fair share of these — they are virtually irresistible to anyone interested in, or owning, antiques. However, they are all liable to lead their readers into the same trap. They purely report on the price realized at auction or, in the case of many American guides, the prices asked by dealers 'across the nation'.

Fair enough, you say, so what's wrong with that?

The guides usually report only on illustrated items culled from auction catalogues — their artists draw the items which have been featured in these catalogues and the caption reports the price realized. No mention is ever made of authenticity or condition of the item. Was there a strong ring operating and/or little public interest? What was the weather like on the day — thick fog or heavy snow? There are dozens of conditions which can influence the price paid.

You only have to look at the pre-sale estimates published in many sale catalogues and compare these to the actual results to see that the auctioneers frequently get their educated 'guesstimates' just as wrong. There is even the case when the item reported does not even sell and is 'bought in' — the knocked-down price then becomes the 'official guide price' for that lot. With anywhere between five and twenty-five per cent of auction lots not being sold and bought in, this results in a fair percentage of 'official prices'.

18th century elm and yewwood Windsor chair with pierced splat. (Locke & England) $370 £220

Let's take one example . . . here is an illustration of a windsor chair taken from a well known, top selling, 'official' price guide.

An attractive and fairly rare chair; it has all the desirable features — gothic style, crinoline stretcher, cabriole legs all in yew wood. Obviously a fine chair. Sold by a highly reputable firm of auctioneers for the princely sum of £220.

Now . . . just suppose you find that this description (and illustration) matches that old chair up in the spare bedroom. You decide to sell. You are offered, say, £300 by a dealer. Should you sell? The official (sic.) price guide says yes! You would be wrong. Your chair is probably worth at least four or five times that listed in the guide. Why?

The price guide did not mention (because it clearly did not know) that the chair illustrated was virtually brand new from the seat down and had been 'dropped' into the auction. How do I know that it was brand new? It was my chair. I entered it into that auction because it has an excellent reputation of not accepting 'trade lots' and getting good prices. The work on the windsor obviously didn't fool any members of the trade present since it didn't fetch anywhere near the price of a properly restored piece. The chair had been restored but not distressed.

My guess is that it was either bought by a private customer who didn't realize the amount of work already done, or by a dealer who would then really go to town with the chains and other distressing tools. It raises an interesting question though . . . why did the auctioneers choose to illustrate it? Did it fool them?*

*Why did I sell my chair just to prove a point? Not only was it mostly 'new' it was also chronically uncomfortable!

buying

Success in antiques can be quantified as probably ninety-five percent good buying. Not only buying at the right price, but also the right material which will satisfy the particular needs of your trade and private customers. Given a normal market situation, selling the right stock at the right price has never been a problem. There are many different sources for goods, but the main prospects can be categorized as follows:

1 The antique trade

2 Antique and commercial auction sales

3 Privately (in the home) (reached by advertising and direct mail)

4 Privately (in the shop)

5 Antique fairs and car boot (garage) sales

6 Commercial shops and premises

7 Estate agents and lawyers

the antique trade

Buying 'from the trade' means, at one end of the scale, the exclusive emporia of London's Bond Street and New York's Madison Avenue to the junk shop in provincial back streets. Many a 'rare lot' has started its trade life on a market stall and ended up in the exalted environment of the Grosvenor House Fair.

You can buy at trade prices at most antique shops by the simple expedient of saying the magic words, 'What's the trade on this?' If the 'retail' price is clearly marked you can usually expect no more than ten to fifteen per cent discount. If the prices are marked in code, you will never know if any discount has been allowed. If you think the 'call' could become regular, you might like to ask various prices and try and crack the code (see 'Price Codes').

The real test is whether you think you can make a profit — the paltry ten per cent (or whatever) small discount is not intended to be your profit, purely a gesture. Many dealers sell only to the trade and are generally much easier to do business with.

There was once a time when you had to produce a dog-eared card to qualify for trade terms. Those days are long since gone. It is now sufficient just to say that you are 'in the trade' to get whatever discount is available.

A theory about trade buying you might like to put to the test . . .

Assuming you are dealing in middle-of-the-road Victoriana, would you shop 'up' or 'down'? That is, would you expect to find regular supplies of stock with a decent profit margin in junk shops or at the better end of the trade? My theory is 'the better the shop, the better the price' provided you want to buy your material and not his.

To explain. A dealer specializing in fine Georgian furniture has to make a bulk purchase of, say, a complete houshold to get his lots. He will then have bought Victorian and other items which he will not wish to display in his showroom. They must be sold quickly. On the other hand, if you find a nice Victorian credenza in a junk shop it may well be the best thing he has had for months. He will have had every price guide dusted off and will ask its top quoted price.

I can remember finding a rather fine carriage clock on a piece of carpet in the Rome flea market. It was surrounded by bits of old gas cookers and what looked like the innards of an Alfa Romeo gearbox. The price demanded was in excess of the identical clock in Bond Street or Madison Avenue.

17th century oak child's wainscot chair.

auction sales

Auction sales include not only so-called 'antique auctions' but all public auctions where you can reasonably expect to find 'goods' — from tiny local charity auctions right up to huge commercial sales of factories. However, whether the sale is tiny and conducted by the local vicar or a gigantic commercial event lasting several days, the same basic ground rules apply.

First, find out where the sales are to be held.

The major auction rooms advertise in the English national press. Details of most British antique auctions appear each week in *The Antique Trade Gazette.* The smaller sales have to be found by scouring the small ads sections in your local or regional newspapers. Commercial sales are frequently harder to find as their sale advertisements sometimes only appear in their own particular trade journals.

It is difficult to quantify the number of small sales that fail to be included in the established media. It is not unknown for some dealers to subscribe to media cutting bureaux who will scour every last local newspaper and 'clip' any mention of an auction — no matter how small.

The larger British auction firms offer subscriptions for either all their catalogues or specific groups, e.g. furniture, paintings, silver, etc. After the catalogue comes the homework . . . Study the catalogues carefully and mark possible interesting items and do as much research as possible given the individual description provided in the catalogue. Descriptions of the identical article will differ considerably from auctioneer to auctioneer.

Also study the TERMS OF SALE so that you will know **how** you have to pay. Some auctioneers ask for bankers' drafts, certified cheques or cash from new buyers. From a personal point of view, I have never known this rule strictly observed. Also check **when** you have to move your purchases. If the lots you may want to buy are too big for you to handle by yourself, make sure that volunteer or professional help is available on the day.

It's a very good, and probably obvious, rule to move your purchases immediately after the sale.

View with care and lots of patience and allow plenty of time for this. You cannot really view too thoroughly. With big sales, with hundreds of lots on offer, complete viewing is the only way. This is when the homework done

18th century library chair designed to be sat on facing the wrong way. Some examples have a drawer in the base.

beforehand on the catalogue can pay dividends. With commercial sales at factories and mills there may be hundreds of lots of machinery etc. Mark all the lots which may be of interest in advance of viewing. Industrial sales, held in situ, can sometimes spread over thousands of feet of factory floor.

tips on viewing

Don't be afraid to ask the porters and attendants for help and advice. They may be able to advise on probable prices if the item is a fairly regular type in their rooms. Many porters have ambitions to be full time dealers and are keen and knowledgeable. Some auctioneers publish guideline prices or estimates in their catalogues. These should only be treated as a guide to the auctioneer's knowledge, not to the value of the lot!

When viewing furniture, feel free to take out drawers and have a really thorough look inside. Look underneath — always making sure that everything is firmly attached on top, (we have all heard those loud crashing noises at views). Look everywhere — the last thing you want after the hammer has fallen is a surprise! If a piece of furniture is locked, check with the porter to see if he has the keys. It is not unknown for an early prospective buyer to lock a bureau with an especially fine interior and absentmindedly put the key in his pocket. However, don't assume that every locked item hides a treasure. I must admit that I have frequently paid over the market price for a locked tea caddy which rattled. A Georgian silver caddy spoon was often responsible — but not always!

It sometimes seems that everything which can be removed or wrenched off is fair game in a sale room. Finials, keys, decanter stoppers and the like are all readily removable at an auction view. Your problem will arise when there is something important missing from your lot which was there at the view.

Always check to see if the 'set' of chairs, etc., really is a set. Some auctioneers describe groups of chairs as sets when they patently came from different sources. These are also frequently described as 'composite' or 'harlequin' sets.

Always check the height of chairs in sets — legs can frequently be broken or badly repaired. This is especially true of 'country' chairs like Windsors whose legs may have suffered over the years with continual washing of stone floors.

If there is insufficient room in your catalogue to make proper notes on interesting lots, make a separate list together with lot numbers. If you are new to auctions, you really can't make too many notes and comments. In the thrill of the chase, lots have a habit of looking a great deal more desirable than they did in the cold light of the view. Mark your prices against the lot numbers — preferably in code in case anyone looks over your shoulder or borrows your catalogue.

It's probably very wise to set your bidding limits firmly before the auction starts and try not to exceed them by more than a hundred per cent!

on the day . . .

Some buyers prefer to stand well to the back so that they can see who is bidding ('I'd like to see you about that lot afterwards') and also to see if the bidding is not being 'trotted' by an over enthusiastic auctioneer. Other dealers prefer to be positioned well at the front and be very mobile, continually up at the rostrum handling all and any lots on offer.

The actual act of bidding is again a very personal thing — the only rule is no rule. Anything goes from winks to wildly waving umbrellas. The most important thing is to make sure that you are seen, and understood, by the auctioneer. Regulars usually have their own signs and methods — the only univerally used sign is the 'throat cut' motion of the hand indicating a bid increase by half the previous bid. If the bidding is going up by hundreds, this motion would indicate a bid of fifty.

Here is one little hint which can be used when bidding against an inexperienced amateur or in an auction where your strength and interests are not known. Set your bidding limit and just keep your (gold pen) in the air with the attitude that you will not lower it until the lot is yours. This leads to your opponent's bid always being immediately 'topped' and can have a most demoralizing effect, especially against the inexperienced or bidder lacking in confidence. This simple ruse will not work against representatives of the Getty Museum.

With inexperienced and/or amateur buyers, their confidence is at its lowest in the heat of the auction and they can be very receptive to outside influences.

During the actual sale, if you are in any doubt about the lot on offer, walk right up and have another look whilst the bidding is in progress — it will be too late when the hammer falls. Actually, as a ploy, it is no bad thing to take a close look and then walk back to your place either

18th century miniature dining chair intended for a child with its stand which can double as a table.

shaking your head or muttering something like 'wrong, completely wrong'. This can really instil doubt in the opposition's mind.

Don't, whatever you do, fall for the oldest mistake in the book: that if you pay more than an experienced dealer you must be all right. Nothing could be further from the truth.

Don't be afraid to ask questions between lots — better a question than a missed bargain or a mistake you may have to live with.

It is customary, by the way, to address the auctioneer as 'Sir' if you speak to him during the sale.

commercial auctions

With either **commercial** auction sales or specialist **antique** auctions the same ground rules apply.

The biggest difference with sales of commercial premises or factories is the sheer size of the operation. In an antique sale the goods on view are usually contained within one large room or hall, or at worst within the confines of a marquee or large house.

The site of a commercial auction could well be spread over several thousands of square feet, or even acres, and every inch has to be covered looking for potential goods.

It was common practice in late nineteenth century England for the management of textile mills, factories and old industrial concerns, to furnish their own offices and boardrooms in the highest quality furniture of the day. This was as much a reflection of their commercial achievements and status, as an insulation from the primitive working conditions enjoyed by their employees.

A Georgian cock-fighting chair. Almost any chair made to be used 'backwards' is termed a cock-fighting chair in the trade.

Today, when these businesses fail or are 'rationalized' the auctioneers are called in to dispose of the assets. They frequently remove some of the more obvious pieces of Victoriana and Edwardiana to their own sale rooms to be included in antique auctions. The cataloguing is then passed over to the commercial specialists — who are more used to machine tools or weaving looms and may be quite content to catalogue furniture as 'woodwork' and leave it in situ. This generic term can frequently cover a multitude of antique furniture which has been passed down from the board room or main offices, over the years, to the shop floor. It is perfectly feasible to find Victorian, Edwardian or even earlier, chairs, cupboards and desks, tucked away in timekeepers' huts, foremans' offices, canteens, and stores.

the ring

There is hardly an auction sale free of this (illegal) practice. It is the one aspect of the antique trade which captures the attention of the popular press, and sensational headlines frequently result. However, it is very much part and parcel of the normal everyday life of most dealers although officially frowned on by their trade associations. I have a sneaking suspicion that if every member who had ever taken part in a settlement or entered into a pre-sale agreement were expelled, their annual general meetings could comfortably be held in a telephone box!

The reason for the popularity of the ring is not solely financial. Dealers are, in the main, a fairly convivial lot and mix socially. It's hardly surprising that this friendliness spreads to the sale room. As the antique trade buys the vast majority of goods sold at auction there is a natural tendency to stand together. It's certainly also a great deal more profitable. The dealers are the only people at an auction who have any real idea of the value of a lot — why should they, they would argue, let the auctioneer or the public in on the act?

The ring works quite simply. The dealers in the knock or settlement take turns at bidding during the sale. The idea is to avoid expensive competition between themselves and to buy the goods as cheaply as possible. They may take turns at bidding to avoid the appearance of a ring and each settles his own account with the auctioneer's cashier after the sale. A second 'auction' is held afterwards, either in the local hotel bar or, if the ring is small, in the obligatory smoke-filled Volvo.

One dealer member acts as auctioneer and another as treasurer. Each 'lot' bought by the group is auctioned again and the highest bidder 'holds the goods'. The difference between the price paid in the real auction and the ring price goes into the kitty and is divided amongst those taking part. It's therefore very possible to attend sales and take away 'wages' at each one without ever taking home any goods.

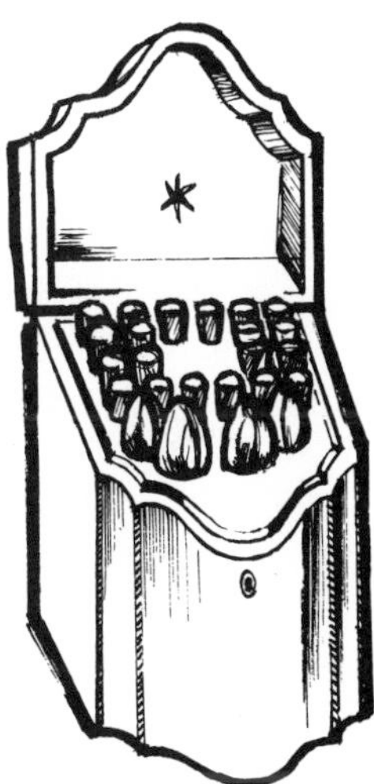

Open 18th century mahogany knife box showing the flatware in place.

This practice usually lasts a fairly short time as those dealers who want only hard cash and no goods to re-sell are not popular and may well be excluded from future arrangements.

If there have been some 'fine' pieces bought by the ring, the small fry dealers take part only in the first settlement. A second 'auction' is then held by the more important (a euphemism for 'richer' or 'bigger') dealers present and the real money then changes hands.

In a big 'collective' sale there will be several rings operating. Silver, furniture, pictures and carpets will have their individual rings or settlements. Only the more important dealers cross the ring boundaries.

On rare occasions the auctioneer himself is a full member of the ring.

When there are only two dealers either in the original ring or left at the end of the settlement auction — the matter may be finally settled by either 'giving or taking' a sum of money.

The common belief is that the ring is bad because it denies the seller the market price for his goods at public auction. The real culprit must be the auctioneer who has been entrusted with the fair and just disposal of the property and should know the correct price and refuse to sell under that figure. Just about the only time the seller really benefits from the activities of the ring is when a wealthy dealer falls out with the established ring and takes them on in auction. This can lead to pride taking over from commercial sense and prices soaring sky-high — bearing no relationship to the current market values.

The hard facts are that the trade provides the vast majority of income to all auction houses — large and small. They could not survive solely with private buyers and must encourage the trade. It's fairly common practice for an auctioneer to give a 'quick knock' to a regular dealer (and therefore valued customer) who is having an unsuccessful day. This can be sad if it happens to be your property he has just given away.

It's also true to say that the vast majority of items sold in general house-contents' auctions are trade lots and would never be bought by the general public.

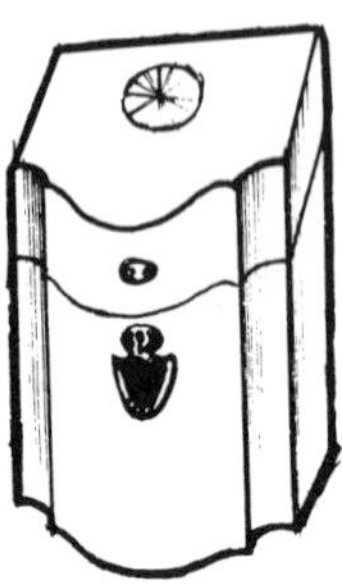

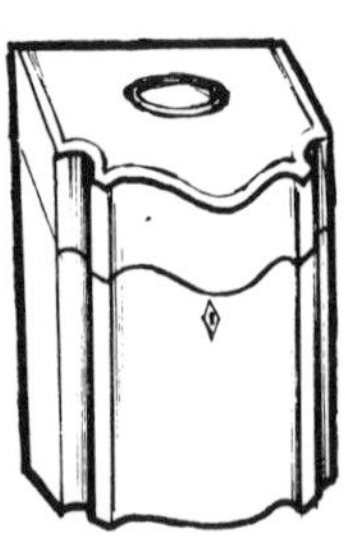

18th century mahogany knife boxes illustrating three shapes.

The really exciting way to find antiques is to buy privately. First you have to get the calls. This means:

advertising for antiques

The accepted way to get private calls is to advertise in your local newspaper. Local classified or lineage newspaper advertising usually appears under the heading 'Articles Wanted' or a similar section; in a local newspaper, the advertisement need not be large — it should however, be **regular** and **interesting.** Local newspapers are usually very well read. This means that even the smallest lineage advertisement will be noticed. Far better to be small and appear every night than save up for a half-page display advertisement once a year.

Antiques are generally sold for a specific reason at a specific time. If your advertisement is not there 'on the night' you may well lose the opportunity. As an everyday regular advertiser I was frequently told by other dealers that advertising is very expensive. The usual remark was 'You must spend a fortune on advertising every night. I tried it a couple of times last month and didn't get any replies.' They missed the point. Advertisements have to be regular.

ADVERTISING IS ONLY EXPENSIVE WHEN IT DOESN'T WORK!

Try and give your few lines some **personality.** Tell the world about yourself and what a nice person you really are. After all, you are asking someone — possibly someone old and nervous — to invite you into their home to look at, and buy, some of their treasured possessions.

To take a very simple example, which of these two advertisements would you respond best to?:

J. SMITH PAYS SPOT CASH
FOR OLD FURNITURE
Telephone 978-3423

JOE and MARY SMITH
deal in lovely old furniture
They would be happy to call on you
(at any time to suit you) when you have
any treasures that must find a new home
Write to us at:
The Old Antique Shoppe · High Street
or telephone 978-3423

The second example will certainly cost more but should be much more productive.

The content of the advertisement should be varied each night to maintain interest. If you have a story to tell about the way you do business, tell the readers.

Similarly, a little humour is never out of place.

If you have an old clock for sale, please tick here ☐

These suggestions only apply in a local media situation. They would be totally inappropriate in the national press, etc. The same ideas can be applied to local radio spots.

'funny ads'

As I have said, the traditional source of antiques is the straight 'Wanted' classified advertisement in the local newspaper. However, many people are suspicious of dealers in general (we have all seen those advertisements which say 'no dealers' as if their money was somehow tainted). Other methods may have to be employed.

I am not advocating the following practices but they are used and you should, at least, be aware of them.

The problem is, as ever, finding 'fresh goods'. How to ferret out these elusive lots which have resisted normal advertising and other methods?

Small classified advertisements can sometimes be seen like these:

Student requires old picture frames and desk

Now, this could be a perfectly genuine advertisement from a starving student. I suspect dirty deeds however. The thinking behind it is that anyone who has old frames may also have old pictures to fit them. Who could overcharge a charming earnest young student?

Doctor moving to district requires large bookcase for documentation purposes

Everyone trusts a doctor. Every dealer loves a big bookcase.

Elderly Couple would like to buy genuine feather mattress

It's enough to bring tears to your eyes. The principle is the same as with the picture frames advertisement. Anyone with a feather mattress still in the house must have other old things.

The sad thing about advertisements of this type is they really do work. People are taken advantage of, and goods are bought — under completely false pretences.

direct mail

Very few dealers use any modern marketing methods to get goods. They much prefer the old established traditional methods of **the auction sale** or **the trade call.**

The 'Old Furniture Bought for Spot Cash' leaflet, which drops through the mail-box occasionally, invariably comes from the lowest orders of the trade — the Knockers (see 'Knockers'). The art work and presentation of these leaflets is always poor — usually just line illustrations cut from the pages of buying guides, roughly pasted into place and poorly printed.

Yet, leaflets for house-to-house distribution, produced with some taste and style, can be a useful source of stock. They should illustrate the various items wanted in a simple outline form with specific detail. In the examples I have illustrated here, the drawings are intended to have strong outlines but not too many details. We are trying to get over a shape rather than a specific item. I have found that when the illustrations were too 'exact' some potential sellers did not respond as their chair, or whatever, was not quite the same.

Any good print shop will provide the leaflets — distribution is the next step. Combine the leaflet with a letter — this enables you to pin-point your approach to your market.

You should not attempt to blanket a whole town. Rather, select the areas you want to reach and pitch your letter accordingly. If the houses you mail are low on the socio-economic scale you should use a different approach and probably ask for different goods than if you are going up market. You will have to produce this letter in your own style. In my experience the friendly chatty approach works well in one area and the more formal in another.

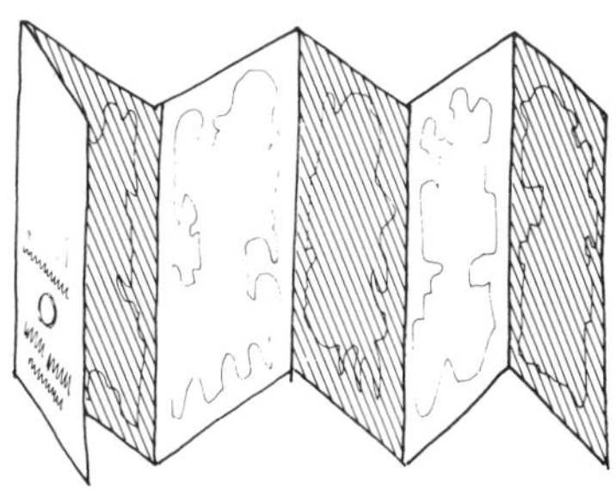

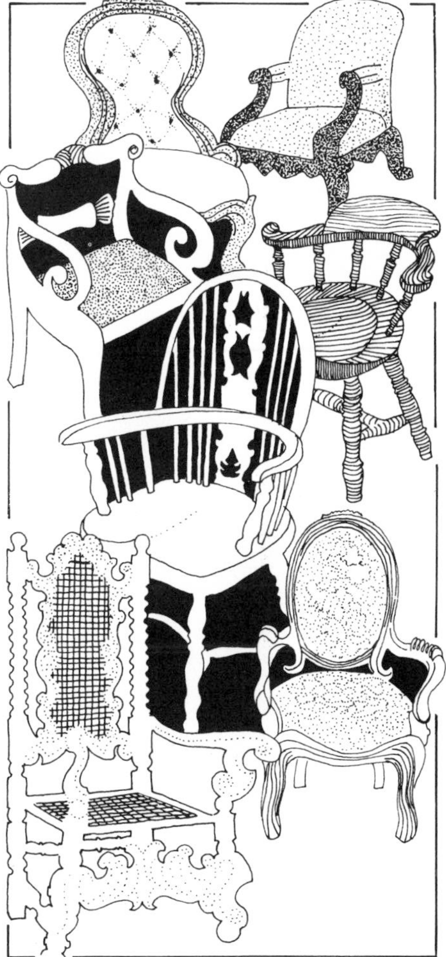

Pages from a well illustrated "Antiques Wanted" leaflet for house-to-house distribution.

direct mail distribution

There are various methods:

1. Do it yourself — the best way, always. Always keep a supply in your car and cover a street or a road, when you have time to spare. Remember to cross the street off your distribution map.
2. Take a sample to a local newsagent and agree a rate per hundred to be delivered with his newspapers.
3. If the newsagent isn't interested, try the milkman.
4. You **could** use a professional delivery service but they may well not be interested in small numbers.

Whichever method you choose, remember to include a checking method to ensure that all your beautiful leaflets have not ended up in a waste bin.

anatomy of a private call

You will get the 'call' in one of several ways. By letter, or telephone following your advertisement, recommendation, or direct mail response.

If you are in conversation with the seller prior to calling, this is an opportunity to engage in some dialogue and discover in a subtle way the reasons for the sale — Where did they get it from? Have they bought it recently? Do they like it? Does it fit in with the rest of the things in their house? All these factors have bearing on the sale and the price which will be asked or expected.

The first 'phone call is another opportunity to ask — quite bluntly — if they intend calling in another dealer. If the answer is 'Yes', this can have a direct bearing on your approach. One reaction could be the suggestion that they get the other dealers in first, as you would rather be last. The inference is that you will pay the highest price. If you are last, you can always pay the most once you discover what the other bids are. The real risk is that they find an early offer quite satisfactory and let the goods go.

This 'I would rather be last and pay most' approach indicates your own confidence and ability and willingness to pay the best price. There is obviously a high element of risk in allowing another dealer into the call before you. One other real risk is that the piece being offered may very often not be the item that is finally bought.

To illustrate the point, a dealer friend of mine recently had a call offering a chest of drawers. During the telephone conversation the seller described it and it was obvious that it was a cut-down Edwardian or Victorian chest of dubious value. The dealer's immediate reaction was that the seller should try another dealer who was less fussy about the goods he bought. Then previous experience prompted him to say, 'No, I had better come and look myself.'

The chest was, as he had suspected, a cut-down example. But he did buy a rather nice bureau and a set of dining chairs, which had not been mentioned in the first conversation. He left the chest of drawers behind!

tricks of the trade

There are numerous tricks of the trade employed by dealers, all of them based on commonsense observation, and on the fact that people are initially suspicious of strangers invited into their home, and the dealer's personality and behaviour will have to allay these fears.

One oft exploited trait is the universal desire to show off possessions whether for sale or not. A classic example — although it does not specifically apply to antique furniture — is frequently used by knockers or dealers in jewellery. The principles, however, are applicable to any antiques.

The scenario . . . A dealer is called to appraise and offer on a selection of jewellery: he understands that only a few pieces are to be sold. In conversation he discovers which pieces are prized for sentimental reasons by the owner. He selects one of these sentimental pieces, usually of very little value, places it in the hand of the owner, closes her fingers around it, and says, 'Promise me you will never sell this. It is extremely valuable, and you should keep it in a very safe place. It is the nicest (ring) I have seen in years.'

This confirms the owner's belief in one of her favourite possessions and establishes the dealer as someone who shares her own taste. He is, therefore, to be trusted. Having once established his credentials he is in a much better position to offer for the more valuable parts of the collection. On a subsequent visit, this sentimental object is again brought into play.

'You still have that beautiful ring, haven't you? I have been doing some research. Can I see it again? No! No! Of course I don't want to buy it, I just want to see it.'

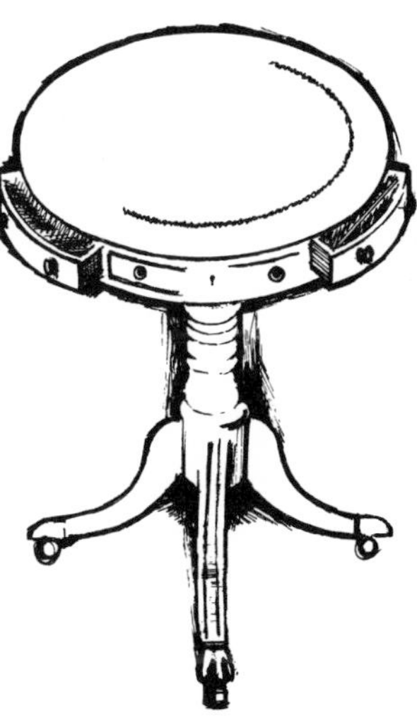

A small 18th century mahogany Drum Table with a leather and cross-banded top.

Now, this is where the psychology comes in.

A mere male would probably go and bring the ring for further inspection, most women however, will invariably bring their entire jewellery box and search through it in front of the dealer. This presents another opportunity to reaffirm the 'value' of the sentimental piece, and make further buys from the collection spread before them.

Another dealer I knew always made a great play of asking the seller what he expected to get for the goods. This naturally resulted in the reaction that they were not going to put a price on something which they were attempting to sell. My dealer would suggest that he would write down his price and then they would be free to quote their asking price. Great play was made of writing down something — usually on a cigarette pack. The little-bit-suspicious seller was then encouraged to quote his price.

'I **thought** you knew what it was worth,' cries the dealer, producing the cigarette pack with the identical price written in pencil.

It was not until after several calls where the same charade was performed that I knew how this mental telepathy was performed. My dealer friend had once been an amateur magician and used the (apparently) common trick of a short pencil lead under the finger nail to write down the correct price after it was announced! I am quite sure that if I ever had the sheer nerve to try this I would proudly produce a scribble of pure gibberish!

how to behave

How you behave when going to someone's home to buy obviously depends on your own personality and methods. Some dealers favour the aggressive method of waving bundles of money about — others take the softly-softly approach. I can only describe the methods I used . . . which certainly worked well for me!

Never be in a rush — always be prepared to sit down and enjoy a conversation and a cup of coffee. Not only is this polite, especially with the older generation, but it can pay real dividends. It stands to reason that the more you know about the situation the better you can provide the solution.

A fairly classic case must be the dealer whose habit was to rush in, quickly size-up the furniture on offer (in this case, a very nice set of ten single dining chairs), make an acceptable offer and pay cash. Then away with them in the trusty Volvo. This man mentioned to a fellow dealer that there was 'plenty left to be bought' as **he** had what he wanted. The colleague followed up the call and bought the remainder of the house contents. Over a cup of tea, he asked if there was, perhaps, anything else for sale.

The lady thought for a moment. 'Only a couple of arm chairs in the bathroom.'

The two carvers missing from the set of ten singles!

The real punch-line to this story is this. Our dealer didn't rush round to the original dealer to sell him the two chairs. He waited for a few days, took out a second mortgage on his house, and then bought the ten to make up his set!

This little story points up the moral: always take your time on a private call.

Taking this simple theory a stage further, the 'conversation period' allows you to find out discreetly how the pieces are valued or 'reckoned' — how much money is required for any specific purpose, etc. This information can really make a dramatic influence on your offers. I was once offered a huge oil painting by an amateur dramatic group. When I asked how much was wanted they didn't know . . . but they wanted to buy some timber. How much would the timber cost to buy? They knew that cost — and that was the price of the painting!

There are few hard and fast rules to be made about buying antiques privately. Everyone has to develop their personal approach and technique. Some highly successful dealers never buy in this method but prefer buying at auction and from the trade. The rewards of 'fresh goods', possibly bargains and the thrill of the chase are all part of the attractions of this method of antique buying. The argument against would include the high cost of unsuccessful calls and low conversion rate.

There is one golden rule well worth remembering when buying furniture from a private house:

If, for any reason, you cannot physically take your purchase at the time of buying — make an excuse: 'I want to see if it matches my other furniture,' and take an important part away with you. Drawers, a pediment perhaps, will prevent the seller asking for (and accepting) a higher price after you have left.

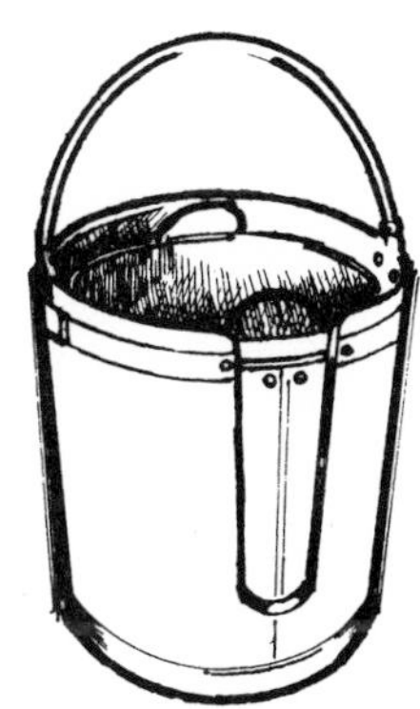

18th century brass bound mahogany plate pail with liner.

Price guides have been known to play an important part in private buying, especially when the quoted prices are in the buyer's favour. Some less than scrupulous dealers have been known to use an old guide with a rather newer dust cover prominently displayed around it!

Think carefully before you turn down any private call. You have spent good money on advertisements looking for goods and here you are, saying, 'No thank you, that's not for us,' or 'that has no value.'

However, these are genuine snippets from conversations which I have overheard in other dealers' shops when the 'phone rings . . .

'Could you value a brass coffee pot with a sort of curly spout? It's covered with decoration. Someone said it was from Benares in India.'

Even the most inexperienced dealer knows exactly what that particular coffee pot looks like and what it's worth — nothing!

On average half, or even more, of the replies you may get to your advertisements are (apparently) for things you don't want. If the description is good over the 'phone, you will know just what they have for sale. Even when the description sounds interesting you may be disappointed when you actually see it.

To illustrate the point . . . I can remember a call from a country pub asking me to go and value just a Benares coffee pot. The landlord called about three times over a period of two weeks or so. Each time I promised to go but never did. The fourth call came one evening when I was just about to go out for a drink in the country. Yes, I would call that evening . . .

The coffee pot was exactly as he had described — worthless, a Benares pot exported in their millions every year from India to every souvenir shop in the world. The story could come to an end there. However, over a drink or three, it transpired that the landlord and his lady wife had a problem. They both 'liked a drink' but the pub had very few customers. It soon became clear that the contents of the pub would have to be sold to pay for their habit. A sad tale, but, on the plus side, the entire pub and its — seldom used — guest bedrooms were full of the highest quality period furniture. Every room had a beautiful chest of drawers, a couple of commodes, period wing chairs, even pole screens. No mention had been made in the telephone conversations about their wealth of antiques — the coffee pot valuation had just been the pretext.

Our publican friend wanted to sell just enough to pay the brewers on the following Friday. He did sell enough that night . . . and every other Thursday night for the next few weeks until the cupboard was bare. A tragic situation but a really superb private call and all because someone appeared to want a valuation on a worthless coffee pot. (I never did buy the pot!)

buying in the shop

As this little guide is primarily concerned with antique furniture you might be inclined to think that only very small pieces of furniture will be brought into an antique shop and offered for sale. However, whilst this is true in the majority of cases, it is certainly not unusual to find substantial pieces of furniture roped to a roof rack being hawked about in the trade.

Buying in the shop has numerous advantages, not least of which is that the dealer is on his home ground, the resident expert, and should be, at least in theory, in command of the situation.

To simplify the example, let us assume that the item on offer is actually produced from a case or a shopping bag. Let us assume it's a rather nice little ivory and tortoiseshell tea caddy.

The life and times of a little Tea Caddy.

The knocker calls and persuades the little old lady to part with her pretty trinket box for a few pounds. The friendly neighbourhood antique dealer won't provide sufficient immediate cash profit so it is then taken next door to Messrs Knock and Ring, the Auctioneers and Valuers.

The priorities are to assure the seller that he will do best to sell it to you — now — at your price. It is all too easy just to make a spot assessment of your buying price, make your offer, and then see it disappear out the door with the words, 'I'll go away and think about it.'

The odds are against you ever seeing that particular caddy again.

The first thing to do is to try and get the seller into a room free from interruption or outside distractions. Having a one room shop makes it extremely difficult to conduct any meaningful negotiation in front of third parties. If you are forced into this situation you are almost certain to be watched (and listened to) by any other dealer in the shop, who will then try to buy the caddy at a marginal profit having seen the ridiculously low price you paid for it.

If you cannot provide a separate room for buying, at least try and screen off a portion of the shop so that you and the seller can be afforded some privacy.

Assuming that you and the seller are now sitting down, the caddy in front of you, where to begin?

Entered, without reserve, into their forthcoming 'collective sale of Antiques and Objects d'Art', it is catalogued as 'a rare and important Tea Caddy in ivory and tortoiseshell with un-marked silver mounts, cut corners, English, late 18th century'.

It is a very good ploy to ask if he is in any hurry as you would like to make a detailed examination. This is unlikely to be refused as the seller is quite delighted to have a proper (free) appraisal of his treasure. This gives an opportunity to offer a cup of coffee. The coffee must be scalding hot and its arrival should be delayed until you make a signal to your assistant. Why? If you feel that the seller and his caddy are going to slip away from you it will be most unusual for your visitor to leave his drink untouched. He will probably sit and finish it, giving you breathing space to increase your bid and save the situation.

As the caddy is being ostensibly examined there is the opportunity to flaunt your expert knowledge, perhaps pointing out some of its exciting features, and possibly, only possibly, some of its defects. This preamble allows for polite conversational questions like — Have you had it long? Where did you get it? If so, how much did you pay for it? This is not in the form of a Gestapo interrogation but is couched in conversational terms of sheer academic interest. All this builds up the picture of the perceived value to the seller of the caddy.

The ring is at the sale in full strength and, with little public competition, the little Caddy is knocked down to their nominee for rather less than our knocker had been offered by the local dealer . . .

Afterwards, at the settlement in the pub, its auction price is increased by over 200%.

I touched briefly above about mentioning any defects. Many dealers like to 'knock' goods offered to them. They will complain about everything; about size, the feet, the shape, the wood, the finish, its unfashionability; almost every aspect or feature comes in for criticism. I have always found this negative approach rude, unrewarding, and totally, completely unsuccessful. You are, in fact, telling the seller that he has no taste, knowledge, perception, and should be ashamed to own such a thing.

Far, far, better to praise it — although it will certainly have some shortcomings. Praise its wonderful polish: 'You must have looked after this for a long time.' This seemingly innocuous question will immediately determine the period the seller has owned the caddy and can be a pointer to his appreciation of the present-day value. Having praised the caddy to the hilt the seller will be positively glowing with pride and enthusiasm and your (possibily very low) offer may well be accepted. It is hard to visualize a situation where a dealer can make anything other than an apparently reasonable offer having spoken so highly of its numerous merits. How can he refuse such an offer from such a charming and knowledgeable dealer?

As you will see, the techniques employed in a shop situation are just as varied and as subtle as in a client's home. The obvious priority is to get the potential seller tucked away and to prevent him leaving your premises until you have successfully concluded the deal.

It is carried off to grace the spot-lit windows of a Bond Street antique emporium. Its ticket price would have kept our little old lady in tea bags for the rest of her life.

If you are unsuccessful in buying the caddy and feel that you cannot raise your bid to a successful level without appearing to be a complete rogue, you must then let the owner go. However, as he is escorted to the door a helpful suggestion can be made.

'Why not try so-and-so along the street. He is a very good buyer of tea caddies. He has a big personal collection. Why not try him? Perhaps he could do better.'

As he leaves in the general direction of your suggested 'good buyer', you can then make the quick 'phone call to tell him that he can expect a gentleman in a brown overcoat bearing an ivory and tortoiseshell tea caddy and the figure you have offered for it. Obviously the next dealer either offers slightly more — which is the safe option — or the risky path, slightly less, hoping that he will come back to you to accept your price. In either event, the caddy is then 'knocked out' between you and the other dealer afterwards. A disgraceful practice — but it happens!

In the case where you are offered goods unseen and arrangements are made for you to call and see the items for disposal, it's a golden opportunity for you to establish your credentials and position as a prime buyer. The better the impression you make at this stage the less likely the seller is to call in another competing antique dealer.

the knockers

At the bottom of the antique ladder are the knockers — a band of dealers who travel the length and breadth of the country knocking on doors — any doors — offering cash for old furniture. Most will knock on any door offering to buy old furniture. They will try any likely door from country cottages to cathedrals. (Honestly! I once met some Irish knockers who had just pulled some 'gear' from Newcastle Cathedral!)

I never had too much luck with knockers.

Some dealers appear to have an inexhaustable supply of fresh goods from a never-ending chain of knockers spanning the country. One dealer friend, a charming lady who specialized in musical boxes, even had a knocker working palaces in India buying broken musical boxes and automata!

When a new knocker appeared I always got the impression that I was being offered the junk and the best 'gear' would come next time. All I had to do was buy the first lots or I wouldn't get a chance at anything else. Knockers are always full of stories about wonderful antiques they have seen — all they had to do was get enough cash for 'this little lot' and then get back to the 'wonderful private call'. Somehow the second 'good lots' never materialized no matter how much was paid, first time round, for the rubbish.

You really appreciate the way knockers work when you get 'the call' for the black marble clock or the huge sideboard. You know before you go on the call what is going to happen but you can't afford not to follow it up, just in case.

The scenario is nearly always the same — the details may vary . . .

A knocker calls and gets into the house. Great interest — not to say enthusiasm — is expressed in some piece of furniture or other antique. Frequently something quite large.

The script . . .

'That is a really superb piece. Worth a great deal of money. Quite the best example I have ever seen. The Americans (or Arabs) are paying a fortune for these now. I will give you £5,000 for it. Can I bring my friend to see it — he's a real expert and I may have undervalued it . . . it won't go in my car . . . you will want time to empty it . . . can I come back tomorrow. Here is £50 as a deposit as a gesture of my good faith . . .'

Then comes the punch line . . . 'I could use that little table (or whatever). I can pay £25 for it.'

The victim is already mentally spending the £5,000 and is quite happy to part with the little Regency brass-inlaid work table for £25 because tomorrow . . .

The knocker walks away with a table costing £75 (£25 plus the £50 'deposit') and is never seen again. The trouble starts for the local dealer when, a few days later, no one has returned to claim the £5,000 piece.

The owner wants to realize his good fortune and calls in the dealer. Will he pay more than £5,000? 'No, thank you, sir, it's worth about £50 if you twist my arm.'

But a charming man said, etc., etc., and he even left a deposit.

'So, what else did he buy from you?'

'Just a little table. He said his bed-ridden old mother would like it . . .'

The really sad thing about all this is that the owner will always believe the first 'buyer' and be convinced that all subsequent dealers are out-and-out rogues.

stolen goods

It's a recurrent nightmare to every (honest) dealer that the goods he is offered or buying in good faith are stolen.

Any antique shop is apparently fair game to the thief and the shoplifter and the dealer stands to lose the goods and the cash paid if they are subsequently found to be 'on the list'. He may also be potentially liable to criminal prosecution. There are no simple rules to distinguish the genuine seller and the thief. I had only one basic rule in business: 'Never Buy Carriage Clocks from Scotsmen Smelling of Drink.' (I can say that quite safely as I am a Scot myself.)

I singled out carriage clocks as they are a prime target for thieves and shoplifters due, no doubt, to their high value, compact size and the very handy handle on top!

It's a good start to be suspicious of anyone selling (in your shop) who insists on cash. If you make 'payment by cheque only' the rule you have gone a long way to safeguard yourself.

Thieves can take many guises. They include, in my experience, charming, old white-haired ladies riding bicycles with baskets full of goodies, young gentlemen with indulgent grandmothers who leave them silver candelabra and who are even willing to call back later for the cash and charming gentlemen with the manners and general demeanor of ambassadors. Few thieves wear black masks and striped jerseys.

The temptation is frequently great to buy suspect material as it often follows that the goods being offered for sale are exciting and valuable. This, however, is not always the case. Everything stolen or 'hot' is not always jewel encrusted. I can remember two young men who arrived almost every Saturday morning (for months) at my shop with loads of un-stripped or mediocre quality pine furniture of relatively little value. Certainly not what you would expect any self-respecting thief to specialize in — but, all stolen and virtually un-recoverable.

In all my years' experience of the trade, I found the police to be fairly helpful with stolen antiques but they failed generally in their distribution of fact sheets listing items. These appeared to circulate only locally as if the thieves were not mobile and somehow confined to their own 'patch'.

The original owners of good antiques are also sometimes less than helpful as their descriptions, measurements, etc., are sketchy, if they exist at all, and good colour or black-and-white photographs (lodged in a safe place) are the exception rather than the rule.

antique fairs

garage & car boot sales

All the suggestions made about buying in the trade can apply to these potential sources. Antique fairs have a possible reputation of being generally overpriced. The rule seems to be the grander the fair, the more prestigious the organizer, the more inflated the prices. In theory at least the better the fair the higher the chances you should have of picking up something genuine as the vetting procedures should be more stringent. In practice, however, you may well find that the higher up the fair ladder you climb the more proficient restorer or finisher is employed and the 'well-attended to' furniture harder to spot.

This is not to say that bargains are still not to be had at antique fairs, no matter their level. I can recall a pair of bluejohn candlesticks reputedly changing hands eleven times in the first day of an antique fair at which I had a stand. It seemed a shame to see them finally leaving the front door as everyone appeared to be making a very good living out of them! I mentioned this particular story to a friend who was a television producer and we did some initial research for a programme to be entitled 'If You Marooned Twelve Antique Dealers On A Desert Island, They Could All Make A Profit!'

Buying at **car boot sales,** or **garage sales,** can be a fascinating experience. If they are genuine there is always the opportunity of picking up something nice or at the least saleable. The big advantage of these sales is that the owner must always have an asking price for anything on offer, and you can either pay this or make a bid and it avoids all the time-consuming preamble of the private call.

commercial premises & shops

Old established businesses and shops in virtually every trade are potential sources of good antique material. The only rule which applies here is that you should always expect the unexpected. The tales are legion of walnut kneehole desks being used as work benches complete with a vice attached to the top, and all manner of antique furniture being tucked away in attics and cellars.

Some time ago a legendary figure in the Yorkshire antique trade, Jim Morton, worked for me as a buyer. He had a wonderful nose for sniffing out good gear in unexpected places. Never the sale room or the routine trade call for Jim — he was much more likely to score in a hotel kitchen, a convent attic, or the backroom of a grocer's shop. His favourite modus operandi was revealed to me before he moved on. The technique involved a visit to the reference section of a town's public library and a search through the trade directories of forty to sixty years before. He would make notes of all the old antique dealers, picture framers, restorers, etc., mark these on a town street plan, and then investigate. You will not be suprised to know that a high percentage of these firms had become defunct, or at least, had changed direction and could be written off. He found, however, that, in a small number of cases, widows or relatives were left with the remnants of the business, old stock, and, in some rare cases, complete store rooms locked away and virtually forgotten after their owner's demise.

I am not suggesting for a second, this method as a major source of material, but merely as a system which worked modestly well for one antique buyer. It probably worked best for Jim because it was his theory and he wanted to prove it.

For the last sixty years (if one can judge from books) dealers have been complaining about the lack of stock. I am a firm believer that there is still plenty of superb material just waiting to be discovered and liberated. Over the past few weeks, whilst writing this section, I have

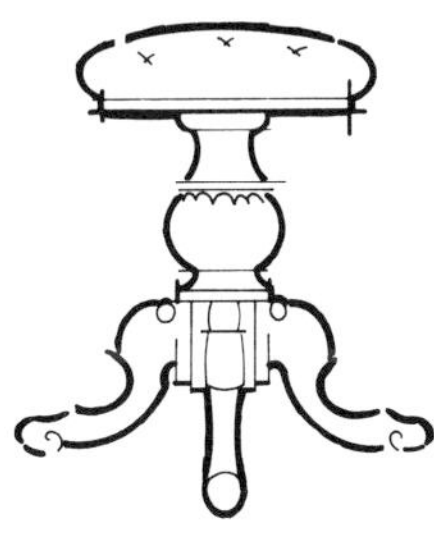

found, without especially looking, an early mahogany secretaire being used to store seeds in a nursery (the knobs on the small interior drawers replaced with knotted string), a fine partner's desk in the stock room of a wholesale stationers and a rare mechanical dining table upside-down in a country stable only yards from a major antiques market. I especially like old country garage and filling station offices. Even machine shops and timekeepers' offices can also regularly hold their quota of antiques.

Over the years I have found the most productive commercial premises to be grocers, chemists and printers but virtually any business formed before the turn of the century is worth a visit. Country and small village grocers are often a useful information source — who is about to move, when and where.

estate agents and banks

Antiques frequently come on the market for various reasons. Two of the most common are when moving house, or disposal of effects or estate on death. In both these cases estate agents, lawyers, or trustees will become involved.

Estate Agents frequently have arrangements with auctioneers or have their own antique sale facilities. It is still, however, worthwhile contacting all these on a direct mail or personal basis, and offering your services, either as buyers of the best, or as a house clearance service.

This latter service should not be neglected as it is frequently the source of very fine goods not recognized by the family solicitor, or whoever is responsible for moving the 'best'.

Lawyers and banks (acting as trustees) are frequently responsible for disposing of household effects. The first approach here is the formal letter setting out the services you can offer. Dealing with banks and solicitors you have to offer something which will make their life easier and less complicated. They are probably bound by professional ethics which dictate that they be seen to get the best possible price for the beneficiaries of the estate. To satisfy this, usually means that the goods are sent for public auction. However, many homes are, to say the least, unsavoury, and many a lawyer and his clerk will take one sniff and opt to leave it to the antique dealer. If the dealer has a strong stomach and is willing to get his hands dirty the benefits can be considerable.

Without dwelling too much on the unsavoury aspects of the trade, I have known a house clearance where the furniture and contents were moved out into the back garden and the neighbours then complained about the smell! Every dirty neglected house does not necessarily mean a host of treasures, but the sheer lack of cleaning frequently indicates that nothing has been thrown away.

get the goods home

Before considering the various sources of buying antique furniture, make sure you are fully prepared before you go on the road. You never ever know what you may be offered!

There's a lovely story about Duveen. His Hispano Suiza had broken down somewhere in the middle of France when he was approached by a stranger who said 'You are Mr. Duveen, the world famous art dealer. The Russian court jewels are hidden only a few kilometers from here. Would you like to see and perhaps buy them?'

For more humble mortals here's a typical checklist.

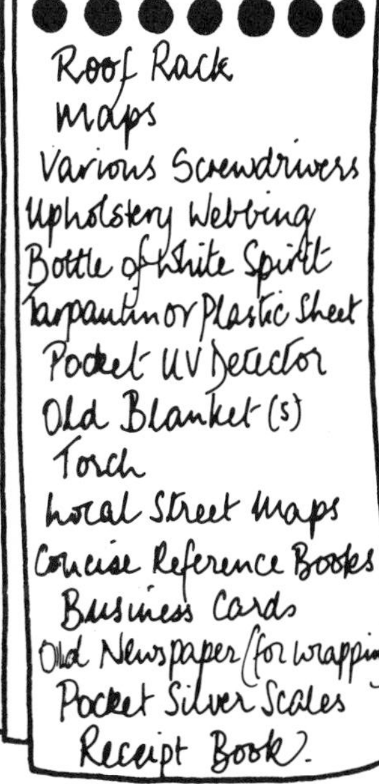

White Spirit is excellent for bringing a very dirty oil painting to life if you want to see what's under all that old varnish. A pocket UV detector is useful for 'seeing' cracks and repairs in porcelain and also serves to 'blind 'em with science'.

The choice of Reference Books depends on your own special interests but the basic list should always include:

Watchmakers & Clockmakers of the World (Baillie)

Marks & Monograms on Pottery & Porcelain (Chaffers)

English Goldsmiths & Their Marks (Jackson.) (Dover)

Guide to the Antique Shops of Britain (Ant. Collectors Club)

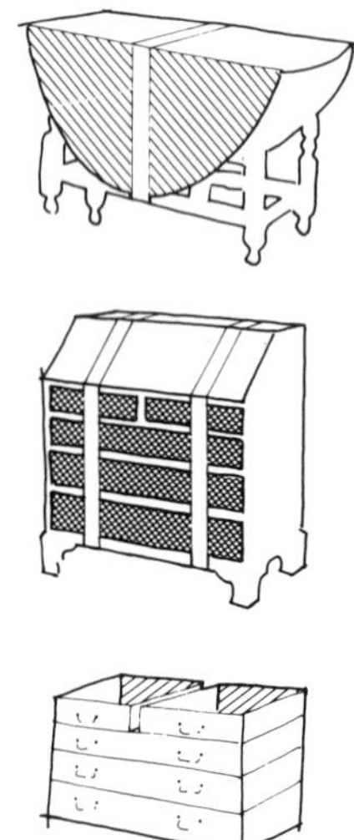

Getting your furniture home is really a matter of commonsense. However here are a few tips which may make life easier.

Always tie flaps on tables and bureaux fall fronts before attempting to carry or load. Large drop-leaf tables are almost impossible to carry or load unless secured.

Always remove all interior drawers from furniture before moving or lifting — especially important with bureaux or secretaires. Alternatively, fill the interior space with crunched-up newspapers or a blanket.

Remove all drawers from large pieces of furniture; it's a good idea to stack them in all the right order and replace them when the carcase is loaded and then all tied together.

Many large pieces of furniture can be 'split' — the diagram illustrates a breakfront bookcase and its many (possible) component parts. Always remove the shelves first and remember to save the little wooden pegs used to support shelves and tie them to the bookcase. Also keep all the large (original) screws which held the whole piece together.

Never lock any drawers or doors — double check to see that all keys are removed and then tied to the furniture, better a lost key than a locked drawer or bureau with no key.

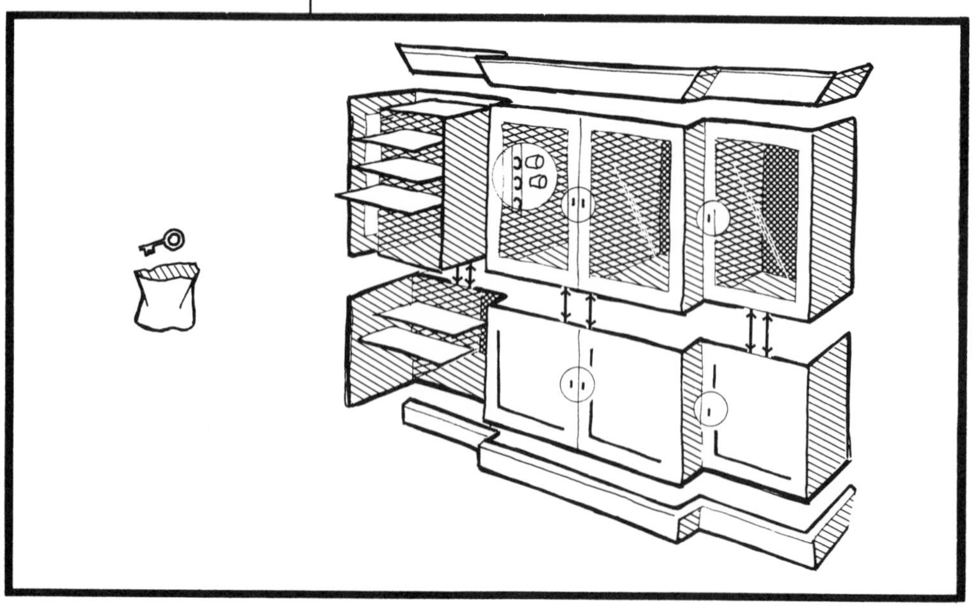

When using a roof rack, make sure the load is very securely tied and covered — then make sure that the roof rack is still attached to the car! Extra weight can frequently relax the brackets which normally secure the rack to the car.

Upholstery webbing is best for securing furniture. Rope can do horrible damage to furniture by rubbing or chafing. It also shrinks and stretches when wet then dry. Never ever use elastic 'octopus' ties!

Never, never, tie on someone else's load. You will be blamed when the whole thing falls off. The rule also applies to customers loading their car. Give as much advice as possible and help by all means, but never do the whole job!

Before setting off home it's a good idea to angle one of your exterior car mirrors to point up at the load on top. You can keep an eye open for flapping tarpaulins or sheets which always attract the attention of police. It also helps to remind you that you have a load on top before you drive into your garage. Having once caught and demolished a twenty-foot high cherry tree in full bloom in a friend's drive with the legs of an upturned dresser base . . .

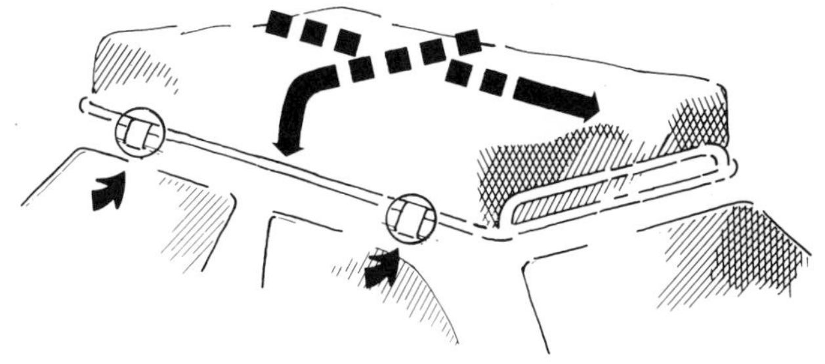

1 dealing

Selling is traditionally considered to be the easy part of antique dealing — the clever side is buying the right goods at the right price. It's an old adage that if a good dealer asked you the price of anything in your shop, he ought to be able to buy it! I am not talking about the type of buyer who is always looking for a bargain or a 'steal' but a regular established trade dealer. To say that you paid too much for something is a lame excuse and only indicates your own inexperience.

Success in antiques can be quantified as ninety nine per cent good buying. If you can buy well, you are almost home and dry.

So you want to **start antique dealing . . .** from where . . .?

There are lots of options:

1 From Home

2 Market Stalls

3 Antique Markets

4 Antique Fairs and Fleamarkets

5 From a Shop

from home

I suppose many dealers start from home initially. On the plus side it has a lot going for it. At the start everyone is full of excitement and enthusiasm and can't get enough of 'the business'. You can spend the day buying and selling — at home — or out 'on the road'; the evenings poring over auction catalogues and old issues of antiques magazines — absorbing everything. Overheads are very low if you are using a spare room, garage or even outbuildings and you can work at your own pace with no set opening times.

At first it can be great fun having customers and other dealers calling. 'Come in and have a coffee or a drink . . .'

There is no better way to find out what is happening in the trade. Who got what at which auction. Who got his fingers burnt with a 'hot lot'. The gossip in the trade is widespread and frequently vitriolic. All great fun and also very good for business. The problem starts when you get better known and more successful and attract more and more people. The business is in very real danger of taking over your entire life. Not only is it taking over your complete day but the kitchen or living room is full of dealers who obviously have no other homes to go to.

It may well be that this lifestyle will suit you and your family very well but you should be warned that this is what could, and frequently does, happen.

Other problems which occur when dealing at home can include little things like planning consent for commercial premises and difficult neighbours who don't always appreciate vans and dealers' cars coming and going at all times of the day and night.

Provided you can live with the problems outlined earlier, the country house with extensive outbuildings is the ideal in many peoples' eyes. I say outbuildings in the plural as I have always found it essential to have more than one location for stock. There are always goods to be tucked away for a variety of reasons — not ready for sale until researched perhaps, requiring restoration or improvement or being kept for somebody special. Extra room gives the opportunity to provide workshops and also storage space for all the bits and pieces useful for restoration purposes that you will accumulate and not want to sell.

With space to spare it is sometimes possible to attract a restorer, cabinet-maker or polisher with an offer of rent-free accommodation therefore giving you an extra facility on the doorstep. These craftsmen will attract their own customers who, in turn, may be interested in your stock. The same principle applies to furniture brought in for work — some may well be buyable by you if probable restoration costs deter the private or trade owner.

Working from outbuildings requires virtually non-existent interior decoration which is a considerable cost saving. Stock is frequently displayed in a casual rather than a 'showroom' manner which can add to the charm and informality of this method of selling.

One disadvantage of operating from a country location is the lack of passing traffic (compared to the city site) whether they be potential buyers or sellers. Advertising to attract people to visit you can be highly expensive. You have to make a very definite statement in your advertising which indicates what you and your stock are all about.

An 18th century Irish brass bound mahogany peat bucket.

Other openings for antique dealing include:

2 market stalls

Nothing more than commonsense, a good nose for a bargain and a tolerance of your neighbour's organic vegetables are needed.

Although I have had no experience of market stalls on a first hand basis — except as a buyer — everything that has been said before now probably applies. Every market seems to have its own personality — it would perhaps be best to visit several times before embarking on the big adventure. Whereas antique 'smalls' are usually the rule in street markets, furniture need not be ruled out — but it does seem rather a lot of trouble!

3 antique markets

Semi-permanent antique markets are found throughout Britain. Usually a collection of small open-fronted stalls; frequently only about six feet by four feet, (two metres by one-and-a-half metres) or thereabouts. Many open on a varied number of days each week depending on the potential audience. Some markets, usually in London and the main provincial cities, are totally professional in their attitude and well worth a visit. The stall holders are on hand during opening hours, know their individual stock and are prepared to deal.

However, the majority, in my personal experience, are usually deserted or their stall holders are buried deep in paperback books and it always seems a shame to disturb them. I really wonder why they bother . . . ?

If you are considering this type of sales outlet as a starter in the trade, visit the market of your choice a few times and see if you approve of the attitudes. If you favour the latter type, maybe just to 'start', take ***War and Peace*** with you.

With market stalls payment is usually on a week to week basis — however, with antique markets take care to read all the small print before you sign, committing yourself to a lengthy contract or lease period.

4

antique fairs and fleamarkets

Here again, all the above suggestions can apply. Check out the fair or fleamarket first. See who is selling, and what (if anything) — and always speak to as many exhibitors as possible. Note what they are offering and if they are happy with the organization and their business.

Slightly higher up the antique social ladder are the **touring antique fairs.** These touring 'circuses' may 'travel' a hard core of dealers adding others from time to time. At these middle ground fairs, there is frequently a veneer of respectability and they may boast a 'vetting committee'. This purports to check all exhibits and confirm that everything offered is genuine and within laid-down datelines. These guidelines may vary for furniture, pictures, jewellery, etc.

If you visit one that you like, check with the organizers on availability of stands, dates and costs. Check out if there are any 'extras' (lighting, insurance, etc). Ask to see their rules for dates so that as little as possible is 'thrown off' your stand by the dreaded vetting committee. The success of these fairs depends very much on the experience and advertising ability of the organizers. Again, as with any other venture, you must speak to other exhibitors — tell them you are considering a stand at a forthcoming fair. What do they think about the way the fair is run and is business good? How many fairs have they done with this group?

At the top of the tree are the rarified number of antique fairs really worthy of the name. Usually exhibitors are invited or, at least, have to be introduced to the organizing committee. In general terms, dealers taking part will have established businesses and enjoy some reputation. This is not to suggest that all the exhibitors are saints but the visitor has a reasonable chance of buying something genuine — frequently at a heavenly price!

An 18th century English brass bound mahogany plate pail (used to carry hot plates to the dining table).

5

from a shop

The location you choose for your antique business will dictate, to a great extent, the style of your business. If the location has been thrust upon you, you will have to overcome any inherent difficulties.

All seems rather obvious? — To explain in more practical terms:

It was Conrad Hilton, the founder of the international hotel chain, when asked the three most important criteria for the site of a new hotel, replied 'Position, Position and Position.'

Obviously, you can have your antique shop in virtually any position (one new antique shop in York has just opened in an old tram drivers hut!) It's up to you to make the business.

One primary decision to be made early on is — do you want to sell exclusively to the trade or only to retail customers, or try for a mixture of both?

If your knowledge of antiques is limited and your business experience likewise, the easiest option is to be primarily retail. In this case the majority of your customers will not know a great deal more than you do. You have the edge of being the resident expert. There is certainly a great deal less pressure selling to the general public as you will have time to research your buys in depth and make a considered judgement about possible selling prices, etc.

Selling to the trade, you certainly have to be faster on your feet. If you happen to be buying in the trade or at auction you are in a much more exposed position and have to make decisions about immediate quick profits and the like.

If you have a shop selling to either group, you have an opportunity to express your personality and style. Assuming basic business acumen, I think that style and taste are probably the two most important factors contributing to the success of an antique shop — whether trade or retail. It's that certain look which attracts potential customers to your shop window and says 'that looks worth a call.'

It's style which attracts the casual browser or passer-by and taste and business accumen which transforms him or her into a customer. 'Style' is just about as hard to define or quantify as 'taste' — either you have it or you don't. Both can transform a simple (frequently inexpensive) item into something which looks really superb. Both make a very definite statement in your window (and in the shop) and reflect the type of business you operate.

I think the only way to illustrate this is to take some examples: the back-street semi-junk-near-antique shop usually doesn't have any real style in this sense. Everything is thrown in the window or, worse, 'arranged' on rumpled blue velvet. The hand-written note on the door says it all: 'Back in ten mins'.

At the other end of the antique spectrum is the ultra smart shop possibly in an ultra smart village or in the prime city site. The walls are lined with beige hessian or watered silk, there is one single piece of furniture in the window, an ethnic basket or bowl filled with beige dried flowers or gourds and a plaque proclaiming membership (allegiance) to one of the trade associations.

Of the two extremes, the junk shop can be considered the more fascinating — the second to have, certainly, more style. My ideal shop would be a mixture of both style and fascination — a window display created like a still life painting, a subtle mixture of tones and textures, the whole softly lit by well placed lighting. It sounds all very pretentious but it should perform a definite purpose. The mixture indicates the breadth and variety of your stock and interests and the design should lead the eye into the shop so that the entire show area is part of the display.

trade attitudes

Many trades and professions have a 'them and us' attitude. None more so that the antique trade. Apart from used car dealers, the antique trade is one of the few businesses which actually buys from one private individual and sells, in theory anyway, to another. It is perhaps indicative that in Britain, Her Majesty's Customs and Excise officers treat both used car dealers and antique dealers in the same special tax scheme.

One of the reasons that many dealers would rather buy in auction is that it cushions or isolates the buyer from the seller. The stories are legion of the seller who finds his or her prize (but sold cheaply) heirloom offered in the local dealer's window at several times the price paid. Another good reason why many dealers use simple price codes to disguise their buying and selling prices.

The 'them and us' attitude even extends to the antiques themselves. Many pieces are 'trade lots' and some are condemned to be only 'private' until fashion changes or desperation for stock catches up.

It is a sad fact that many dealers are totally comtemptuous of 'private customers' — they are frequently categorized as 'time wasters' and 'messers' and positively discouraged from buying in many establishments. To be fair, some private 'customers' do not help. I have been told on more than a couple of occasions when offering help 'No, thank you, I am just killing ten minutes until my car/taxi/bus, etc., arrives . . .'

The big advantage of trade customers is that they, generally, know what they want to buy and the price they are willing to pay. Private customers, in the main, do not! The trader can make up his mind in the second. To illustrate the point . . .

I had just received a very fine brass corinthian column standard lamp back from the metal polishers and I put it straight into my window. It looked quite fabulous!

A couple were examining the lamp as I re-arranged the window. They came in.

'How much is the lamp?'

I mentioned the (very reasonable) price.

'That's exactly the price we thought . . . we just missed one about four years ago and have been looking ever since.'

A quick sale, you say? They looked at each other.

'We'll go away and think about it!'

I must admit I took great delight in selling it to the first trader who called in a few minutes late. Such are the ways of the private 'buyers'.

the ethics of exporting

One way or another, most of the antiques sold in this country will end up going abroad. Along the way, knockers, dealers, auction houses and packers will all have their share of the profits. It's a frequently heard criticism of the antique trade that 'everything goes abroad'. The hard fact is that this has been the case for the better part of this century — before then the trade was very much the other way!

It is certainly a sad fact that so many examples of our heritage and past go abroad. However, it is also true that few antique businesses in Britain could survive selling to British private customers. The saddest fact of all is that the average British individual is just not interested in buying antiques. The combined efforts of the major auction houses and the media in the coverage of internationally important items sold for huge sums has implanted in the British mind that antiques are 'expensive'. The superior attitude of some members of 'the trade' to less-than-knowledgeable customers has also done nothing to rectify this situation.

trade attitudes to new dealers

Some dealers seem to take a delight in sowing seeds of doubt in other dealers' minds — frequently those new to the trade. The new — much prized — and highly 'reckoned' piece of furniture is examined — the response can vary . . .

'You haven't got much money in this have you?' (said with a trace of pity in the voice . . .)

'Do you think it's right?'

'The restorer has been at this . . . is he new?' (no good!)

'It's been very well attended-to hasn't it?' (well or badly restored)

'I've seen this before, haven't I?' (the inference being that the piece has been around the trade for ever)

'Do they (the top and the bottom) really match?'

One lesson in this department — If you, as a dealer, find something in a new dealer's shop which has not been priced correctly — in other words, the steal of the century — pay the asking price and please don't try and knock it down any further. If you do, it will be remembered for ever when the dealer finally finds out what it was really worth?

If, however, you are a private customer — all is fair!

price codes

Most antique dealers who sell mainly to other dealers use price codes to mark their stock. These codes usually indicate the purchase price, export trade price, home trade price and retail price. Two different codes are sometimes used for buying and selling prices to further protect the information. These price codes are usually very simple. Many are based on a ten digit combination, e.g. GILT FRAMES:

G	I	L	T
1	2	3	4

F	R	A	M	E	S
5	6	7	8	9	10

adding value by provenance

In the notes of various furniture types and styles I have not made any detailed mention of historical facts, mainly for the very good reason that there are a great many excellent scholarly books on antique furniture in print which concern themselves almost solely with this aspect. I have only mentioned an historical fact when it can influence or can have a very direct bearing on the value or desirability of the piece in question. In other words — where these facts make the item easier to sell or more profitable.

Many dealers, especially those who specialize in antique fairs, use exhaustive and lengthy descriptions of their furniture on display. One bearded dealer, rejoicing in the nickname of 'The Badger', could fill a whole sheet of closely typed description for every table, box, desk or whatever in his display at the drop of a caddy spoon. It's certainly possible to find out interesting or fascinating facts about furniture and its original use or development and these can only add to the interest (and price) and should be encouraged.

If a piece of furniture has any proven (or even suspected) provenance this should also be described as fully as possible — it's nice to know that the little lap desk was (supposedly) carried at the Battles of Cripple Creek or Waterloo although this does not, necessarily, add to the value. Proved beyond reasonable doubt, it is then up to the buyer to decide the extent of any premium he is willing to pay.

Even dubious or fragile provenance should be mentioned. As a piece changes hands any historical 'fact' becomes diluted and credibility should be retained as long as possible. I once bought a musical box which was reputed to have been the property of Charlotte Brontë. When I came to sell it, all I got in return for this information was knowing smiles — no premium price.

It is no bad thing to have a fair repertoire of popular historial anecdotes. These can be trotted out in conversation and quickly establish the buyer or the seller as an expert.

adding value by work

Value can be added to a piece of antique furniture by careful restoration, cleaning and polishing, etc. Value can also be added to otherwise plain and mundane pieces by the addition of fancy or elaborate brasswork. New pleated silk can transform work-boxes and work-tables, screens and chiffonier doors. When combined with new brass grills or galleries the sale value of the piece is dramatically increased. The moral or ethical implictions of this 'improvement' are best left to the individual.

adding value by exposure

Value can also be added in a much more subtle way. Furniture which is featured in advertisements — usually in antique magazines or in fair catalogues is frequently offered at a premium. Some exhibitors have been known to feature every piece on their stand in this way so that every customer goes away happy. They have their genuine antique plus a catalogue!

Much the same thing applies to photographed pieces in auction sale catalogues. Photographs in catalogues certainly appear to influence private buyers . . .

'It must be good, its photograph is in the catalogue.'

Furniture featured in dealers' advertisements appear in the antique press.

The norm for the trade is to choose exceptionally fine examples from their stock. This is intended, no doubt, to illustrate the high quality they normally try to maintain.

However, the item illustrated is frequently sold by the time the magazine appears, given that the advertisement went to press some six to eight weeks before publication date. One dealer in York took a different approach. He used his advertisements to feature furniture which he could not move from his showrooms but which invariably did sell on publication.

restoration

When to restore? As with most other aspects of antiques there are no clear set rules. Sometimes you have to restore. In other situations 'restoration' could, just as easily, ruin the piece of furniture.

The whole question of restoration is full of potential dangers and imponderables. Academic purists are frequently quoted to the effect that only some twenty-five per cent restoration is permissable. In an ideal world, no doubt, this would be true. Unfortunately dealers usually have hard cash tied up in a piece of furniture. They are faced with the moral dilemma — should they leave it in a corner, un-restored and un-loved and contributing to their bank borrowing, or restored and sold? Most dealers do not take too long to resolve that question.

If you are selling to the trade remember that many dealers will not buy restored furniture whilst other will not buy anything that 'needs work'. Only the very experienced (or foolhardy) private customer will buy furniture that requires extensive repair. Dealing in furniture, you have to ask yourself whether it is better to restore or not. Leaving ethics to the rich purist, which path makes most commercial sense?

Selling 'in the rough' or unrestored, the percentage profit on the price paid will be almost certainly higher, quicker and safer than with restoration involved. After adding restoration costs the eventual ticket price should be considerably higher but the percentage profit margin may be lower.

Before embarking on any restoration, remember **the first profit is always the best profit.**

Assuming you are not in Bond Street or Madison Avenue, you may find high quality pieces of furniture easier to sell unrestored and at a higher percentage profit. Most 'good' dealers prefer to buy 'fresh' unrestored goods. This way they can have their own favourite man do the

Raw materials are the life blood of any restorer. Here, York restorer Rod Dunning examines the tip of his personal timber iceberg. A good restorer will have a representative collection of old seasoned woods, drawer linings, chest backs and the like to draw upon. However, with rare woods he may have to call in a few favours from friends in the trade or contact specialist suppliers to obtain suitable replacements.

The finest restorer needs sharp chisels, the correct raw materials, years of experience and a fair touch of genius. He will have to replace pieces, large and small, and leave no tell tale traces. The original furniture maker in the 18th century never had this problem!

When a lock, hand made screw or even a nail has to be replaced — it must be the genuine period article. Your restorer can't just call on the friendly local hardware store and buy one from stock. He will have his own personal collection, built up over the years, to draw upon or use as reference material. He will certainly be able to buy period 'style' metalware but this will receive a great deal of further treatment before being used.

When a piece of furniture is to be restored, a thorough examination is required before work actually starts. The full extent of the work required has to be determined, any special materials, brass and metal work to be ordered (or found) and potential problem areas identified.

work and they know the extent and quality of the work done. The piece, when fully restored, can then be offered with a higher degree of knowledge and, therefore, confidence. The only real question is the quality of the restoration. Good restorers are hard to find and harder still to get work out of.

First of all, the quality of the piece will probably dictate the restorer used. In that ideal world again, the dealer would have access to several restorers. For the 'shipping goods' he would use someone cheap and cheerful and save real 'artists' for the finer quality pieces. Paradoxically, the higher the quality of the restorer's skill, the more 'questionable' work he will be asked to do. When you have someone who can produce repairs or alterations of undetectable quality you can see the ethical problems arising.

Should you find a restorer who can produce such undetectable work — what can you reasonably ask him to do? That 'set' of five chairs . . . how much more valuable they would be if they were 'restored' to their original eight! The 'single' chair transformed into the missing 'carver'. The permutations are endless. Faced with an excellent 'improved' set of chairs, many dealers will turn a blind eye and quick profit.

Frequently the restoration or improvement can be achieved by the simple removal of a feature which dates the piece perhaps twenty years or so too late (see chiffonier illustration). Pieces destined for private homes are frequently 'flashed up', altered and 'improved' to the dealer's every whim and to suit his particular market place.

I can well remember selling a fine Cuban mahogany chest to a dealer friend. It had just been 'pulled out' of a country house stable and its brushing slide was completely missing — only the front remained. Within a couple of days I found it in his showrooms for sale. I must admit to being a little surprised at the speed of its restoration and couldn't resist pulling out the slide . . . The first thing I noticed was the prevailing smell of shoe polish. The 'slide' was, in fact, a piece of brand-new pine, coloured with brown shoe polish. I pulled it a little further and found that the rear portion of the slide hadn't even been coloured! This type of so-called restoration is totally unacceptable — the chest sold later that same day into the trade!

finding a restorer

How can you find a good restorer? There is no easy way. It's a sad fact of the antique way of life that if he is any good, no-one is going to tell you about him. The good restorer is an asset to be carefully nurtured and kept well hidden from view. When asked directly by a private customer for the name of a restorer I have known a dealer recommend someone that he would never dream of using himself. He possibly felt that he had to appear helpful and would avoid, at all costs, revealing his personal restorer.

Restorers can be very, very slow. This fact, coupled with the fact that very few seem to work through their backlog in any logical order, means that your furniture may well disappear for some considerable time. However, there are few pleasures in the antique trade more satisfying than the first sight of a well-restored piece of furniture which you had originally bought as a bundle of firewood. Slow is relative. All restorers are slow but some are slower than others. Few can be described remotely as quick.

I once bought some furniture from a lady and asked her the usual dealers' question on a 'private call'.

'Is there anything else . . ?'

She thought for a moment.

'I do have rather a nice corner cupboard but it's at the restorers. Come to think of it, it's been there for nine years!

This time scale is, I hope, unusual. However, be prepared for months rather than weeks if the restorer is especially busy or has 'strong' regular trade customers.

is restoration expensive?

Expensive is a relative term and has to be equated with the commercial or intrinsic value of the antique.

The physical cost of restorations falls into three main catagories: time, materials and fittings.

The time costs naturally depend upon the hourly rate charged and the speed at which the restorer works. Needless to say, all the materials used in restoration have to be paid for. You can opt to supply the genuine old drawer linings or whatever from your stock or the restorer can be asked to supply from his. Either way it costs money. Not only money, of course, but the actual physical use of finite resources on a piece when you both might need them for an even more important job the following week.

Brass 'cabinet furniture' or handles may have to be bought or even made. It pays to be familiar with the catalogues of the leading brassware suppliers to the trade. These publications are usually extensively illustrated and should be studied. When you are offered furniture with missing, complex or unusual fittings it is as well to know immediately if they are available 'off the shelf'. Their availability will influence your offer or your decision to 'leave well alone'.

Even brassware bought from specialist suppliers will frequently require a degree of work before being acceptable. The good restorer will do considerable work to alter colour, wear and even design to make them match or look totally authentic. 'Off the shelf' handles, for instance, will spend hours on the electric buffing machine to really smooth down their edges to wafer thin proportions until they almost merge with the wood — just as they would if they had been polished daily for a couple of hundred years.

If the missing handle cannot be matched directly from the catalogue, the nearest alternative style may have to be cut and altered to match. With unusual cast brass handles and mounts to find, these may well have to be duplicated using the lost wax method from specialist brass founders. New steel locks or machine cut screws should never be used. Every restorer worthy of the name has numerous little tin boxes and drawers full of the genuine period articles and will have to be persuaded to part! (Some restorers have been known to use new reproduction style steel fittings. Car brake fluid can then be introduced to the scene to provide an extraordinary over-night rusting effect!)

All these factors combine to make it difficult for a restorer to give you a firm estimate of costs before starting a job. One can sympathize with him in this respect as he will never really know what he is going to find under the surface. The worst thing he can find is that a less-than-excellent restorer has been there before him.

When the final cost is known and it's wildly over your highest estimate, there really isn't much you can do about it. The last thing you want to do is fall out with a good restorer over something as trivial as money. All you can do is to pass the extra cost on if you are selling or, if

you are 'keeping', just hope that it 'comes into price' with natural inflation. If it is any comfort, even an expensive restoration can look reasonable with a year or two under its belt.

Very few restorers deliver on time. Very few ever do work in any logical order. The importance of the customer and/or the weight he carries are nearly always the deciding factor. Some restorers acually keep especially good pieces back because they add prestige to their premises. You might think that, like a big box of chocolates, they couldn't wait to get started on a particularly fine piece. Many, however, prefer to live with it for a while and really absorb all its subtle features.

So then, what can be considered 'good restoration'? There really shouldn't be a distinction between degrees of restoration. There should only be restoration which is totally undetectable to the experienced naked eye. Any restoration which can be detected is best described as 'wood butchery'.

For all their faults and foibles, I have the greatest possible respect for the good restorer. He may not be able to design a fine piece of furniture to save his life, but he has to be a far, far better craftsman in every respect than the original maker in the nineteenth century. All the original craftsman had to do was work at a leisurly rate with large, well seasoned pieces of fine timber. The modern restorer may well be given a 'bag of bits' and asked to produce something which looks as if no-one had touched it — ever! His greatest compliment must be that no-one knows he has ever touched the piece.

He is an essential link in the antique chain but seldom receives his due. He can earn a good living but rarely figures in the same income (not tax) bracket as most of his dealer clients. Never one to avoid a sweeping generalization, I have never known a restorer worthy of the name who advertises for work! The 'business card' entry in antique trade directory pages is possibly permissable, but advertising for general consumption should perhaps indicate some caution.

foreign restoration

Antique dealers and enthusiasts on holiday always look for the 'antique quarter' and many find English goods on offer there . . . they may find them restored or improved to suit their particular market place. Pieces bought for specific export markets frequently require rather special restoration treatment . . .

Big mahogany partners'desks bound for Germany, for instance, will be highly polished and leathered using vivid colours that would never grace a St. James' club. The gleaming desk is then smothered with polished brass fittings. In general terms, furniture destined for German dealers must look expensive.

With goods for the Italian trade it would be almost impossible to provide the finish required in England. Goods are sold here, 'in the rough', and are made suitable for the demands of that market totally in Italy. The plainest, most ordinary Victorian chiffonier could end up in Rome, with a polish like a Rolls Royce, brushing slides everywhere, coloured tassles hung from at least three keys, scalloped, gold embossed leather trim on the shelves and, perhaps, gilded brass scenes of a Greek goddess driving a chariot pulled by six horses applied on each front panel. An extraordinary object, certainly, compared with the staid original, knocked from a Yorkshire front room, but really quite fun if not taken too seriously.

One of the unique aspects of Italian 'restoration' or, rather, 'improvement' is that everything happens totally in the open, quite frequently in one street. In one single shop in the antique district you can see the original furniture just out of the container from England. Next door the cabinet-makers are roughly cutting slots and fitting the brushing slides, the leathers and the tassles are hanging in bunches in another shop further along the street. The friendly neighbourhood polishers are applying coat after coat of shellac to the most mundane pieces of mahogany to achieve that uniquely Italian finish.

One specialist shop in every antique street will be an Aladdin's cave of highly gilded brasswork of the most ornate design and complexity. In the final showroom the finished piece, fairly dripping with extras, and looking enormously expensive and impressive awaits its eventual home in a Roman villa or apartment.

care

With almost all matters of care of antique furniture, I believe very strongly that any treatment other than very simple (and potentially harmless) cleaning is best left to experts. If you do want to try your hand at simple improvement, there are numerous books on the subject which deal with the treatment of almost every aspect of furniture and fittings care.

In my career in the trade I think I managed with the following contents in our 'care cupboard'

Reviver

OO Wire wool

Soft shoe brush

Scratch cover

British Museum leather polish

Coloured and natural wax polish

The furniture reviver was always made up for me by a local wood-carver. It always came in Schweppes' Indian Tonic Water bottles which, somehow, added to the mystique and potency. When applied to dirty or dry furniture (using cotton wool balls in most cases and OO grade wire wool with very dirty furniture) the effect was magical. Tired, dry timber gained new life and patina almost immediately. This reviver is simple and easy to use, really does work and can do no harm to old furniture or a delicate patina.

He never would tell me what was in these mysterious smelly bottles so I contacted the original source, the Conservation Department of the Victoria and Albert Museum in London and they recommended:

The potion used by the conservation department of the V & A to clean and 'revive' newly received dirty and neglected furniture is:

2 parts: Methylated Spirits
2 parts: Vinegar
2 parts: Pure Turpentine (not substitute)
1 part: Raw Linseed Oil

The mixture will separate when not in use and should be thoughly shaken every time before use. Apply some cotton wool to the mouth of the bottle and shake the mixture onto it. Apply to a small area in an unobtrusive part of the piece as a test. The reviver will remove old and dirty wax — right down to the original shellac or varnish finish. If, however, there is no protective varnish the reviver could do severe damage to the object. An experienced polisher will be required to put matters right.

Use only on small areas at a time and clean off immediately with another cloth. Never allow the reviver to accumulate or to lay on the surface. The constituents of the mixture will separate if not kept moving and, individually, do damage to the surface. The reviver only works as a mixture. Every trace must be removed with a clean dry cloth otherwise you will be left with a nasty sticky surface.

Leather on antique furniture can also get tired and dry and this too can be quickly and simply improved by a wonderful potion known as **British Museum leather polish.** I almost looked forward to buying something with dry leather so that I could use the amazing polish. When applied with a soft cloth it soaks in immediately and makes even the most crumbly leather soft and supple again within seconds. A real pleasure to use! Any large chemist will mix it — the recipe is:

Lanolin (anhydrous)	7 oz (avoir)
Cedarwood oil	1 oz (fluid)
Beeswax	½ oz (avoir)
Hexane	11 oz (fluid)

It was originally formulated by The British Museum for the restoration of old leather book bindings. Every aspiring antique dealer needs a selection of old 'bindings' (never 'books') to set off a bookcase or other piece of library furniture. (Never sell your collection of leather bindings — you can never have too many!) A tip — don't buy too much at one time. The hexane quickly evaporates in use and the residual sludge is of little use for anything!

Coloured wax polishes are excellent for quick simple scratch cover jobs, as are some of the branded products on the market.

Modern synthetic adhesives are probably the most efficient glues ever invented. **NEVER USE THEM.** If you have to glue a piece of antique furniture, always use a simple animal or vegetable glue which can be easily removed when the next owner comes to repair it.

Tea caddies

Jargon

This section is not intended to be a complete glossary of antique furniture terms — but rather a descriptive listing of some of the terms used by the antique trade.

Apron

apron, the; frequently shaped, lower front on a piece of furniture — usually associated with commodes or bow fronted chests of drawers.

armoire; name given to large French wardrobe, usually with two arched and panelled doors, over drawers. Frequently in pine or fruitwood.

arrangement; agreement between buyers at an auction; alternative name for the ring. As in, 'Is there an arrangement?'

astragal; the fine wooden moulding into which is set the small panes of glass in a cabinet. Also known as 'glazing bars'.

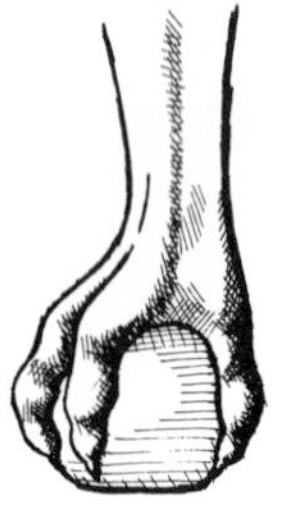

Ball and claw foot

auction rate; the number of lots usually sold per hour. The rate is required to be known so that dealers need only return from refreshments in time to bid for their particular interests. A good auctioneer will sell at one hundred lots per hour. In commercial sales, beware of 'stand on' lots when calculating potential number to be sold in an hour (see 'stand on').

back pocket; cash payment.

ball and claw foot; a style of foot originated in England in the eighteenth century — derived from oriental designs — of a round ball held in an animal's claw.

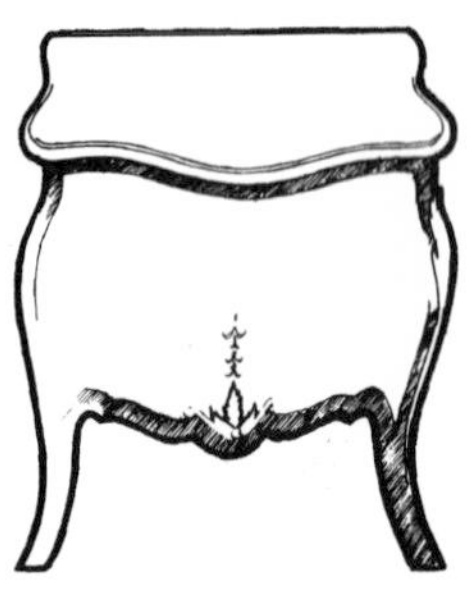

Bombé

banding; a strip of wood laid into another for decorative effect, either the parent wood or another type and colour. See also 'cross-banding'.

beading; half or quarter-round wooden moulding.

bids off the wall, taking; auctioneer's expression indicating bids from thin air for a variety of reasons, usually to bring bidding up to the reserve price.

blind; usually in describing a cabinet or bookcase door. 'Blind' means the panel is made of wood, as opposed to glazed.

bombe; usually a bureau or commode with a bulging rounded front, frequently also serpentine. Still made today in Italy in huge quantities and imported into England to be veneered.

Bonheur du jour

bonheur du jour; any very small desk or table with cabinet or open shelves.

book, the; The record of bids, totals for division at a settlement or knock. As in, 'Who is keeping the book?'

bought in; (or **buy in**); if a lot at an auction sale does not reach its reserve price the auctioneer may 'knock it down' to a fictitious buyer to disguise the fact, since too many unsold lots might damage the credibility of the auction house. Usually the same fictitious name or series of names are used. The disposal of the lot may well be negotiated after the sale or offered again at a later auction.

boulle; a method of decorating furniture with strips of fine brass filled with tortoiseshell. Invariably French.

bun foot; a flattened ball foot widely used in England in the seventeenth century.

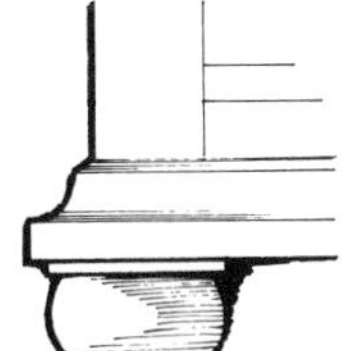

Bun foot

burr; markings in wood, where branches had grown. Usually increases value and desirability of the piece.

butler's tray; a shallow tray in mahogany on a folding stand. The most desirable is an oval flat tray with four folding wings.

Butler's tray

butterfly joint; a joint, shaped like butterfly's wings, used to join two pieces of flat wood end to end.

breaker; piece of furniture, any period, virtually impossible to restore, or worth more as raw materials for restoration.

bridle joint; the particular point at the top of a table leg set into the top frame.

Bridle joint

broken set; number of matching chairs, less than the original number (dining chairs are frequently numbered on the rear rail of the frame), e.g. three single chairs and a carver (elbow).

buy at the table; buy in auction rather than at the settlement.

caddy; a small lockable box designed to hold, usually two, varieties of tea, and a mixing or sugar bowl — from a Malay word for a weight in the tea trade.

cab leg; trade contraction of cabriole leg.

cabinet furniture; handles, escutcheons, knobs, etc., for furniture, usually in brass.

cabriole; a shaped leg usually found in Victorian furniture and highly desirable period furniture. Best examples would be in Victorian chairs and period dining, library and windsor chairs. Always known as 'cab' legs in the trade.

call, private; a visit by a dealer to a private house to buy antiques.

call, trade; a visit to one antique dealer by another, a 'good trade call' is a form of praise indicating a dealer, prepared to 'deal'.

candle slides; small slides found in bureau cabinets, card tables and canterburys to hold candlesticks.

canterbury; a Georgian or Victorian open container designed to hold sheet music.

carcase; the main 'body' or framework of a piece of furniture, e.g. if you remove the drawers from a chest of drawers, what remains is the 'carcase'.

carver; dining chair with arms, frequently slightly larger than other 'single' chairs in set. Also quite correctly known as 'arm' chair. Always three or four inches wider in the seat than single chairs.

Carver

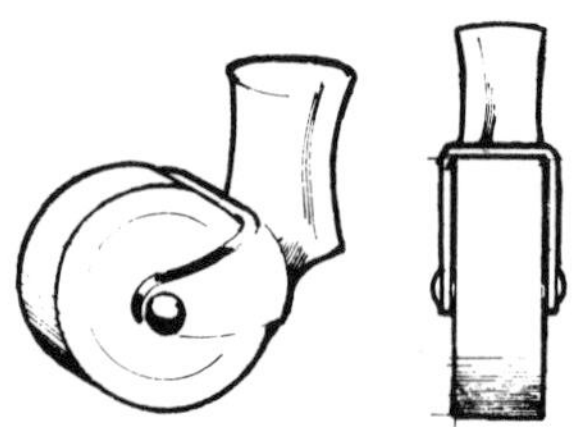
Castor

castor; a small wheel of wood, leather or brass held in a brass 'clamp' to allow furniture to be moved without lifting.

cellaret; a box designed to hold wine — frequently divided into sections to take bottles.

chaser calls; letters or telephone calls, which prove to be false, offering attractive goods, usually from remote country villages, or from addresses a considerable distance from the recipient.

cheap lot; well below market price.

clean piece; in good, clean, condition, ready for sale without work, polishing or restoration.

clean house; used as a recommendation that the (frequently upholstered) furniture came from a house which could be described as 'clean'.

Compendium table

cock beading; a small protuding moulding on a drawer front.

codes; any method of price coding.

coffer; a kist, marriage chest, or box.

collective sale; an auction sale where lots have been gathered from various vendors (sellers).

come into price; an item bought too expensively . . . which has to wait until demand, inflation or fashion brings the price up to the level asked.

compendium table, (games table); an eighteenth century or Victorian table containing a variety of game boards and counters. The boards usually inlaid with rare or coloured veneers. The counters in natural and stained ivories and bone, some counters in (imported) mother-of-pearl.

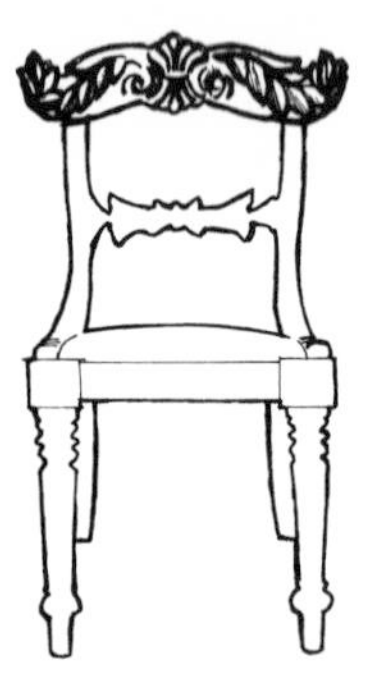
Cresting

composite (set) of chairs. A collection of chairs which bear more than a passing resemblance to each other. Expression frequently used in auction catalogues to describe four or six chairs as a 'set' but not made at the same time, or as an 'original' set.

consul table; a table designed to stand against a wall, frequently without back legs.

cresting; the carving on the top rail of a chair.

deceased effects; an all too frequent expression seen in some dealers' advertisements, e.g. 'deceased effects cleared'. Much the same meaning as 'house clearance' — everything is bought in the household when the owner dies.
In the 'good old days' the undertaker was frequently an antique dealer as well and took furniture and effects in lieu of payment for the funeral. Many older dealers tell tales of buying the furniture surrounding the open coffin!

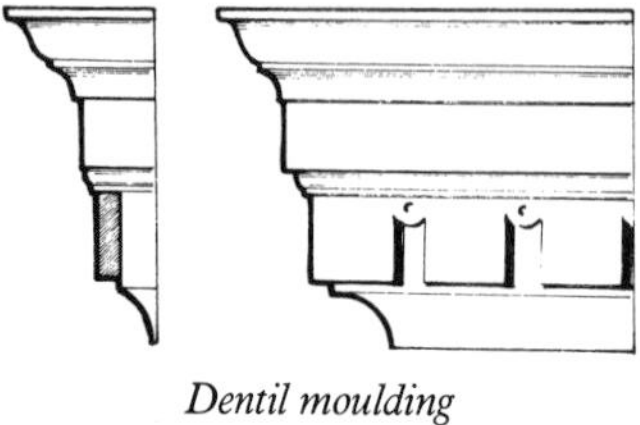
Dentil moulding

dentil moulding; series of small blocks forming a decorative frieze.

distressing; method of making newly restored wood look somewhat older! Chains, bags of keys or nails, etc., are amongst the 'tools' used in distressing.

dividend; the 'split' of proceeds between members of the ring, settlement or knock.

dovetail joint; a method of joining two pieces of wood together at right angles by wedge shaped joints, usually seen in drawers. A useful dating clue to furniture — dovetails are either hand or machine made.

Dovetail joint

dowel; a wooden peg used to fasten furniture together.

draw leaf; the leaf of a table, usually hidden within the carcase of the table, which can be 'drawn out' to add length to the table.

dresser; piece of furniture consisting of a base (a mix of drawers, cupboards, and in the case of some Irish examples, a chicken coop, with an open rack above to hold and display kitchen pottery, etc.

dropped in; at auction, placing an item for sale, usually by a member of the trade, perhaps pretending to be a private vendor. In the picture trade, frequently done to establish (by buying in by the seller) the 'price' for an artist — usually when the seller has a collection by the same, hitherto unsold, artist.

dumb waiter; stand containing either two or three circular revolving trays.

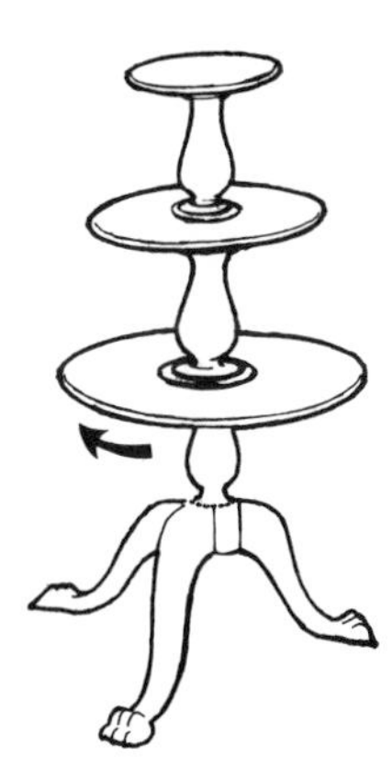

Dumb waiter

effects; as in 'deceased effects', all the goods and chattels in a household.

elbow chair; alternative name for carver. The usually larger dining chair with arms in a set. Sold individually as a 'desk' chair.

exotic (woods); zebra wood, amboyna, partridge wood and the like.

flashed-up; decorating with fancy brasswork, over-polishing, adding decorative grills, galleries, new leather — usually to a plain piece of furniture which 'needs help'.

fluting; rows of parallel concave carving or moulding — the opposite to reeding.

'fill it up'; expression used in auction to indicate a bid to next round number, e.g. if the last bid was ninety-five, the auctioneer might ask you if you wished to 'fill it up' — make your bid a hundred.

finial; a decorative turned urn or pinnacle on a cabinet, bookcase, pillar, etc., in wood, ivory, bone, etc.

Finial

finger joint; the wooden hinge mechanism of the 'moving' leg in a card or tea table, (see also 'knuckle joint').

fresh goods; antiques bought (usually privately) and not previously 'seen' by the trade — as with goods bought in the trade or at auction. A dealer, offering goods bought privately, gains a reputation as a source of 'fresh goods'.

fruitwood; cherry, apple, pear, etc.

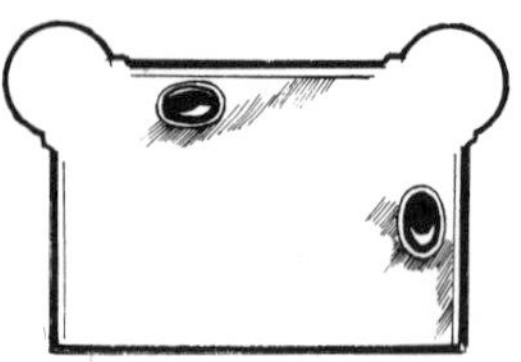

Guinea pockets

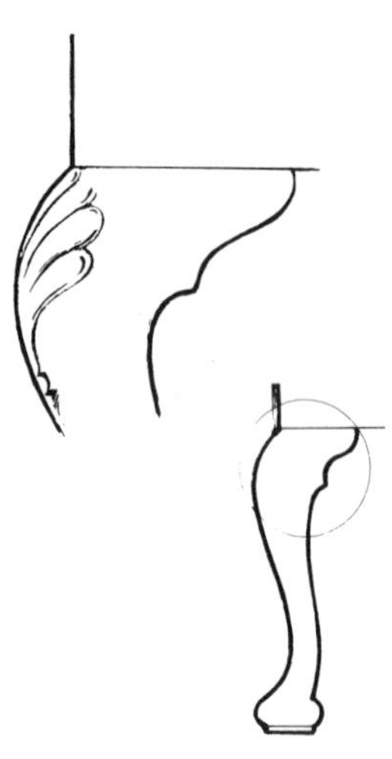

Knee

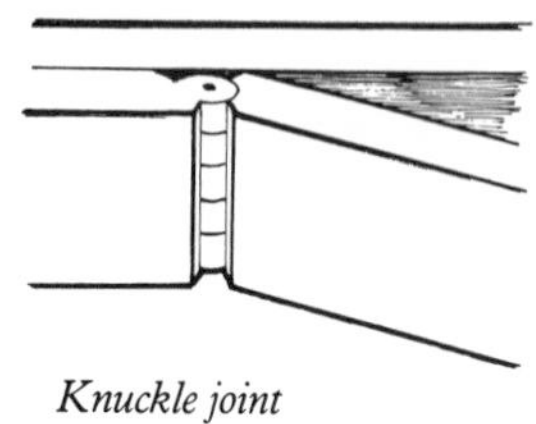

Knuckle joint

gear; general name used in the trade for antiques of all descriptions.

give or take; a situation at a settlement when the goods are left between only two dealers. One or the other offers either to give or take a sum of money, the other participant can either accept or increase the bidding until one or the other accepts the price.

glazing bars; see 'astragal'.

goods; general name used in the trade for antiques of all descriptions, (see 'gear').

guinea pockets; shallow dish shapes (usually in mahogany) set into the green baize of card tables, used to hold gaming tokens. Named after the English guinea coin.

hawked about; (or hawked around), a piece taken from dealer to dealer for sale.

hold the goods; ring member who ends up at the conclusion of the second auction actually carrying off the lots.

hot goods; overpriced goods — usually in the trade or shop.

hot lots; overpriced goods bought in auction.

house clearance; the purchase of the entire contents of a household — usually including the clearing-up and disposal of all the residual (un-saleable) rubbish — this latter task frequently being passed to a third party further down the antique social ladder.

house sale; auction actually held on the house premises — perhaps in the house or outbuildings or in a marquee in the grounds.

important; dealers' euphemism for expensive or overpriced.

improved; additions or alterations made to a piece of furniture to improve its value.

joints; (in furniture). The commonest, dovetail, mortise and tenon, are best described in the illustrations.

knee. the curved, frequently carved, top of a chair or table leg.

knock, the; the ring or settlement.

knock; to knock; to find fault with something or everything about a piece of furniture.

knock-out; yet another name for the settlement.

knock, in the; members of the ring or settlement, as in the question, 'Are you in the knock?'

knocker; dealer who knocks on private house doors (uninvited) attempting to buy antiques (modern equivalent of a 'rapper').

knuckle joint; the wooden hinge mechanism used to pivot the 'moving' leg in a card or tea table, (see also 'finger joint').

list; a list issued by local police listing goods stolen.

lost wax process; the simplest method of copying individual brasswork, the wax copy being burnt off by the addition of the molten brass.

lots, trade; an antique usually only bought by a dealer, not by a member of the public or goods entered into auction by a member of the trade.

market price; the current trade or retail price (depending on who is speaking to whom!)

marquetry; inlaid woods of different varieties and colours to make a geometric or pictorial design in furniture. Many such woods are dyed or 'shaded' by immersion in hot sand.

marriage; a piece of furniture in two parts, sold as one, which were not made at the same time, usually associated with bureau bookcases.

messers; either a dealer or member of the public who can't make up their mind whether to buy or not — messing about.

'needs work'; requires restoration, repair or polishing, etc.

ogee; a handsome curved foot, frequently found only in the best pieces.

ormolu; in trade terms, any gilded brass fittings, usually associated with French furniture.

parquetry; inlaid woods gaining effect with variation of grain direction.

patina; name given to the combination of dusting and polishing acquired over many years which achieves a deep 'natural' polish. Patina (or, the lack of it) contributes greatly to the value or desirability of any piece of furniture. As easy to recognize as it is hard to describe. The only metaphor I can think is the visual comparison of the paint on a Ford and on an Aston Martin.

pediment; the moulding or decorative feature topping a piece of furniture, frequently a bookcase or cabinet.

period; can be used as 'Victorian period', 'Edwardian period'. However, when used as an adjective (a period chest) it means, in fact, that the chest is pre-1830, or in other words 'antique' in the purists' vocabulary.

pie-crust; decorative carved edge to a circular table top. A genuine pie crust should always have been carved out of a solid top. Any sign of added timber to create the depth to allow the crust to be carved should be treated with great suspicion.

potential; as in, 'This piece has potential.' Meaning it can be improved after restoration or 'treatment'.

premises, on the; auction sale held in the house or works.

price codes; any method of disguising price paid, etc., on price ticket by means of an alphabetical or numeric code.

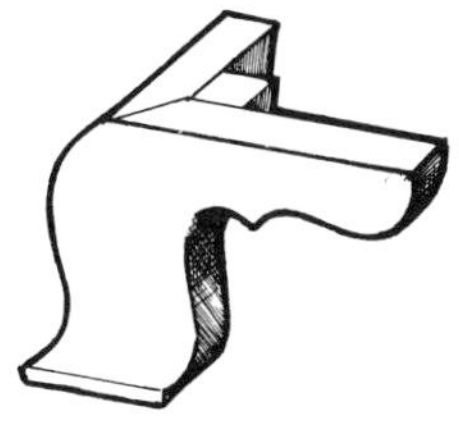

Ogee foot

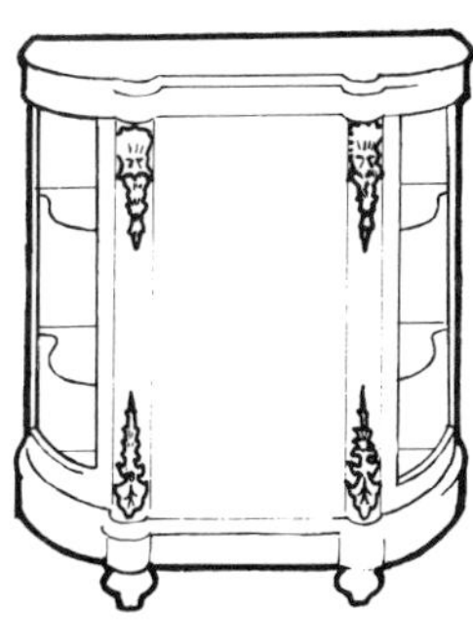

Ormolu

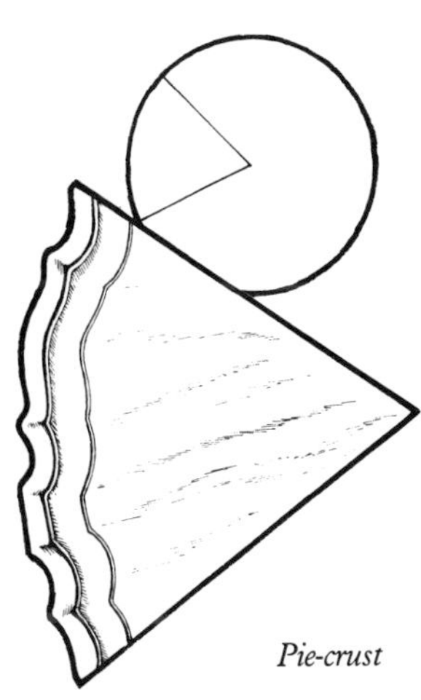

Pie-crust

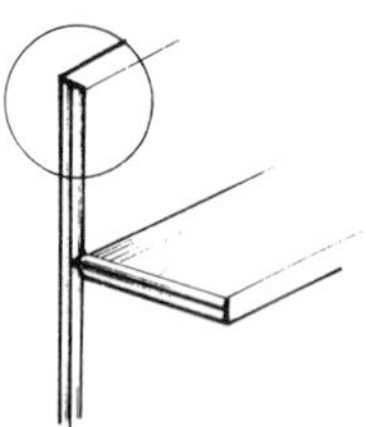
Reeding

price, come into; time taken for an over-priced item to arrive at market price (e.g. sale with a profit in it . . !)

private call; a visit by a dealer to a private house to buy antiques.

provenance; the authenticated history of an antique.

pulled out; buying 'goods' from a private house, as in, 'Pulled out some good lots today.'

quality goods; high quality antiques.

rappers; old name for knocker — as in raps (knocks) on any door.

reckon; to 'appreciate' the true value, as in, 'Does he reckon it?' 'Is it reckoned?' — is the true value appreciated.

reeding; lines of parallel convex wood carving, see illustration. (Opposite to fluting — which is concave).

right; opposite of 'wrong'. Genuine.

ring, the; collection or group of dealers who buy collectively at public auction, also known as the knock, settlement, arrangement. A term hardly ever used in practice but only in newspaper or media reporting.

Settle

rooms, the; conversational description of the two main London sale rooms, Christies and Sotherbys. As in, 'Did you buy it in the rooms?'

rough, in the; a piece of furniture in original un-restored condition but needing polishing or restoration.

running-up (at auction), the artificial bidding — usually by the seller, to create a high public price (frequently in the case of picture dealer who has a collection by the same artist and needs to establish a market price). Or, to drop one's own goods in auction; running-up refers to bidding for the goods, hoping to drop them on the competition.

serpentine; curved front to a chest or commode.

settle; as in, 'Are you going to settle?' Translation: 'Are you taking part in the settlement?'

settle; a wooden high backed seat for three or four, frequently with a hinged seat hiding a chest from which it was derived.

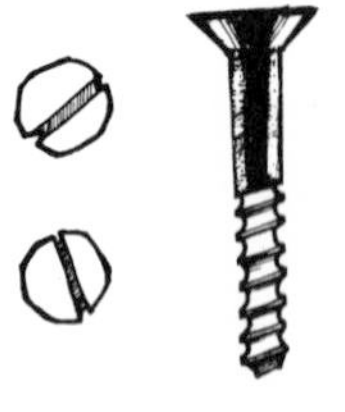
Screw

settlement; a group of dealers who buy collectively at public auction also known as the knock, arrangement or ring by the media.

scheme 3; a reference to the British Value Added Tax Scheme, meaning payment in cash, no receipts, etc., therefore no tax.

screw; the important screw to the antique dealer is the hand-made or hand-cut variety which will prove the age of a piece or can be introduced to a fake. Before the mid-eighteenth century screws were generally found only in firearms.

shipping goods; antiques, Victorian, Edwardian and later furniture intended for export, usually in group lots or mixed container loads.Not considered by the trade as being suitable for private sale in UK.

single; a dining chair without arms, usually narrower than the arm or carver chair.

skiver; thin 'skin' of polished, usually coloured, leather, used to cover top or writing surfaces in furniture. Frequently tooled in gold. 'Thin' to fit flush with crossbanding veneers. Usually 'laid' on a smooth bed of plaster-of-paris.

spade foot; a tapering four-sided foot usually found on dining chairs and sideboards.

splat; the central upright rail of a chair back, frequently pierced, carved or decorated.

stand on; expression used in auction to indicate willingness to take following (usually identical) lots at the same price as the successful first bid, e.g. if there are ten lots each containing the same item, the successful bidder for the first lot would be given the option of 'standing on' to take his choice (or all) of the following lots at the same price. The auctioneer should indicate before offering the lots that he is willing to entertain this method. This should be kept in mind when calculating number of lots to be sold per hour — 'stand on' lots can be very quick!

stretcher; supporting rail between chair or table legs.

stripped; a piece of furniture, usually pine, from which the original or later paint has been removed, usually by caustic soda or slivers of freshly cut glass.

strong; a dealer who is buying well in the trade or at auction can be described as a 'strong buyer' or 'so-and-so was strong today at the sale'.

stuffed over; upholstered furniture where the covering is over the chair seat frame and/or back frame, effectively hiding the construction.

tallboy; tall chest of drawers, usually in two parts, or an unusually tall single chest of drawers (in American: high-boy).

tambour; thin strips of wood glued to a fabric base making them flexible — rather like the 'roll' top on a roll-top desk. Some commodes could be described as 'tambour fronted'.

tarting up; making a piece look rather better, polishing, 'surface' restoration.

tickle; to buy a bargain, 'got a great tickle yesterday'.

top-rail; the topmost cross-piece on a chair back.

Tottenham Court Road; a disparaging term used to describe period-design furniture produced in the first quarter of this century.

trade; the antique trade.

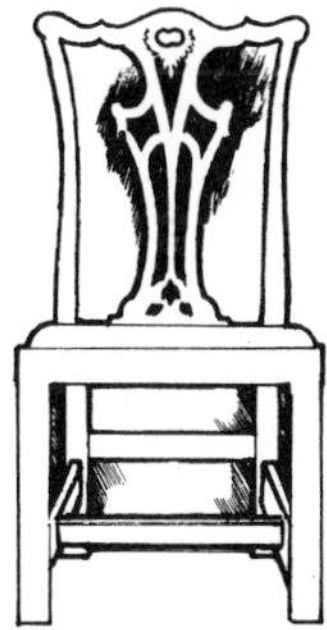

Single chair

Spade foot

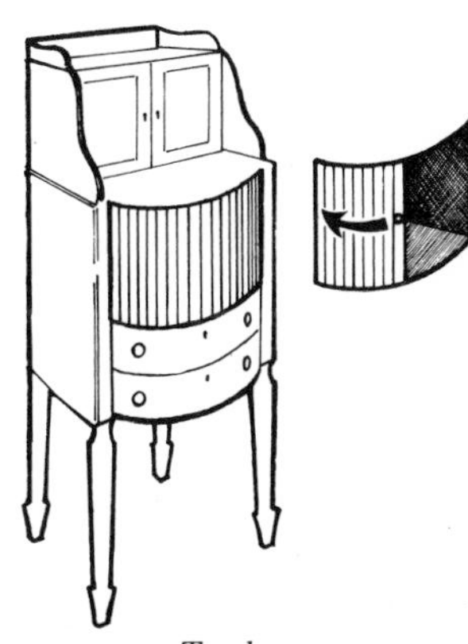

Tambour

Triple top table

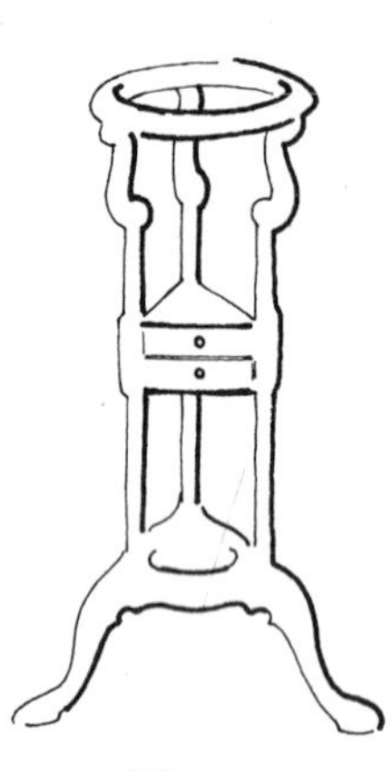

Wig stand

trade call; a visit to one antique dealer by another, a 'good trade call' is a form of praise indicating a dealer prepared to deal.

trade lots; description given to goods at auction considered to have been entered by another trader; also goods usually for trading-on to another dealer — not to a member of the public.

trade, what's the trade on this?; frequently heard expression in the antique trade; translation: 'How much is this (piece) to me, as a fellow dealer?'

triple top table; a rare and very desirable table with a series of folding tops; turn over once and it's a tea table (polished top), turn over again and it's a games table (baize lined top — perhaps with guinea pockets). Usually associated with the first half of the eighteenth century but later examples (sometimes with cut corners) can be found.

trotting; at auction, the auctioneer taking fictitious bids to raise the price to the reserve, or higher.

un-stripped; piece of furniture, usually pine, painted and saleable only (to the public) when the paint is removed by 'stripping' — commonly by caustic soda. Furniture offered 'un-stripped' may well be done so for a good reason! The paint could hide a multitude of sins, previous stripping by blow-lamp, for instance, and consequent scorch marks.

veneer; a thin layer of wood — usually attractively grained, applied to a carcase of solid, less expensive, wood. Rule of thumb — the thicker the veneer, the earlier the piece.

wages; small profit, to 'take wages' on a piece, is to ask small profit, say ten to twenty per cent.

well attended to; extensively restored, not necessarily well done — in fact, rather obvious 'restoration' work. Much used by media antique expert, the late Arthur Negus.

well-reckoned; the market price is appreciated or known and a 'top price' asked.

well seen; a piece which has been offered for sale in the trade for some time. The opposite of 'fresh goods'.

wig stand; either a wooden mushroom on stand designed to hold a wig when not in use or a basin used to hold the actual wig stand, the china bowl catching the powder for re-use.

women's shops; a rather unkind description applied to some shops which always seem rather over-full of little pieces of furniture, lots of colourful china and dolls on every chair.

work; as in 'needs work' a piece of furniture requiring restoration, repair or polishing, etc.

wrong; opposite of 'right'. Not genuine!